POPULAR CULTURE
IN AMERICA

Maurice Kish *The Tunnel of Love* (oil on canvas)

POPULAR CULTURE IN AMERICA

PAUL BUHLE
EDITOR

University of Minnesota Press   Minneapolis

Published by the University of Minnesota Press
2037 University Avenue Southeast, Minneapolis, MN 55414.
Published simultaneously in Canada
by Fitzhenry & Whiteside Limited, Markham.
Printed in the United States of America.

Most of the essays in this book closely resemble
their original *Cultural Correspondence* form.
However, the following have been considerably
reduced for space reasons: Franklin Rosemont's
"Free Play and No Limit" and "Surrealism in the
Comics I"; R. Crumb and Bill Griffith's "As the
Artist Sees It"; Philip Lamantia's "Radio Voices";
Michael E. Starr's "Prime Time Jesus"; and James
Spady's "Black Music."

Library of Congress Cataloging-in-Publication Data

Popular culture in America.

Includes index.
1. United States–Popular culture–History–
20th century. 2. American literature–20th century–
History and criticism. I. Buhle, Paul, 1944–
E169.12.P64 1987   700.973   86-7117
ISBN 0-8166-1408-3
ISBN 0-8166-1409-1 (pbk.)

Contents

Paul Buhle

Comics

Radio and Television

Recent Literature

Envoi: Humor as Popular Culture Wisdom

Acknowledgments

I wish to acknowledge my fellow editors of *Cultural Correspondence* for their years of steady and often thankless effort. In chronological order of their participation, they are: Dave Wagner, Daniel Czitrom, George Lipsitz, Edith Hoshino Altbach, Ron Weisberger, Sam Hunting, and Marcia Blair. Many other friends helped in various ways, from contributing an occasional $25 to assisting with production. Morris Edelson printed nos. 1–2 and typeset most of no. 5, Kathy Shagass laid out no. 5, and Penelope Rosemont nos. 9–14.

Special thanks go to the small circle of steady correspondents, especially Jay Kinney, Dan Georgakas, Stan Weir, and Franklin Rosemont (who also edited nos. 10–11 and the Surrealist Section of nos. 12–14), and to the wider circle of irregular letter-writers and phone-callers. Their advice and good wishes encouraged me to bring out the magazine in the face of steadily rising prices, vanishing independent bookstores, and flagging social idealism.

Without the help of the University of Minnesota Press staff, the contents of *Cultural Correspondence* could not have taken on new life in this book. I wish, especially, to express my appreciation to Marlene Tungseth, Diane Lunderborg, and Gwen Willems.

Introduction: The 1960s Meet the 1980s

We are now almost a generation past the high points of the Vietnam War and the accompanying protest movement. The Woodstock Nation has long since dispersed and its veritable opposite number, Archie Bunker, only appears in reruns. Popular culture's contemporary terrain is the depoliticized middle ground of MTV and Steven Spielberg. Never has the real past, in this accelerated society, seemed more distant or its Reaganesque evocation more blatantly deceitful.

And yet, we have our own self-constructed cultural history available at the flick of a switch. Bruce Springsteen wins the heart of a nation at political conservatism's high tide with his honest lyrics about blue-collar dignity in now-diminished hometowns. Television, with its recycled plots and its cable access to infinite residuals, as well as films, clothes, even sports (with their statistical obsession) seem to be meditations upon times gone by. "Maybe everything that dies, someday comes back," muses Springsteen about Atlantic City, and we understand the phrase in a double sense. A society that never accepted the past as definitive, which believed itself to

Paul Buhle

be a new beginning for civilization, has at least *this* shared past. The collective cultural experience probably means more by now than our common feeling for, say, the Constitution. And in a more disquieting sense: the specter that haunts us, as always in America, is not really some war-ravaged or poverty-stricken past, let alone some mythicized national pride, but our defiled hopes in technology, mass politics, and mass society. We are all part of the social aching to renegotiate that missed connection between the cultural promise of a richly diverse, democratic society and the reality at hand.

By the 1970s and 1980s, in what may be known as the "age of the cassette," critics who had reached early middle-age were self-conscious products of that mass culture, with special reasons to believe in its social influence. Their identities had been formed and transformed by the television they watched, the top-forty music they heard, even the comics they read. Advertising, that symbol for everything corrupt in mass society, had actually conspired with the decisive sexualization of popular music and with the cachet of recreational drugs. Television had brought the horror of America's Vietnam engagement (and its effects, such as the 1968 Democratic party convention) into the living room. "Celebrity," the synthetic creation of hero status, had given the counterculture a Bob Dylan or a John Lennon to pronounce vague but emphatic alternatives to the apparently collapsing system.

Soon enough the media pronounced the revolution finished, the social movement dead, and the values of consumer capitalism strengthened by the experience. Erstwhile activists found themselves locked inside an America grown cold but not entirely without consolations now more and more exclusively cultural. Springsteen, Jimmy Cliff, and television's "Rockford Files," vernacular postmodernism all, suited them as well as the protest literature of a Nadine Gordimer might have served an entire earlier intellectual generation at a similar hiatus.

Popular Culture in America is a contribution to collective self-understanding, a "sampler" of popular-culture scholarship rooted in the social experience of the 1960s. Its contents originally appeared in *Cultural Correspondence* between 1975 and 1983. Scholars and journalists have written on at least some of the subjects discussed here, but our authors and artists share a premise still slow in denting formal criticism. American culture, at its best, has ever been the genius of the ordinary writ large. We have no other aesthetic sources. As in every society, people use the mechanisms and symbols accessible to them to make sense of their lives and to resolve—realistically or fancifully—the contradictions that beset them. For a variety of historical reasons, ordinary Americans have had a unique opportunity and a unique need to make the most of popular culture. Our purpose as intellectuals has been, then, to clarify the implications, good and bad, and to speculate about the ways in which these human and technical resources can be used to help push democracy toward its logical conclusions.

The writers in this volume condemn the manipulative qualities of commercial culture. But they just as vehemently reject nearly all of what has passed for Marxist (or liberal or conservative) orthodoxy on popular culture. To make their point, they seek out the exemplary moments when Mikhail Bakhtin's description of the Rabelaisian world of mass carnivalistic creativity takes new life in modern conditions or when Walter Benjamin's expectation that audience and artist will blend into one another is briefly realized. Our scholars often place themselves—their own lives—within the material. They make no claim to be definitive and have no intention of precluding the reader's own judgment. This is, as one contributor says of a Saturday morning 1940s' children's drama, a game anyone can play. They are seeking to establish an attitude, to begin once more at the beginning of understanding.

The foundation of all cultural criticism, Daniel Czitrom reminds us, rests upon the intellectual's ambivalent wish both to preserve an aesthetically meaningful culture and to uplift the masses.[1] The two terms of the duality have entwined themselves around the rise of interpretation and of radical politics, sometimes shifting sides, sometimes merging only to separate again. Modern culture, acting upon the intellectual, has pulled him or her one way and the other, from the vision of culture renewed to the vision of culture debased and barely surviving the masses' own degradation. The newer criticism, child of a romanticism as all-embracing as the original, is heir equally to both sides, both views. Its proponents and teachers include Novalis with Rousseau, Pound with Breton and Charlie Chaplin.

Matthew Arnold exemplifies the ambivalence at its historic origins, in the intellectuals' response to the early Industrial Revolution. Because Arnold considered culture's pursuit of perfection the substitute for religion lost to secular humankind, this aristocrat of taste grasped the fundamental logic of our fascination with mass culture. No matter that his imagined "sweetness and light" failed utterly to incorporate the blood and bowels of a real popular culture. Arnold had a mission: to make self-conscious the cultural developments already taking place and to make possible a worldview no less suited to the emerging environment than Homer's was to the ancient Greeks or Dante's to his contemporaries. Although Arnold repulsed the claims of philistine industrialists, he also denied the reductionism of the Left. Jacobinism viewed culture as "an impertinence and an offense," but precisely because culture holds something beyond the reach of the political process, it "really does the world and Jacobinism itself a service." Through culture's ministrations, radicalism had a future larger than mere economic triumph.[2]

On the other side of the class line from Arnold, contemporary socialist movements arose. New prophets preached the vindication of the protean mass driven or lured into the cities, confined to industrial drudgery, and palliated with cultural innovations. By Arnold's time, this population had already responded enthusiastically to feuilletons, stage shows, and penny sheet music. The mass thereby struggled for identity, as Martha Vicinus says, in a world beyond its control.[3] Socialist sentiments predicted the birth (in Marx's phrase) of a "new society within the shell of the old." But socialists hardly less than genteel critics eyed the actual culture suspiciously, increasingly so as eclectic utopianism passed into ordered, Marxist-influenced political movements. During the last quarter of the nineteenth century, the ascending socialist parties transformed religious iconography, folk melodies, and familiar national watchwords into the symbols for political mobilization. But they accomplished this wonder almost unconsciously, driven by the insight that only such adaptations could wean workers and their families away from the social institutions of the Right. Marx, Engels, and other early theoreticians viewed these experiments with undisguised anxiety. As concerned with class autonomy as Arnold had been with elite culture's autonomy, they felt an instinctive revulsion toward sentimentalism, toward the irrationalism and the foggy implications of the unknown emerging culture.[4]

The United States, with shallow historic traditions and a vibrant commercial culture, naturally became the prime site of unanticipated consequences. The absence of a feudal-historic past fixed dominant ideologies of the nation, for centuries after the colonial origins, to the Mosaic world of mythic paradise lost and (at least potentially) regained. This vision never suited the material realities, and it failed notoriously to address the curious limitations of American culture. A vibrant popular literature, organized sports, theatrical amusements, and music grew up with the first rudimentary appearance of mass leisure. But these amusements had a kind of inherent sub-rosa status, culture sanctioned neither by religious ethos nor by dominant economic classes. No dignity for an art representative of those classes, no European-style aesthetics, could possibly develop here. De Tocqueville, among others, noted the paucity of aesthetic achievement relative to the actual triumphs of democratic social life. The peculiar avant-garde, mentally restive transcendentalists, could not for all their brilliance reconcile the actual with the ideal or even inscribe an organic American worldview upon their own creations.

The kind of cultural fulfillment envisioned in Walt Whitman's *Democratic Vistas* foundered on the rock of commercial expansion, which made the craftsman a mere factory hand and the farmer a producer of cash crops for far-away markets. History had not delivered either a Garden of Eden with restored Adamic virtues or a nation of verse-singing artisans sure in their destiny. Instead, America had become a society already rich by existing world standards, bloated with corruption and sundered with assorted classes, races, and languages. Only commerce and culture brought these worlds together. Industrial democracy declined, in spite of heroic resistance, while the scale of production steadily widened.[5] But a crude cultural democracy burgeoned and it was as rich, diverse, and unself-conscious as the society around it.

According to Warren Susman, a revolution of sorts had already taken place. The "culture of abundance" had permeated middle-class society and moved steadily through the social fabric. Plenty, play, recreation, public relations, and celebrity tended to replace older key values such as hard work and self-denial. "Creating wants" became a major enterprise, even amid mass poverty; products of the culture, whether attainable by ordinary people or not, became advertisements for the society and were widely believed to be representative of the American way of life.[6]

The continuously revolutionized means of communication, a vital element in this process, set off public excitement and – for the first time – stirred scholarly curiosity. Major American intellectuals such as Charles Horton Cooley, John Dewey, and Robert Park envisioned programs through which a new social order could be engineered along functional, rational lines. The ordinary participants in the culture, by contrast, lived with and fostered cultural change through new entertainments such as the "movies," which found their earliest enthusiastic audience in immigrant neighborhoods, their matinee idol in the Little Tramp.[7]

There was something inherently radical in this departure – more than a hint of that new society within the shell of the old. But how could it be politically mobilized, brought to self-consciousness? Socialists, Wobblies, and, later, Communists had no better notion than the social scientists. Individual artists, cultural rebels squarely in touch with popular sentiment and committed to social transformation, probed the possibilities in an uncertain searching. Greenwich Village bohemians in 1910–25, Harlem intellectuals such as Claude McKay and Langston Hughes, activists of little-remembered ethnic cultures in their final American renaissance, radicals in Hollywood and on the stage, all worked instinctively with the tastes of their constituencies, the available technology, and the market reality. These varied intellectuals and culturalists willy-nilly took part in what Susman calls the "discovery of the idea of culture and its wide-scale application [as] a critical tool that could shape a critical idea."[8]

The delineation of this idea, almost as much as the utopian aspiration that lay behind it, remained unrealizable. Generations of rebels went down in political defeat, shorn of their illusions in the democratic process and in the collective model of foreign societies (most especially, the Soviet Union). Cultural criticism became the prerogative, the occupation, of peculiarly distaff radicals increasingly soured on all utopias. Clement Greenberg's 1939 essay, "Avant-Garde and Kitsch," defined one pole of the critique. The avant-garde, the West's unique creative invention, was being overwhelmed, swallowed up, by *kitsch*, pseudo-art for the masses. Neither folk culture nor European high culture could exist anymore, except in the museum sense. American popular culture increasingly resembled, in its manipulativeness and absence of humanistic values, totalitarian Stalinism. The struggle for freedom was a holding action, these critics suggested.[9]

Theodor Adorno, Max Horkheimer, and Herbert Marcuse of the exiled Frankfurt School defined the other pole. More dialectical in their treatment of civilized tradition, defiant in their idealism, they understood that culture's debacle had been inherent in the development of the West, the accompanying depersonalization actually a fulfillment of tendencies inevitable in the original division of mental and manual labor. The steady mechanization of work and leisure simply provided the means for realizing the inherent logic of the system. Adorno's famous self-criticism indicated that criticism itself was an evasion of the fundamental issue, reinforcing by its effort a passive, purist aestheticism. "What appears to be the decline of culture is its coming to pure self-consciousness," therefore, the illusion grown to larger-than-life size. Popularized in Herbert Marcuse's *One-Dimensional Man*, this exile's view seemed to portend a seamless web from which the very idea of escape had become treason to consciousness.[10]

Such a mordant expectation seemed to many intellectuals an apt response to the world situation after Auschwitz. But the older utopia of popular life made fresh claims upon consciousness. Postwar prosperity fostered a wide mass audience with money to spend and plunged the nation into a veritable golden age of popular culture. If by any critical standard the bad became worse, the very volume opened up new space for much of real value. Whereas Adorno condemned jazz—to his European taste, animalistic and degrading—contemporary European sophisticates increasingly admired the black contribution as the most authentic American art form. And whereas Edmund Wilson condemned the detective genre, Camus proclaimed the American detective the key inspiration for existentialism, the avant-garde philosophy of the age. Ordinary Americans, if they had read Adorno's attack upon cartoons as violent, degrading, and antidemocratic, could nevertheless see for themselves the continual victory of the underdog (mice over cats, and cats, squirrels, or rabbits over humans) through antics that resembled all the tricks used by the lower classes throughout history. Country music, black urban blues, film noir, and early television all bristled with their own contradictions, contesting intellectuals' claims to the end of history (or ideology), stirring their publics to new levels of expectation.[11]

Perhaps, as some historians argue, the political stasis of cold war America displaced social criticism into the entertainment itself. At any rate, the criticism that the "TV generation" first experienced came packaged as entertainment rather than erudition. Harvey Kurtzman, likely the most exacting comic-book editor in the industry's history, put together in *Mad Comics* a savage critique of those genres available to children and adolescents—that is, comics (then at an all-time peak in sales and variety), television, popular film, and yellow journalism. Ernie Kovacs, grand experimenter with television technique, practiced a similar style of analysis in his satirical gibes at the emerging commercial mannerisms. Soon adolescent sophisticates could imbibe Tom Lehrer, Jules Feiffer, and Lenny Bruce—immanent criticism with the kick of a mule.[12]

By contrast, they did not find much use in the cultural criticism available at the nearby public library. For more than thirty years, critic Gilbert Seldes's *The Seven Lively Arts* (1924) stood alone as a sympathetic treatment of popular culture, recognized but not taken particularly seriously. Communications research proceeded quietly during the 1930s and 1940s along sociological lines. According to Paul Lazarsfeld, a leading figure in this development, the cold war and then the Vietnam War put this initial research on hold. More likely, the vibrant elements of contemporary culture, from Jackie Gleason to rock and roll, remained on such different wavelengths from the reigning critics (and U.S. intellectuals in general), that no framework yet existed for interpretation except the unarticulated guidelines of artists and audience themselves.[13]

Mass Culture: The Popular Arts in America (1957), the earliest anthological classic, had, then, a curiously belated quality of intellectual discovery.[14] Only the rise of mass education made mass culture a "social issue" negotiable in the campus textbook market. Most of its contributors expressed their personal distaste or betrayed the uneasy feeling that they *should* feel distaste. Clement Greenberg complained, in the pages of the most prestigious liberal-socialist journal of the country, that even criticism of *kitsch* constituted a surrender to its repulsive charms. Young sociologist Herbert Gans could answer only that intellectuals had both right and duty to investigate something so socially important. "It is not the quality of the work that social scientists study," Gans argued, "but the ability of the work to attract the choices of the audience, and the reasons for it"–a characteristically value-free claim that shed a solemn light upon the minimal advance of a sympathetic interpretation.[15]

Events rather than intellectual inspiration moved the critical agenda forward. From one standpoint, the shift of consumerism into high gear, with 1950s' teenagers as the ideal constituency (treasured by society, endowed with cash, and striving for self-definition through product-identification), demonstrated the masterful power of the commodity. From another standpoint, the breakdown of racial insularity afforded new cultural input at just the moment when the ideology of home and family had seemingly reached its outer limits. Rock music, especially in its rawer forms, asserted group identity against the propriety of existing aesthetic and disciplinary codes. This revenge from the presumed beneficiaries of cold war prosperity coincided with a growing sense of unease that would take a variety of forms during the 1960s.

The Civil Rights movement, placing the stamp of indigenous radicalism upon a compelling religious zeal and a tenacious folk cul-

Paul Buhle

ture, soon inspired a burst of youthful idealism across the nation. Whites who discovered their generational identity through black music felt a unique resonance in antiracist appeals. Political involvement and personal change had already been linked; as the 1960s progressed, no one could say which was more important for the rebellious college students, which cause and which effect. After 1967, radical arts, sexual emancipation, clothing styles, and the vision of imminent political transformation marched together in a mass-culture reprise of old-fashioned political bohemianism.[16]

The conjunction of Marshall McLuhan and the "media politics" of the later 1960s confirmed for many younger intellectuals (and nonintellectuals) the correctness of their instincts. By insisting that the print media had transformed Renaissance Europe and that electronic media would likewise transform the modern world, the Canadian conservative broke down the final barriers of intellectual resistance against careful attention to popular culture. Nearly every home in the U.S. had at least one television set by 1960 and access to national network news by 1963. The nightly "body count," the surging antiwar movement, the ghetto riots, and the Kent State Massacre all made the catchphrase "The whole world is watching" seemingly determinative proof of the media's many-sided impact.[17]

The dampening of expectations (or fears) raised by social conflict and dramatized or even (contrary to McLuhan's definition of the "cool medium") heightened by television did not quell the flow of cultural discussion. On the contrary, description and debate of popular culture became almost a national craze. Again according to Lazarsfeld, and this time more accurately, the discussion suspended at the beginning of the 1950s amid heated political issues reopened with the eclipse of social confrontation and the appearance of new technological accoutrements such as cable television and inexpensive cassette players.[18] As later dramatized by the counterposition of driving 1960s' music and somnambulent Yuppie confusion in the hit film *The Big Chill*, key symbolic cultural tastes almost froze in time so as to maintain the illusions of a vanished authenticity. Subsequent social life, for millions among the largest and most prosperous generation in U.S. history, became a commodified meditation on an unforgettable past.

Introduction: The 1960s Meet the 1980s

A marked breakdown of linear fashion in music, clothing, and interior design soon emerged—not as a mere remixing of antique fads but as a conscious recuperation of styles with their original ambience, a postmodernism of the mass consumer. The proliferation of flea markets, the salvaging and sales of every remotely defined "collectible," offered a particularly manic expression of the impulse to recover something lost in the junkyards and attics of American consciousness. Likewise, and on a scale dwarfing all similar phenomena, television syndication brought Lucy and Ralph Kramden into the world of "All in the Family" and "M*A*S*H," themselves soon to join the artifacts infinitely accessible to the culture consumer.[19]

A noteworthy mea culpa by literary historian-critic Leslie Fiedler in 1970, regretting his own (and, in effect, his entire generation of critics') condescension toward popular culture, meanwhile suggested a changing academic atmosphere.[20] Instructors were no longer embarrassed to show historic popular films in class as documents worthy of serious consideration. Dissertations began to appear on popular-culture topics in American Studies, History, English, Sociology, and other fields. The Popular Culture Association's yearly conventions began to look more like Star Trek "trekkie" gatherings of fans and stars than like the MLA.

One particular scholarly development steered refugees from 1960s' activism toward 1970s' scholarship. Social history absorbed the tensions of the period by overthrowing the cold war, unitary view of the American past as the democratic triumph of a middle class and pluralist but essentially assimilated, homogenized society. A more complex interpretation, incorporating anthropological definitions of culture and fresh interpretations of women, minorities, and the working class, came to the fore. Newer studies stressed less the traditional institutional delving of parties, unions, or famous men than the way the masses of ordinary folk lived out their lives, how they understood their world and their prospects. Documentation led to the recovery and interpretation of forgotten song lyrics, slogans, little signs of self-consciousness and discontent, and collective resistance, whether in times of open conflict or of simple endurance. The developing view required no Marxist *telos* to render the

Paul Buhle

lives of the subjects worthy of understanding. Should the history of the human race end in disaster, past efforts to achieve dignity and to make life full would lose none of their real importance. More to the point, the eventual rebuilding of a force for democratic social change demanded an understanding less remote than Marxism and less superficial than the hastily developed slogans of the 1960s. "TV generation" radicals-turned-scholars naturally approached the problem from a distinct viewpoint: Sartre might have called it the search for a techno-organic method.[21]

Here, in the dual experience of historical insight and updated culture critique, can be found the definitive roots of *Cultural Correspondence* and of this anthology. The original editors had long mulled over the influence of comics, popular music, good mass-market films, interesting television, and factory-made hallucinogenics on their own personal development. They watched the less self-conscious younger generation come of age in the heady later 1960s, with the semidetachment that Adorno described as the natural stance of the critic. They instinctively inclined, by virtue of taste and political commitment, toward a certain fondness for the Springsteenesque blue-collar culture roiled by suburbanization and the effects of Vietnam but still surprisingly intact and full of rich memories. The collapse of the New Left presented them a political fait accompli. But they looked around themselves, at their experiences and understanding, for a conceptual way out.

From a Hegelian standpoint, history did not stop. Therefore, the socialization of leisure, like the socialization of labor that Marx had posited, necessarily contained a dynamic for transformation. By reexamining a maligned, misunderstood past and present through a fresh perspective, they might save the philosophical kernel of Marxist socialism from its increasingly archaic shell and, in so doing, turn the Frankfurt School on its head. The aphorism in Adorno's final and most personal text, *Minima Moralia*, would come to mean its opposite: "That there is no longer a folk does not mean . . . as the Romantics have propagated, that the masses are worse. Rather, it is precisely in the new, radically alienated form of society that the untruth of the old is first being revealed."[22] The old untruth exposed a new truth. Mass culture had educated the masses, in some way not yet fully understood. Founding coeditor Dave Wagner, struggling in our first issue with the possibilities, sought abstractions equal to the concept:

That mass culture . . . is, taken as a whole, a total response by Capital to the historical possibilities of the specifically modern mass which it first creates and which now continues to create itself.

That the culture of the masses in its quotidian is objectively and historically concrete; that is, both in its aspect as the subjectivity of capital objectifying itself for consumption . . . and in its aspect as a response to the demand for objective and historical self-recognition by the mass in its daily life.

That the mass concretizes its demand for objective self-recognition first in the interstices of daily life, i.e., mass cultural production . . . and later by endorsing its own creation in their mediated or alienated forms as capital appropriates their movement in its interstices with the movement of its own subjectivity (i.e., the market).

That the objective recognition of their own subjectivity on the part of the masses is covert, disguised and mediated by individuality in the process by which it continually moves in this guise toward the overt form of universal subjectivity.[23]

The difficulty of phraseology indicates not only a close (perhaps overly close) reading of Hegel but also the degree of intellectual isolation in this particular approach. Young social historians, lively exmilitants, feminist scholars, and others shared the general sentiment but shied away from philosophical conclusions; the philosophers, even the radical philosophers, possessed a cerebral and Euro-centered conception that forebade equal time between Husserl and Stevie Wonder. The cultural journals, Old Left-gone-Center (the *Partisan Review*) and the newer crop of post-New Left products, stayed with close literary studies and treated mass culture, when at all, with a certain disdain.

Fortunately we had a personal inspiration among the first rank of radical thinkers and cultural critics, our own philosopher-king of mass society. C. L. R. James—pioneering West Indian novelist, distinguished forefather of Pan-African history, famed cricket historian and critic, advisor to Third World heads of state—had made alliance with us a few years earlier. *Radical America*, our common meeting ground, served for a time as the unofficial journal of Students for a Democratic Society and of James, our "discovery," a Marxist of no compromise with class society of any kind and no compromise with cultural philistinism of any kind either. Probably no stranger combination could be found in the strange 1960s than this septuagenarian "Black Plato" (as the press would call him later) and we youngish, ruminative rock and rollers.[24]

James based his unquenched revolutionary optimism on what Frederick Engels had called "the invading socialist society," the appearance of advanced social relations within the existing order. The old forms of radical expression—reform politics, unions, state ownership of production in some countries—had, James argued in the 1940s–1950s, become part of the logic of continued capitalist (or state-capitalist) development. New forms of self-expression arose from the social relations that ordinary people had established within their workaday lives. No one could predict the new phase, he preached, but closer observation of ordinary people, respect for their effort to understand and change the world around them, would permit an adequate view of the emerging possibilities. That meant for him, avid cricket fan, Calypso-lover, and (in his old age) television watcher, a constant eye upon the dialectic between mass politics and culture. For us, his disciples, it meant observation of our own immediate environment.

An earlier and more numerous set of James's disciples had in early 1950s' Detroit published a newspaper called *Correspondence*. Named after a 1920s' Left attempt to foster direct "workers' correspondence" in the pages of a mostly ethnic radical press, the James paper sought to speak for and through the average blue-collar reader about the mundane questions of life, from television, sports, and husband-wife quarrels to such weighty subjects as current race problems and world politics. *Cultural Correspondence*, originally conceived in the three-decker urban district of Somerville, Massachusetts, had no such class pretensions. But we sought a common understanding among like-minded types in our political circles, people whose experiences roughly bridged the intellectual and blue-collar worlds.

We believed at first that a political revival would lend an immediate practicality to, as the subtitle read, our "strategic journal of popular culture." Alas for such illusions. *Cultural Correspondence* soon became a laboratory to study mass society but without the required institutional base to sustain any new school of thought. Strictly speaking, we lived up to our title (future editor Jim Murray would say, "Culture is what we live, Correspondence is what we seek") by achieving a political community of sorts, amid continued disintegration of the larger political milieu. Realistically we had an ephemeral magazine on our hands. Had we been Germans, we might have continued somehow mining the veins of dialectical philosophy, applying the results rather abstractly to the subject. But, as middle Americans, we found our contribution through our indulgence of the particular.

A post-New Left generation, a little too young for the activist 1960s but moved by the same democratic impulses, had meanwhile proceeded to their dissertations, where (unlike ourselves almost a decade earlier) they felt free to study a wide variety of popular-culture phenomena, from nurse novels to sitcoms. Sharp observers of the particular, unburdened by any political hangovers, they added fresh inspiration to our pages. Their generational kin, still in school or just interested in our approach, became the largest portion of our readership, which peaked at around 3,000. Together we explored subjects of common interest until cash and energy ran out.[25]

Cultural Correspondence had arrived and, in the form we intended it, also departed too early for its own good. By the mid-1980s, these younger scholars and the burgeoning journalists of popular culture constituted a critics' group of significant size and sophistication, if little mutual contact. Readers of the *Village Voice*, *American Film*, even the *New York Times* could find a sustained, serious, and frequently sympathetic treatment of familiar *Cultural Correspondence* subjects. Instructors in television and other courses had a handful of good, accessible books to assign, with more on the way. Some of the books' authors, more of the emerging schol-

Paul Buhle

ars, and a handful of the journalists in fact grew and grew out of that old *Cultural Correspondence* milieu. We had brought them together, helped crystallize an intellectual development in the making. In a nutshell, we had arguably been the first political journal of culture to assume its readers (and writers) *watched* television; a small point but one with large implications.

On the other side of the question, as Fredric Jameson has argued, the ultimate disintegration of modernism's aura has served to dispel the last illusions of an old-style avant-garde. As Jameson says, "aesthetic production today has become integrated into commodity production generally"—indeed, become a necessity of the ever-expanding consumer market.[26] The much-deplored blending of advertising and art likewise "deconstructs" ideological design and makes both accessible in new ways. The very arbitrariness of the self in a society on the verge of technological transformation and/or nuclear doom prompts the shared insight that our collective view of identity is a successive series of self-determinations. The triumph of the merchandizer, from the Oval Office to the corner video shop, has certainly flattened our reality. But the flatness permits a wide perspective. By Adorno's formula, capitalism has become obvious in what it always was; the great change lies in the people who have grown up with a kind of perceptual, cognitive sophistication previously inconceivable.

The appearance of new-style cultural criticism, thousands of copyshop "punkzines" radiating rearranged images of daily life, offers recent proof. Published by energetic postadolescents, the "zines" (adapting their nomenclature from the mimeographed science-fiction "fanzines" of the 1940s–1970s) neither dispute the triumphal consumer ideology nor lay social hopes against war and ecological Armageddon. Rather, they arbitrarily assign new values in the original Dada fashion, by counterposition and subtle alteration, exposing an immanent reality behind the advertisers' sales-logic.[27] Nearly a century since the beginning of the process Warren Susman described as the sea change of modern culture, arcane magazine advertisements for dish detergents, army life, or machine tools offer premium artistic raw material.

This is emphatically not the historical sensibility envisioned in the original *Cultural Correspondence*. But the punkzines, like the popular-culture scholarship, are stepchildren of our intentions nevertheless. As Perry Anderson has written, the crisis of twentieth-century radical theory has been marked by steadily advancing penetrations into the subject, to the point where—notably in poststructuralism—we have "subjectivism without a subject"—a maze of unsolvable mysteries about humanity and society.[28] If this so-called crisis of historicity has become absolute, the reduction of all social evidence to popular images irreversible, then the images must perforce finally be seen as more than arbitrary blips on the screen of modern consciousness. *Cultural Correspondence* no. 1 set forth the notion that the very devastation of "timelessness" previously reserved to bourgeois art now freed the products of mass culture for a new kind of historicity, their real relations with the lives of their users now transparent symbols of larger meanings.[29]

Cultural Correspondence was only a rudimentary beginning. Nevertheless, we advanced the effort to untangle the knot of commodity fetishism, to posit a socialization of culture similar to the socialization of labor a century earlier. That we did so in a particular way—not through abstractions but through the pleasures of ordinary people's lives—speaks to our origins and training. If the "new society within the old" can still emerge from under the shadow of nuclear war and ecological destruction, its images will surely be found here.

Notes

1. Daniel Czitrom, *Media and the American Mind, from Morse to McLuhan* (Chapel Hill, 1982), 33.
2. "Culture and Anarchy," in *Poetry and Criticism of Matthew Arnold*, edited by A. Dwight Culler (Boston, 1961), 425.
3. Martha Vicinus, *The Industrial Muse: A Study of Nineteenth Century British Working-Class Culture* (New York, 1974).
4. The most updated treatment is in Horst Groschopp, "Kulturarbeit und Kulturarbeiter in der Geschichte der deutschen Arbeiterbewegung vor 1914," in *Der Sozialistische Kulturarbeiter, Mitteilungen aus der Kulturwissenschaftlichen Forschung Nr.12* (Berlin, 1983), 5–52. See also S. S. Prawer, *Karl Marx and World Literature* (London, 1976); Paul Lafargue, "Appendix: Marx and Literature," in Karl Marx and Frederick Engels, *Literature and Art: Selections from Their Writings* (New York, 1947).

5. See, for instance, Herbert G. Gutman, *Work, Culture and Society in Industrializing America* (New York, 1976).

6. Warren I. Susman, *Culture as History: The Transformation of American Society in the Twentieth Century* (New York, 1984), xxiv.

7. Robert Sklar, *Movie-Made America: How the Movies Changed American Life* (New York, 1975), chap. 1.

8. See Susman, "The Culture of the Thirties," in *Culture as History*, 173–77.

9. Clement Greenberg, "Avant-Garde and Kitsch," in *Mass Culture*; Irving Howe, *World of Our Fathers* (New York, 1976), 598–607.

10. Max Horkheimer and Theodor W. Adorno, *Dialectic of Enlightenment*, translated by John Cumming (New York, 1972); Theodor W. Adorno, *Prisms*, translated by Samuel and Shierry Weber (London, 1967), 24.

11. *Cultural Correspondence* founding coeditor Dave Wagner captured this line of thought best in his "Interview with Donald Duck," *Radical America* 7 (Jan.-Feb. 1973), in which the famous duck (as a retired Hollywood progressive) genially takes apart Adorno's mistaken views. See also George Lipsitz, *Class and Culture in Cold War America: "A Rainbow at Midnight"* (S. Hadley, Mass., 1982), chaps. 9–10.

12. See Paul Buhle, "Harvey Kurtzman: Interview," in "Jewish Humor," edited by Paul Buhle, in a special issue of *SHMATE* 6 (Summer 1983).

13. See Seldes's invaluable memoirs *en passant* in the second edition of *The Seven Lively Arts* (New York, 1957); Paul Lazarsfeld, Introduction to *Mass Culture Revisited*.

14. *Mass Culture: The Popular Arts in America*, edited by Bernard Rosenberg and David Manning White (New York, 1957).

15. Greenberg, "Pop Culture and Kitsch Criticism," *Dissent* 5 (Winter 1958); Gans, "Popular Culture and High Culture Critics," ibid (Spring 1958), 186. See also Gans's full-length version of this defense, *Popular Culture and High Culture: An Analysis and Evaluation of Taste* (New York, 1974).

16. Literature has just begun to appear on the entire subject. See, for example, *The 60s without Apology*, edited by S. Sayres, A. Stephanson, S. Aronowitz, F. Jameson (Minneapolis, 1984).

17. Best conveyed in Czitrom, *Media and the American Mind*, chap. 6.

18. Lazarsfeld, Introduction, vii–viii.

19. The vernacular version of postmodernism has received virtually no attention. See F. Jameson's high-culture variant, "The Cultural Logic of Capital," *New Left Review* 146 (July–Aug. 1984).

20. Introduction to George Lippard's *The Monks of Monk Hall*, edited by Fiedler (New York, 1970 ed.).

21. Along with Gutman's work, cited above, outstanding examples include Alan Dawley, *Class and Community: The Industrial Revolution in Lynn* (Cambridge, 1976) and the essays collected in Hartmut Keil and John Jentz, eds., *German Workers in Industrial Chicago, 1850–1910* (DeKalb, 1983).

22. Theodor W. Adorno, *Minima Moralia: Reflections from a Damaged Life*, translated by E. F. N. Jephcott (London, 1974), 204.

23. Dave Wagner, "Philosophical Steps," in *Cultural Correspondence* 1 (Aug. 1975), 12.

Introduction: The 1960s Meet the 1980s

24. Paul Buhle, Introduction to *15 Years of Radical America, An Anthology*, edited by Paul Buhle, *Radical America* 16 (May-June 1982); and the following interpretive essays on James's cultural perspective: Sylvia Wynter, "In Quest of Matthew Bondsman: Some Cultural Notes on the Jamesian Journey"; Dan Georgakas, "Young Detroit Radicals"; Dave Wagner, "Philosophy and Culture"; and Wilson Harris, "A Unique Marxist Thinker," in *C. L. R. James: His Life and Work*, edited by Paul Buhle (London, 1986).

25. Contrary to expectations and public announcements, *Cultural Correspondence* did not come to an end with the collapse of the old administration. Jim Murray, publisher of the lively cultural commentary *Jim's Letter* and prominent activist in the political arts movement of the 1980s, seized the helm and turned the magazine onto a new course. It has generally ceased to have a historical and scholarly interest in popular culture as such. But it appears just as irregularly as before. *Cultural Correspondence*, New Series, has evolved into a sort of documentary and strategic expression of the political arts movement, with a marked fondness for the original inspirer of the magazine, C. L. R. James.

26. Jameson, "The Cultural Logic of Capital," 70.

27. See, for instance, David James, "Poetry/Punk Production: Some Recent Writing in L.A.," *Minnesota Review* N.S. 23 (Fall 1984); and Paul Buhle, "Invasion of the Punkzines," *Village Voice Literary Supplement* (June 1982). *The Book of the Sub-Genius* (New York, 1983), edited and mostly written by Ivan Stang a.k.a. Doug Smith, is the master text of sanctified advertising and the most available of the punkzine writing and collage texts.

28. Perry Anderson, *In the Tracks of Historical Materialism* (London, 1984), 54.

29. Wagner, "Philosophical Steps," 12–13.

Overviews

Tristan Meinecke *Amerika* (assemblage)

TV Critic's Code

David Marc

Television, for bad or worse, is the national culture of twentieth-century America. To deny the fact is poor research. To ignore the fact is suicidal politics. I, would-be upwardly mobile lower-class New York City graduate student, have personally stood in front of more than one class of Iowa farm-kid freshpersons and, on the first day of class, have lectured on television texts so obscure as to be analogous to the subtle literary allusions of a doctoral level seminar in eighteenth-century literature. I have been not only understood by the class members but taken to task by them for my opinions.

The television critic must take his cues from Whitman. He must go among the people and lend his training and sensibility to the new experiences of life with the machine. What is this machine after all if not merely the latest evolutionary product of the biopool? To ignore television is to follow the heritage of William Cullen Bryant and Henry Wadsworth Longfellow: to write whimsical European lyrics while the vast and wild new environment of the continent—fraught as it is with dangers and possibilities—lies at one's heels. A modern-day Whitman would have to watch television or else be forced to give up his connection to the masses of people who find their wishes, dreams, and role models therein.

Perhaps television has become the "ordeal" of the American scholar, in Van Wyck Brooks's sense of the word. To refuse to watch has become the bottomline of the Old Gentility. To make believe that American television can be measured by the "standards" of the ballets and British stage productions of PBS (laughingly called the "Petroleum Broadcasting System" in advertising circles) is perhaps worse; a tragicomic species of Neo-Gentility. For me, television is organic. It was more "there" than the trees and rivers themselves in the world into which I was born. To reject it out of hand would be historical voyeurism; a kind of bourgeois nostalgia; even nihilism. Would the boost in self-image be worth the loss of my past? If I do not make my past usable, it will continue to use me. The critic born after World War II is born with television, yet everywhere he is in blinders. To confront television has become merely the refusal to deny nature. Television awaits its Wordsworth who can skip through its wavy woods making sense of its light and dark.

Edward Shils accuses those "who know better," and yet still give their critical attention to works of mass culture, of indulging in a "continuation of childish pleasures"; of cultivating an easy connoisseurship that makes them "folksy" and flaunts their rebellion against the rigor and aridity of the "high" culture which their parents, teachers, and the cultural ruling classes once tried to impose on them. As if the parents did not buy the sets that sit in 97% of American homes! As if the "cultural ruling classes" were not the networks and advertising agencies top-heavy with Ivy League graduates! As if the scorn of teachers does not itself signal the highest form of validation in American culture!

It is this kind of patronizing thinking on the part of Shils and others that allows for such an easy alliance between capital and the university intellectual. It has been an inexhaustible source of strength for the networks and their advertisers to be able to tinker so grandly with American culture beneath the upturned nose of the very intellectual who is perhaps the individual best equipped to make an appraisal of their handiwork.

The choice is clear: to turn one's back, like Eliot, on the exasperating present and make of culture study a tiresomely elegant and clever deconstruction of an imagined finite, static whole, locked away in the distant and safeguarded tower of the ivied cathedral, or to place oneself in the shabby livingroom of the present and begin the struggle to make sense of the endless parade of artificed images that relentlessly marches before our eyes. Eliot's primary cultural determinants—religion and ethnicity—pale as cultural indicators in the face of the choices offered by *TV Guide*. Even the more recent cultural signifiers—income, education, occupation, sex, and age— are becoming subsumed in the face of multichannel cable systems, which are attempting to recognize, pacify, and finally obliterate such avenues of identification as viable arenas of individual (human) expression. Yet television, beneath the powerful aura that sends intellectuals scurrying to their fallout shelters, is just a machine; a tool with no mind. The same knife that is flaying apart the cultural guts of America can be used to carve pluralities of artworks.

As Herbert Gans has pointed out, all human beings have aesthetic urges and are receptive to symbolic expressions of their wishes and fears. Will the humanist critic (critic of the humanities) leave the recuperation of these symbolic expressions to the social scientist, whose primary concern is merely to measure the effect of the text on those nameless others "the masses"? If the term humanist means anything, those who accept the label must make their voices heard.

I would submit that all the "validated" empirical analyses of the effects of mass culture on the masses aren't worth a damn because the social scientist is merely playing what has become Madison Avenue's own game—and nobody beats the dealer. Numbers are abstract symbols and nobody can manipulate them with more facility than the corporations whose very existence is predicated on them. Only the personal, critical, autobiographical testimony of individuals impassioned and trained to identify and evaluate the individual texts of authors and their relationships to each other can pierce the relentless, habituating *imago mundi* emanating from the scores of millions of receivers that fill every crevice of the republic with their highly deliberate, humanly conceived sights and sounds. Like Plato, the Catholic church, the Puritans, and the Soviets, the literary elite of the U.S. now trembles with fear that "civilization" (i.e., rational moral standards) can be completely undermined by a medium of expression. If anything, one would think that such a view would make a counterstatement an even more pressing project. But we must also remember that the dime novels that caused such horrors to the New Humanists (most of them far less complex in concept or imagination than many television shows) were eventually recovered by Henry Nash Smith as a fertile compost heap of the national imagination.

Perhaps most important is the fact that television simply will not disappear. Forget that. Instead, its own poets—and critics— must arise, Cincinnatuslike, from the masses and begin the guerrilla work.

Dialectical Tensions in the American Media Past and Present

Daniel Czitrom

In the post-McLuhan era, which is to say, since about 1965, an emerging consciousness of the importance of a strange beast known as "the media" has accompanied the enlarged role played by modern communication in everyday life. Yet so much of the discourse about "the media," in learned journals as well as in informal conversation, suffers from fuzziness, lack of clarity, and a jumble of definitions. Think, for example, of the ways in which the noun "media" finds increasing expression as an adjective, as in "media event," "media people," and "media hype." Think, too, of the various usages of the noun form. The original modern sense of "media" dates, interestingly enough, from its use in advertising trade journals of the 1920s—as in "advertising media."

But today the term is used interchangeably with "the press" or the journalistic profession, especially in the sense of investigative reporting. At the same time, "media" is often used to distinguish nonprint forms of communication, such as film and broadcasting, from print forms. It may connote the larger realms of entertainment and show business. Denunciations of "the media" as too liberal, too permissive, too conservative, or too manipulative invoke the term as a moral or political category. Most everyone engages in damning "the media" for glorifying, exaggerating, or even causing some particularly odious feature of modern life.

Confusion of the singular and plural forms – "medium" and "media" – surely reflects a popular perception of the incestuous relations among the various mass disseminators of words and images. Their contents are remarkably reflexive; each medium is filled with content from and about the other media. The bourgeois commercial nexus at the center of the American film, broadcast, and press industries clearly encourages this situation. It also promotes the sense of "the media" as a total, unchanging, "natural" part of modern life. Indeed, the everywhere-ness, all-at-once-ness, and never-ending-ness of "the media" are powerful barriers to understanding, or even acknowledging, their history.

The fact that "the media" evokes such diverse meanings represents a linguistic legacy of the contradictory elements embedded in the history of all modern means of communication; each medium is a matrix of institutional development, popular responses, and cultural content which ought to be understood as a product of dialectical tensions – of opposing forces and tendencies clashing and evolving over time, with things continually giving rise to their opposite. These contradictions have been expressed, broadly speaking, in terms of the tension between the progressive, even utopian, possibilities offered by new communications technologies and their disposition as instruments of domination and exploitation. A central theme of *Cultural Correspondence* over the years has been how that tension manifests itself specifically through struggles in and over American popular culture.

There is a need to recover the historical elements of an as yet uncompleted dialectic – not only as an aid to understanding the present configuration of American media but also as a possible guide to making sense of the imminent upheaval to be wrought by new cable, video, and satellite technologies. What follows is a historical sketch of some dialectical tensions in American media as viewed from the three related standpoints of early institutional developments, early popular responses, and the cultural history of media content. I have drawn examples mainly from three media whose histories I know best: the telegraph, motion pictures, and radio. Last, I have offered some thoughts on how the historical perspective might help us gain insight into the implications of the latest rash of technological breakthroughs. My interest is less in presenting a static, grand theory than in stimulating discussion and action concerning the new fields of play soon to open up in three main areas: decentralized distribution networks, greater individual control over hardware, and opportunities for innovative programming.

1

Considered as institutions, each of the media evolved from the work of individual inventors and entrepreneurs later subsumed into larger corporate and/or military contexts. The key roles played by small concerns and amateurs in the early history of new communications technologies is too often forgotten. Yet, clearly, the importance of the corporate and military settings for technological progress, supported by large capitalization and highly organized research teams, intensifies the closer one gets to the present.

Samuel F. B. Morse's perfection of a practical electric telegraph was a lonely and poverty-stricken venture. For six years after the 1838 demonstration of a workable instrument, Morse failed to obtain any government or corporate subsidy for his work. The Congress finally authorized a $30,000 appropriation to build the first telegraph line in 1844; but in refusing Morse's offer to buy him out, Congress thwarted his wish that the government control future telegraph development. The ensuing 25 years of wildcat speculation and construction, both fiercely competitive and wasteful, finally ended with the triumph of Western Union—the first of several natural communications monopolies to rest in private hands.

In the case of motion pictures, one finds a larger group of individual inventors and small businessmen acting as catalysts for technological innovation. The variety of cameras and projectors used in the early years reflected the contributions of numerous inventors from around the world. Capital investment in the early years of the industry, as well as its creative energy, came largely from petit bourgeois immigrant film exhibitors and distributors. They were eager to invest in the new "amusement," which was beneath the dignity of traditional sources of capital. With origins deep in the gritty cauldron of urban commercial amusements, motion pictures found their first audiences mainly in the ethnic and working-class districts of the large cities.

Each early attempt at standardizing or licensing equipment, films, and distribution was undermined by successive waves of "independents." The Motion Picture Patents Company, heavily capitalized and dominated by the Edison interests, appeared to be invincible when it was formed in 1909. But it lasted only a few years. The Hollywood film colony, later the symbol of authority and rigid control, was originally founded by independents seeking to escape the grip of the Patents Company. The fluidity of the movie industry was permanently altered when sound was introduced in the late 1920s. "Talkies" helped to solidify the hold of a few major studios since the technological complexity of sound production precluded the sort of independent activity that characterized the early years.

Individual inventors and amateurs figured prominently in the first years of radio as well. Pioneers such as Marconi, De Forest, and Fessenden laid much of the foundation for wireless technology in small, personal research settings. The technological sophistication required for wireless telephony (transmission of speech), as well as the needs of the military in World War I, encouraged more systematic and heavily financed research and development. Still, it is worth remembering that an important part of the strategy of large corporations such as AT&T and GE involved buying out and intimidating individual inventors—the most famous case being the notorious dealings of AT&T with Lee De Forest.

World War I had encouraged a boom in radio research, with close cooperation between AT&T, GE, Westinghouse, and the federal government, and it had directly led to the creation of RCA. But the emergence of broadcasting in 1920 came as a shock. Virtually no one had expected broadcasting—the sending of uncoded messages to a mass audience—to become the main use of wireless technology. By 1926 corporate infighting in the radio world resolved itself, leaving in its wake the basic structure of today's commercial television. AT&T agreed to abandon broadcasting directly, selling its station WEAF to RCA. AT&T won RCA's assurance that it would drop plans to build an independent long line system of wires. In addition, RCA, GE, and Westinghouse set up the National Broadcasting Company (devoted exclusively to broadcasting) and contracted to lease the AT&T web of wires. NBC, with this powerful corporate backing, began offering the first regular national broadcasting over two networks based in New York.

2

The dream of transcendence through machines is an ancient one, and the urge toward annihilating space and time found particularly intense expression with new communications media. Overcoming old constraints of time and space implied a great deal beyond mere advances in physics. Generally speaking, popular reactions to dramatic improvements in communication emphasized the possibilities for strengthening a moral community and celebrated the conquering of those vast social and cultural distances that had traditionally kept the large majority of people isolated.

An especially strong utopian cast marked contemporary responses to the telegraph and wireless. The public greeted the first telegraph lines of the 1840s with a combination of pride, excitement, and sheer wonder. In dozens of cities and towns, as telegraph construction proceeded quickly in all directions, doubters, believers, and the merely curious flocked to get a firsthand look. In 1844 Alfred Vail, Morse's assistant, reported that at the Baltimore end of their experimental line crowds besieged the office daily for a glimpse of the machine. They promised "they would not say a word or stir and didn't care whether they understood or not, only they wanted to say they had seen it." Noting the large numbers of people visiting the first Philadelphia telegraph office in 1846, a local paper concluded, "It is difficult to realize, at first, the importance of a result so wholly unlike anything with which we have been familiar; and the revolution to be effected by the annihilation of time . . . will not be appreciated until it is felt and seen."

Daniel Czitrom

Paeans to the liberating potential of the "lightning lines," stressing the telegraph's inherent possibilities for furthering community, found frequent expression in the spiritual and religious metaphors used to describe its wonders. "Universal communication" became the key phrase in these exhortations; the electric telegraph promised a unity of interest, human beings linked by a single mind. By successfully harnessing the "subtle spark" of electricity latent in all forms of matter, humans became more godlike. "Piercing so the secret of Nature," as one commentator put it, "man makes himself symmetrical with nature. Penetrating to the working of creative energies, he becomes himself a creator."

Successful completion of the first Atlantic cable in the summer of 1858 inspired spontaneous and planned celebrations around the country. Such intense public feeling over a technological achievement appears rather strange to us now; certainly it is difficult to envision such a reaction today. Bonfires, fireworks, and impromptu parades marked the occasion across the nation. New York City held a huge parade on September 1, 1858, described as the city's largest public celebration. Over 15,000 people, from working men's clubs, immigrant societies, temperance groups, and the like, marched in a procession that revealed the strength of the telegraph's hold on the public imagination.

Those who celebrated the promise of "universal communication" frequently expressed a sense of the miraculous when describing the telegraph. They subtly united the technological advance in communication with the ancient meaning of that word as common participation or communion. They presumed the triumph of certain "messages"; but they also suggested that the creation of a new communications technology, "the wonderful vehicle," was perhaps itself the most important message of all.

A more privatized form of utopian response greeted the first wireless devices of the 1890s and early 1900s. In the writings of scientists, amateur enthusiasts, and trade publications, one finds repeated projections of how wireless technology would soon be tailored to fit the personal needs of operators. The English engineer William Ayrton suggested in 1901 that eventually everyone might possess his own wireless transmitter and receiver, so that:

Dialectical Tensions in the American Media

If a person wanted to call a friend he knew not where, he would call in a loud, electro-magnetic voice, heard by him who had the electro-magnetic ear, silent to him who had it not. 'Where are you?' he would say. A small reply would come, 'I am at the bottom of a coal mine, or crossing the Andes, or in the middle of the Pacific.' Let them think what that meant, of the calling which went on every day from room to room of a house, and then think of that calling extending from pole to pole; not a noisy babble, but a call audible to him who wanted to hear and absolutely silent to him who did not.

Today we think of radio as synonymous with broadcasting, but in the first years after the earliest broadcasts, the amateur wireless community scoffed at the idea that radio ought to be dominated by a few big stations. The activity of wireless amateurs from around 1907 through the late 1920s is too often neglected as a factor in the history of radio. The "hams" provided a crucial demand for wireless equipment, supplying the original seed capital and audience for the radio industry. They bought radio equipment and kept up with the latest technical advances before and after the first broadcasting. This group numbered perhaps a quarter of a million around 1920, including some 15,000 amateur transmitting stations.

Throughout the 1920s, "radio mania" remained an active, participatory pastime for millions of people. One had to constantly adjust and rearrange batteries, crystal detectors, and vacuum tubes for the best reception. For numerous radio fans of all classes, the excitement lay precisely in the battle to get clear reception amid the howling and chatter of thousands of amateurs and larger stations. The practice of "DXing," trying to receive the most distant station possible, remained strong for years. As one newly converted radio fan wrote in 1924, the various programs interested him very little: "In radio it is not the substance of communication without wires, but the fact of it that enthralls. It is a sport, in which your wits, learning, and resourcefulness are matched against the endless perversity of the elements. It is not a matter, as you may suppose, of buying a set and tuning in upon what your fancy dictates."

By the end of the 1920s, however, the triumph of corporate-dominated commercial broadcasting radically curtailed this sort of

---

13

radio activity. Broadcasting, originally conceived by manufacturers as a service and a means of getting people to buy radio equipment, eventually shoved aside the very people who had nurtured it. In its mature state, radio succeeded not in fulfilling the utopian visions first aroused by wireless technology but in appropriating those urges into the service of advertising. Commercial broadcasting, first with radio and then television, became the cutting edge of a technologized ideology of consumption. That ideology, which played off of a distorted version of utopian hopes, reiterated a basic message that what one had was never enough. It created the need for products in large part through an appeal to a mythical past – lost community, lost intimacy, lost self-assurance. Consumer goods promised to make one happy by returning what had vanished. Commercial broadcasting needed the advertiser's message to older popular cultural forms made historically specific for the new home environment of radio.

3

The cultural history of modern media – that is, the evolution of their content and that content's relation to the larger popular culture – reveals another set of contradictions. Particularly insofar as popular culture is equated with the popular arts, modern media have operated primarily as business enterprises intent on maximizing profits. Especially within the broadcast media, the authority of advertising has been paramount in setting cultural parameters and promoting the consumption ethic as the supreme virtue. But this hegemony has never been as complete as it seems. The media have not manufactured content out of thin air. Historically, the raw materials for "media fare," as well as its creators, have been drawn from an assortment of cultural milieus.

The cultural histories of film, radio, and television, particularly in their early years, could arguably be written entirely from the point of view of the contributions of immigrants and the media's reliances on older cultural forms adapted to new technologies. The central role played by immigrant audiences and Jewish immigrant entrepreneurs in the rise of the movie industry is well known. Slapstick comedy, raucous, vulgar, and universally appealing, was the first style to pack audiences in – and it was also the first style to be identified worldwide as uniquely American. Only in Hollywood could a Fatty Arbuckle be transformed from a semiskilled plumber's helper into a $5000/week comedy star in three years. When the Warner brothers made the great leap into the sound era in 1927 it was not by accident that they chose *The Jazz Singer* as their vehicle. Its story of how a cantor's son renounces his father's religion for a career as a popular singer essentially encapsulated both the history of the movie industry and the rapid secularization of Jewish life. The early film industry was energized in large part by a projection of the powerful urge toward collective representation so prominent in Jewish culture. The moguls, themselves immigrant showmen, reinvented the American dream with their new medium.

In the case of broadcasting, the exigencies of advertising demanded that programming present the aura of constant newness. Yet the content relied heavily upon traditional cultural forms. Variety shows, hosted by comedians and singers, became the first important style of network radio. Drawing from the vaudeville format, these shows remained quite popular through World War II; many of the stars continued their success on television. The master of ceremonies served as a focal point for activity and as a means of easy identification with a sponsor's product. Most of the variety stars had much experience in earlier stage entertainment; ethnic and regional stereotypes, dialect stories, and popular, long staples of vaudeville and burlesque, easily made the transition to broadcasting.

The characters in radio's first truly national hit show, "Amos 'n' Andy" (1928), were direct descendants of pre-Civil War minstrel show figures. Andy – pompous, domineering, a pseudointellectual – greatly resembled the minstrel "interlocutor," whose job was to direct and control the simple, unsophisticated "endmen," represented by Amos. Freeman Gosden and Charles Correll had spent many years on the minstrel and carnival circuits before adapting the blackface style to radio. The show's reliance on situational jokes, as well as on one-liners, also pointed toward a new form of humor fitted to broadcasting: the serialized situation comedy.

Daniel Czitrom

The history of American popular music in this century offers perhaps the clearest example of how media content has been continually invigorated and revitalized by forms, styles, entertainers, and artists from outside the mainstream. The growth of radio broadcasting and the recording industry in the 1920s hastened the cross-fertilization of popular (but hitherto localized) musical forms. America's rich racial and geographical diversity of authentic folk music–country, "mountain music," blues, jazz–became commercialized and available to much broader audiences. The new media allowed audiences and artists exposure to musical forms previously unknown to them. The post-World War II rise of rock and roll, closely allied to the more general phenomenon of "youth culture," reflected a vital and new amalgam of white country music, black blues, and traditional Tin Pan Alley show music.

Recent infusions of Third World music such as reggae, ska, and salsa point to the growth of an international style in popular music. The disco explosion, beneath all the glitter and flash, is fundamentally based on the popularization of Latin dance and rhythms, spiced with the urban gay sensibility. The power of the recording and radio industries to standardize and exploit popular music, to hype stars and trends, should not be ignored or minimized. But denial of the authenticity at the core of much popular music mistakenly simplifies the complex tensions existing within our popular culture.

4

Before discussing several of the more recent developments in communications technology, it might be instructive to cast a fleeting look backward at two early "media dreamers," Edward Bellamy and Hugo Gernsback. In 1889 Bellamy, America's preeminent utopian, elaborated an idealized vision of future communications in his short story "With the Eyes Shut." He described the dream of a railroad passenger suddenly transported into a whole new world of media gadgets. Phonographed books and magazines have replaced printed ones in railroad cars. Clocks announce the time with recorded sayings from the great authors. Letters, newspapers, and books are recorded and listened to on phonographic cylinders. One can even listen to a play while watching pictures of the players on a slide-projecting phonograph. Everyone carries an "indispensable," a combination tape recorder and phonograph. Bellamy seems concerned that the sense of hearing threatens to overwhelm that of sight. But what stands out in his fable is the limitless choice of programming, in a privatized setting, available to the individual.

Whereas Bellamy's fantasy conjured up images of inexhaustible "software," Hugo Gernsback, science-fiction writer and wireless enthusiast, was captivated by the radical potential of radio "hardware." In the early 1900s, Gernsback tirelessly promoted amateur wireless activity in his own magazines and others'. The culmination of this work came in his book *Radio for All* (1922), which projected "the future wonders of Radio" 50 years hence. Gernsback predicted the coming of television, videophones, telex, and radio-controlled airplanes. He managed to think up some gadgets we seem to have missed: radio "power roller skates," radio clocks, even a "radio business control" console. As the frontispiece to Gernsback's book shows, he envisioned a future where an individual's radio equipment would be at the very center of business and social life.

Atavistic expressions of the utopian urges given voice by Bellamy and Gernsback appear all around us today. Only now, with the advent of new satellite and video technologies, their fantasies have a firmer material base. Of course, Bellamy's "software socialism" and Gernsback's "hardware socialism" hardly appear to be lurking around the corner; corporate capital has enormous resources invested in the expansion of that material base. The press is filled with stories detailing the maneuverings of RCA, Warner Communications, MCA, SONY, and all the rest in the scramble to get a piece of the new action. No one can deny the central position of big capital in the new advances. But recent developments may still promise in essence what they appear to deny in substance.

The acceleration in the evolution of media hardware and software has been fueled, in large part, by the continuing persistence of utopian urges in the population at large. With the imminent spread of cheap video hardware to large numbers of people – for example, video cameras, cassette recorders, and video disc players –

Daniel Czitrom

the potential exists for individuals (and collectives) to become producers as well as consumers. The historical gap in broadcasting between the oligopoly of transmission and the democracy of reception, therefore, may be drastically reduced. What is important to see is the interaction between the corporate giants and the deep and genuine desire on the part of the people to gain more direct control over how they communicate and the content of their communications.

An awareness of the dialectical tensions within the American media can perhaps explain why it is possible to critique the worst tendencies of modern media—banalization, encouraging conspicuous consumption, the trend toward global hegemony—while at the same time offering real hope for its future. It is less important to curb futurist fantasies than to continually work at exposing the too often hidden political and social agenda attending technological progress. The recovery of historical perspective, bringing the contradictions of American media into sharper relief, can perhaps help us to reshape the future of modern communication.

Literary Origins of Popular Culture in the U.S.

A. K. El Janaby (collage)

Horror in American Literature

Paul Buhle

The chief contribution of American literature is horror. From first to last it has illustrated what C. L. R. James calls the uncertainties of life and the ultimate doom of Western civilization's claim to escape the universal human fate. This is a negative romanticism, to be sure, for no more hope is given for the collective promise of the lower classes than for the pretentious optimism of the bourgeoisie. But it contains a revolutionary kernel, nevertheless. In a society infatuated with the illusion of progress, horror speaks to a human essence beyond history. Poet and writer strive to regain their ancient role: the magic storyteller who gains coherence through use of universal symbols, offering a break with current existence and all its limitations.

The depth of horror in the American spirit is shown by the first national literary classic, Michael Wigglesworth's *Day of Doom*, which remained for a century after its seventeenth-century publication second only to the Bible in New England sales:

> *No heart so bold, but now grows cold.*
> *and almost dead with fear*

Paul Buhle

No eye so dry, but can not cry
and pour out many a tear.
Earth's potentates and pow'rful States,
Captains and Men of Might
Are quite abasht, their courage dasht
at this most dreadful sight . . .
The mountains smoak, the Hills are shook
the Earth is rent and torn
As if she shall be clean dissolv'd
or from the Center born.
The Sea doeth roar, forsakes the shore
and shrinking away for fear;
The wild Beasts flee into the Sea
as soon as He draws near.

This reflects, of course, the morbid metaphysics of the Puritans, whose abstract intellectualism and bourgeois expectations separated them from the ritual spontaneity of the European peasant life they willfully left behind. The sense of impending calamity outlasted their specific culture because each succeeding American generation learned afresh that material advancement alone could not satisfy an inner longing for some fateful resolution to the New World quest.

If reason and happiness did not prevail in this most ideal of human experiments, what of human fate? So political (and revolutionary) a personality as Tom Paine wondered anxiously about Dream Life, imagination's rampant run over mental judgment in its hours of weakness. America's first major novelist, Charles Brockden Brown, at the turn of the nineteenth century, put these intuitive fears into several fantastic works, unified by the notion that Americans had escaped the Old World class society only to confront their inner selves—revealing the disastrous quality of sheer human existence and of ideas that (in Brockden Brown's own words) "can be accounted for by no established laws." The American Revolution may have triumphed. But this achievement, too, would pass finally to dust, and in its crumbling reveal a fearful inner decadence. Brockden Brown's confidant, William Dunlop, whose production of

Mathew Lewis's *The Monk* was among the early triumphs of the American stage, foresaw the arena where the macabre spectacle of decline would be played out: the *frontier*, what Dunlop called "the asylum of European crimes."

Here, especially in the Old Southwest, horror becomes popular culture and establishes American literature on its own turf. Here the modes are settled for the horror to follow in all fields. Horror is a blank-faced joke, the joining of the terrible to the hysteria of unreason, the lack of control over human events linking the two together. Here the ghosts play on the ideals of untrammeled individualist democracy, revealing beneath its superficial freedoms the alienated struggle of all against all.

Southwestern writings took the solid ground of the ordinary frontiersman, who described with a straight face the incredibly grotesque of social life and of nature or who casually unraveled a cruel practical joke with what Max Eastman later described as the "perfectly naked angle of meaning"–"cracked," not "talked around" in European intellectual fashion. If this were a barbarian culture, drunkenness and licentiousness along with random violence endemic, what made the pioneer unique was his self-consciousness of his reversion as the basis for humor. Not for nothing had there been 24 American editions of Baron von Münchhausen's works by 1835 and had Daniel Boone sat around the campfire with *Gulliver's Travels*. In the face of the fantastic, the true agony of asocial existence grew more dim, and what Marius Bewley called the "illicit marriage of disease and rippling muscle, or horror and hearty laughter" actually soothed the isolate with an acceptable self-vision.

The ghoul may occupy a special place in medieval popular literature about the violation of the dead, but a random frontier boatsman swears he eats corpses when he's ill. Augustus Longstreet, frontier politician and chronicler, wrote astonishing tales about dinner-and-dissection mixups of the baby in the stew, "Gander Pullings" of humans torturing animals, endless physical and psychological violence. Frontier people talked tall about pulling the stars down from the skies, drinking from the moon, riding lightning and provoking rain, passing consciousness animistically to bears and wolves and in return acting out the ritual barbarity interpreted from animal life. The frontier woman in particular–one-eyed, hairlipped, wooden-legged–defied all the traditional sanctity of civilized character. Like Lottie Richards, who personally "carried twenty eyes in her work-bag that she had picked out of the head of certain gals of her acquaintance," she was as bestial as her mate, infinitely more savage than the Amerindian "savages" she did her share to eradicate. Behind the violence and mockery of civilized ways, cultural historian Constance Rourke perceived, lay the same emptiness of feeling that drove the Puritan to apocalyptic religion and Captain Ahab to stark madness: "Anger, love, hatred, remorse were absent; fear alone was revealed, but only in a distant and fragmentary fashion, only to cast away with laughter. If it created unities, the resilience of the comic spirit seemed a destructive agent, so blank were the spaces where emotion might have appeared."

The great writers–Poe, Twain, Bierce, even Melville–might disavow the heartlessness of the frontier. But they could not escape the alienation of spirit, the essential loneliness that animated its sentiments. Each found the means to confront that emptiness and search out a road of escape, of transcendence, or of ultimate acceptance that nothing fundamental in the human condition could truly be altered.

In the last decades of the nineteenth century, "local color" writers spoke with new vividness about the American decadence. In the West, Ambrose Bierce sketched out a comic diabolism that deprived the Civil War of its crusader's mission, the "winning of the West" of its pseudoheroic spirituality, the entire American Dream of its claim to virtues and happiness. The land the pioneers had left behind, New England, sported a weird sentiment in its emptiness, where the brilliant Mary Wilkins Freeman depicted her heroines as almost ghosts already, deprived of true human contact. As Lovecraft said, the landscape had become one where "mere grotesqueness is very common; sly, malignant madness sometimes lurks around the corner." At the highest level of social critique, Bierce summed up the apocalyptic view of the future. His short story "Ashes of the Beacon" looked to the future American revolution amid the "noise of arms, the shrieks of women and the red glare of the burning cities." American political pretensions were to be crushed and obliterated by history.

This is the final horror and the final drawing of the political implications that had been centuries in the making. The intended American escape from the Old World past to the frontier, the search for a timeless small-property Republic, proves to be not only an illusory but a mad and self-destructive concept for those who believe in it. Pessimistic about alternatives, writers of the political catastrophes etched into American self-consciousness the portent of a true twentieth-century dilemma: socialism or barbarism.

Ricardian socialist George Lippard's *The Monks of Monk Hall* (1845) set the guidelines for a "political" horror in America. The day would come when Independence Hall would be torn down and replaced by a palace for the wealthy, and the American flag would be exchanged for a banner of crowns and chains. The heavens would weep and the constant refrain "Woe to Sodom" would sound in the background. The graveyards would stir, and the dead would rise en masse to avenge the ruination of the republic by the avarice and cupidity of individualistic striving. Dedicated to Charles Brockden Brown, and set in Philadelphia where the first workers' general strike had risen and failed to alter the course of economic events, *Monks of Monk Hall* depicts only catastrophe ahead.

Ignatius Donnelly's *Caesar's Column*, Jack London's *The Iron Heel*, and a dozen other less notable works carry the catastrophe closer to our own world of international class conflict. Socialist novelist George Allen England, in his *Darkness and Dawn* (serialized just before World War I in *Munsey's Magazine*), conveyed the expectation of disaster in contemporary popular literature. At a time when socialists are on the verge of creating a new society, the entire society is blotted out (England's commentary on the world conflict?), and hero and heroine find themselves alone in surviving a vast and mysterious destruction. Only after trials and agonies, stumbling through laughable architectural wreckage and inhuman mutation, does the couple help to found a new order in which all is pure and socialistic. The moral: first Armageddon, where America pays for its sins; afterward, with luck, the rebuilding on a new and more universal basis.

Free Play and No Limit: An Introduction to Edward Bellamy's Utopia

Franklin Rosemont

Looking Backward opens in 1887. A wealthy young Bostonian retires to his bedroom in a secret basement vault that he has had specially constructed to shut out street noise. He is a chronic insomniac, and so has engaged a hypnotist to put him to sleep. He wakes up in the morning—113 years later.

Like Rip Van Winkle, Julian West finds the world in which he awakens very different from the world in which he fell asleep. The intervening years have witnessed nothing less than a "complete transformation in the human condition,"[1] the result of a thoroughgoing social revolution that has realized, for the first time, full human equality. In abolishing private ownership of the means of production, society has also done away with social classes, exploitation, poverty, hunger, war, sex slavery, racial discrimination, slums, crime, jails, money, rent, banks, charity, corruption, taxes, advertising, housework, politicians, merchants, servants, lawyers, the army, the navy, and the State Department.

Government itself scarcely exists, its functions having been reduced to the coordination of industrial production and distribution. There is very little disease, insanity, or suicide, and virtually no legislation ("we might be said to live almost in a state of anarchy"). Churches have all but disappeared. There are no locks or locksmiths, and no safes ("because we have no more thieves"). Coercion is a thing of the past; everything has become "entirely voluntary, the logical outcome of the operation of human nature under rational conditions." Working hours are short. Work itself has been greatly simplified and, as far as possible, rendered attractive. Vacations are ample; emigration is unrestricted. In the new society of the year 2000, "liberty is the first and last word."

All this has, in turn, fundamentally transformed the human personality. "The conditions of life have changed, and with them the motives of human action." In Bellamy's utopia there is no more selfishness, greed, malice, hypocrisy, apathy; no more "struggle for existence"; no more hunger for power; no more anxiety or fear about how to satisfy basic human needs. "The highest possible physical, as well as mental, development for everyone" is the aim of the new education. Everyone is happier, healthier, brighter, friendlier; more active, more adventurous, more creative.

"Perhaps the most notable single aspect of the Revolution" was "the elevation and enlargement of woman's sphere in all directions. . . . Since the Revolution there has been no difference in the education of the sexes nor in the independence of their economic and social position, in the exercise of responsibility or experience in the practical conduct of affairs. . . . In every pursuit of life . . . [women] join with men on equal terms."

Moreover, "the sentiment of brotherhood, the feeling of solidarity, asserted itself not merely toward men and women, but likewise toward the humbler companions of our life on earth and sharers of its fortunes, the animals. . . . The new conception of our relation to the animals appealed to the heart and captivated the imagination of mankind."

The 113 years also have seen, thanks to the revolution, an unprecedented flourishing of science, technology, and the arts. Bellamy differs from many utopians in his confidence that modern technology can be conquered and put at the service of human desire. His forecast—in *Looking Backward* and its sequel, *Equality*—of such

27

things as automobiles, radio, television, helicopters, air-conditioning, and waterbeds, has ensured him a permanent place in the history of science fiction. Interspersed through a charming love story and an unremitting attack on capitalism and its institutions, these inventions doubtless added to the appeal of his utopia.

Its appeal was, in fact, extraordinary. Indeed it is generally acknowledged that *Looking Backward* was the most widely read and influential book of the late nineteenth century. It provoked vigorous debate in newspapers and magazines, in classrooms and living rooms, in union halls and saloons. It fascinated both the "man in the street" and the "leading intellectual." Because of *Looking Backward*, said Vida D. Scudder, "the fading emotions of the old Abolitionist era flamed again." A broad movement sprang up, for the purpose of realizing the dream set forth in Bellamy's book. More than 150 Bellamy clubs were formed around the country. Eugene V. Debs and Daniel DeLeon were among countless thousands who entered social radicalism through the door that Bellamy opened. J. A. Wayland, founder and editor of *Appeal to Reason* – the most widely circulated socialist periodical in U.S. history – gave *Looking Backward* credit for having "popularized socialism, made it interesting, and started millions to thinking along lines entirely new to them."

A number of American utopian novels had appeared before Bellamy's, but except for Nathaniel Hawthorne's *Blithedale Romance* (1852), none had made a lasting impression. *Looking Backward* put utopia on the map of the U.S. It started a vogue for utopian romances that ran through the 1890s and well into the following century. If it is still unclear to what degree it influenced Mark Twain's *Connecticut Yankee* or L. Frank Baum's *Wizard of Oz*, its impact on many other works – including William Dean Howells's *A Traveller from Altruria*, Ignatius Donnelly's *Caesar's Column*, Frederick Upham Adams's *President John Smith*, and Charlotte Perkins Gilman's *Herland* – is firmly established.

Bellamy's influence was not limited to his native land. *Looking Backward* was wildly popular throughout the English-speaking world – in Canada, Australia, and New Zealand, as well as in England; William Morris acknowledged that he wrote *News from No-*

where as a "reply" to it. Tolstoy, finding it "exceedingly remarkable," arranged for its translation into Russian; Maxim Gorky once called the U.S. "the country of Henry George, Bellamy [and] Jack London." Jean Jaurès, the outstanding figure of pre-World War I French socialism, saluted this "American masterpiece" that did "wonders toward dissipating hostility and ignorance against our ideas." The renowned Marxist theorist Clara Zetkin, leader of the German socialist workingwomen's movement, translated it into German and wrote an introduction to it. And, by way of exemplifying the exceptional range of its appeal, Helena P. Blavatsky – author of *Isis Unveiled* and *The Secret Doctrine* – declared Bellamy's work "magnificent" and in harmony with the perspectives of Theosophy.[2]

The history of the Bellamy movement in the U.S. remains to be written.[3] As a link of the older radical Abolitionists and Reconstructionists with the new generation that would form the Socialist party in 1901 and the I. W. W. five years later, its study could teach us a great deal.

Few social movements, if any, have been so colorful, so heterogeneous. Under the banner of *Looking Backward* were Unitarians, Theosophists, trade unionists, populists, feminists, Christian socialists, spiritualists, homeopathists, vegetarians, prohibitionists, members of the Farmers' Alliance, an appreciable number who thought of themselves as Marxists, and several Union army generals – including Arthur Devereaux, "hero of Gettysburg," and Abner Doubleday, the apocryphal "father of baseball." Among Bellamy's adherents were Edward Everett Hale, William Dean Howells, Charlotte Perkins Gilman, Thomas Wentworth Higginson, Lucy Stone, Hamlin Garland, Julia Ward Howe, Helen Campbell, Frances Willard, Jesse Cox, Lucian Sanial, Florence Kelley, Thomas Lake Harris, Solomon Schindler, Laurence Gronlund, Thomas Davidson, Burnette Haskell, Sylvester Baxter, and Clarence Darrow.

Looking Backward was written fast and furiously in the dazzling light of one of the pivotal American labor battles: the bloody

Haymarket Affair and its aftermath in Chicago, 1886, in which a group of innocent labor leaders were framed and hanged at the behest of big business.

The book appeared in a period of unprecedentedly rapid and convulsive change in American society. The Civil War and Reconstruction paved the way for extensive industrialization, which in turn exacerbated class stratification beyond anything even dreamed of earlier in the U.S. To meet the mounting threat posed by the great trusts, workers thronged into the Knights of Labor. The year when Bellamy was readying his book for publication, 1887, has been called "the year of 10,000 strikes."

Historians have debated the background of Bellamy's thought. From book reviews and editorials he wrote for the *Springfield Union* in the 1870s, we know that he was familiar with the work of such utopians as Robert Owen, Frances Wright, Charles Fourier, Albert Brisbane, Etienne Cabet, John Humphrey Noyes, Josiah Warren, and others. Greater than any of these, however, was the influence exerted on him by the Old Testament prophets and the millennial/heretical tradition in Christianity – the Anabaptists, for example.

Bellamy, who descended from a long line of Baptist ministers, sometimes has been called a "Christian socialist," but the tag does not fit well. His early essay "The Religion of Solidarity" is closer to transcendentalism than to any Christian creed. Until the end of his life, he hoped that the remnant of radical egalitarianism in the margins of Christendom would add its resources to the revolutionary ferment. Noting that the church's proslavery position had dealt "a blow to its prestige in America from which it had not yet recovered," he warned that "its failure to take the right side in this far vaster movement would not leave any church worth mentioning." Of course, this warning went unheeded; indeed, some of the most venomous diatribes against his utopia came from priests and preachers. His last book, *Equality*, includes a scathing indictment of "ecclesiastical capitalism." After his death, his works were a major influence on the short-lived Social Gospel movement, but the fact remains: he himself stood with the infidels.

We may glean something of Bellamy's literary preferences

from a passage in *Looking Backward* in which Julian West looks over the bookshelves in his twenty-first-century home and joyfully discovers the works of Shakespeare, Milton, Wordsworth, Shelley, Tennyson, Defoe, Dickens, Thackeray, Hugo, Hawthorne, and Irving. Dickens he admired above all: "He overtops all the writers of his age. . . . No man of his time did so much as he to turn men's minds to the wrong and wretchedness of the old order of things, and open their eyes to the necessity of the great change that was coming, although he himself did not clearly foresee it."

Living most of his life in the small milltown of Chicopee Falls, Massachusetts, Bellamy's personal acquaintance with contemporary writers was limited. It is interesting to note that Mark Twain—who found *Looking Backward* "fascinating"—once arranged to meet with him. Twain's friend William Dean Howells became an active supporter of Bellamy's ideas and corresponded with him for years.

To some extent, he knew the work of Hegel and even that of Marx; his acquaintance with the latter would increase appreciably after the publication of *Looking Backward* when, devoting himself unreservedly to agitational/propagandist work in the service of the revolution, he came into contact with representatives of virtually every radical/revolutionary tendency. Bellamy's critique of capitalism, however, was derived less from books than from the things he saw with his penetrating eye and felt with his dreaming heart.

It is interesting that Bellamy independently arrived at certain of Marx's conclusions using a very different method. But what draws us to a writer, a thinker, an artist, is not so much what he or she shares with others as it is the unique charms that he or she alone disposes. Bellamy's real importance lies precisely in those qualities that distinguish him from all others: his particular moral/revolutionary attitude and its underlying psychological and poetic dimensions. It was these qualities that made *Looking Backward* so vitally a part of its time. And it is these same qualities that render so much of his message as acute and vigorous today as it was the day it was written.

Franklin Rosemont

The esteem in which Bellamy is held even now in many countries stands in marked contrast to the disfavor that has befallen his work in his homeland. Of the pre-World War I radical generation in the U.S., probably a substantial majority were initially drawn toward socialist solutions by *Looking Backward* and the furor it provoked; surely there were few who had not read it or did not at least have a fairly accurate idea of its content. Of today's vastly smaller radical generation, the reverse is true: few have more than vague notions of his work; the merest handful seem to have read *Looking Backward*, and scarcely anyone outside the universities is familiar with his other works.

American Marxists, disregarding the appreciations of Debs and DeLeon, have long treated Bellamy with condescension, as noted by Heywood Broun in his preface to *Looking Backward* in 1931. Notwithstanding Kropotkin's early enthusiasm for Bellamy's work, anarchists have been equally indifferent.

Not that Bellamy has vanished from American bookshelves: on the contrary, *Looking Backward* has remained in print (seven editions are currently available) and is widely accessible even in small-town libraries. The anomaly is that Bellamy now lives almost wholly outside the currents that style themselves radical in this country. He is read primarily as a precursor of science fiction, or as a curious contributor to the "American experience," or as a minor survivor of romanticism in the dawn of American literary realism.

The reasons for Bellamy's eclipse from the spectrum of American revolutionary thought are not difficult to discern. World War I was a watershed for radicals everywhere. As the better-known figures of international socialism (and anarchism) endorsed the expansionist aims of "their" respective national capitalist rulers, the Second International ignominiously collapsed. Then the October Revolution in Russia, 1917, brought enormous prestige to an unfamiliar and rigorous interpretation of Marxism. Draped in the glory of the first conquest of state power by the working class, bolshevism quickly upstaged all other currents of socialist thought. The new movement, priding itself on its "hard line," looked askance at the seemingly naive visionaries who had exerted such influence a few years earlier. Anything tainted with "utopianism" was now automatically suspect. And so, having been the best-known name in American radicalism, Bellamy became taboo.

Those who have monopolized the title of "revolutionary" in this country have been notably zealous in advertising their ignorance of Bellamy, but the apologists for modern liberalism have been no less assiduous in their neglect. Bellamy's indictment of capitalist civilizations, like Fourier's attack, was too merciless and too all-encompassing for it to have proved serviceable, in the long run, to the essentially "civilized"—that is, repressive—ideology of bourgeois reformism. If welfare statists and social democrats now and then lay claim to his legacy, it is precisely in the manner that they claim Marx: by doing violence to the integrity of his views. Contrary to widespread belief, Bellamy was in fact strongly antireformist. Rejecting the notion that reforms were "sufficient methods of overthrowing capitalism," he stressed that "they did not even tend toward such a result, but were quite as likely to help capitalism to obtain a longer lease of life by making it a little less abhorrent." He went on to express his "considerable apprehension" lest the revolutionary movement "be diverted from its real aim, and its force wasted in this programme of piecemeal reforms."

Shortly after Bellamy's death, John Clark Ridpath said: "He who believes in the Existing Order can have no part or lot with Edward Bellamy. He who does not believe in the Existing Order, but fears to disturb it, has no part or lot with him either."

One other reason for the eclipse of Bellamy lies in the name he gave to his system: Nationalism. He meant by this that the whole population of the country would take over the means of production from the capitalists; thus the word had not a trace of its later connotations of jingoistic patriotism and chauvinism. Bellamy at first expressly rejected the names socialism and communism, which in the America of the 1880s still signified isolated and exotic communitarian experiments, often led by eccentric religious sects or small political sects, equally isolated and exotic, such as the German immigrant socialists in New York who were sharply criticized by Marx and Engels for their supercilious irrelevance to the American workers' movement. Seeking a new name for a new idea—one that would not be limited to the needs of any sect but would express the aspirations and interests of all producers, among whom he included workers, farmers, and petit-bourgeois tradesmen – Bellamy selected Nationalism. His reputation has suffered immeasurably because of the totally different definitions that this term later acquired.

Bellamy's system retained the interclassist character common to most utopias, reflecting a specifically petit-bourgeois longing for harmony, free not only of the oppression of monopoly capital but also of the potential uprising of the proletariat and subproletariat – an uprising feared as a vengeful cataclysm certain to be ruinous for all. It was Bellamy's belief that capitalism could be abolished in the U.S. without the violence of class war.

Too many historians have been content merely to note the Nationalist movement's predominantly middle-class leadership and have utterly ignored the extent and variety of its interaction with the militant proletariat. It is thus rarely acknowledged that in the decisive labor struggles of the period, such as the 1892 Homestead Strike, the Nationalists stood with the workers. The protracted drive for shorter hours, the central issue of the class struggle in those years, received Bellamy's support from the start. The fact that *Looking Backward* – the best-selling book of its day – took for granted a much shorter workday surely was an important boost for the Eight Hour movement, just as Bellamy's acknowledgment of full equality for women doubtless contributed to the cause of equal suffrage.

His enthusiastic support for the women's movement contrasts sharply with the masculine arrogance (pathetic disguise of a deep-seated fear) so characteristic of other Left currents, then as now. Most of those who enjoyed the mantle of orthodox Marxism in the U.S. retreated in holy horror from this bold, new current – of women speaking and acting for themselves – and many went so far as to contrive abjectly specious arguments to "keep women in their place." Bellamy, to the contrary, saw the women's movement not as a competitor or a threat, but as a natural and indispensable ally.

Repeatedly Bellamy stressed that it was his aim "to extend popular government, the rule of the people, to industry and commerce." By *Nationalism* he meant "the translation into industrial and economic terms of the equal rights idea, hitherto expressed in terms of politics only." He argued that without equality in industry, political democracy "must forever fail to secure to a people the equalities and liberties which it promises."

This conception of industrial democracy was taken up a few years later by the IWW; indeed, it was the cornerstone of the IWW program. Bellamy deserves greater recognition as a forerunner of the Wobbly theory. In an 1890 article, he wrote that "in the progress toward National cooperation, there shall be a question of an organization inclusive of different trades, and ultimately of one including all trades," thereby prefiguring the central IWW idea of one big union for all workers. It is noteworthy that long after Bellamy had become unfashionable among communists and socialists, his ideas were still seriously discussed in the IWW press.[4]

Close in spirit to the IWW, too, is Bellamy's "industrial army." His "military" metaphor has caused considerable consternation among critics and has been woefully misconstrued by many. The "industrial army" is perhaps not the most appealing feature of Bellamy's system, but one should at least try to see it as it was meant to be rather than to vilify it solely on the basis of *a posteriori* projections. Bellamy's "industrial army" is not military at all, of course, since there are no wars in his utopia–no possibility of wars–and no weapons with which to fight them. His marching bands of un-uniformed working men and women, with their great festivals and musical pageants through garlanded streets and pleasure gardens, have nothing in common with the brutally disciplined troops of any bureaucratic/hierarchical military regime. To find a comparable example in military history, we would have to point to the joyous libertarian throngs who fought at John Ziska's side in the Hussite wars, or to the glorious Durutti Column in the bright early days of the Spanish Revolution.

Not surprisingly, the ideologists of "things as they are" greeted *Looking Backward* with derision. Bellamy was probably the most denounced man of his time. In church and classroom, in "respectable" assemblies, and in the bourgeois press, he was pictured as the devil in disguise.

More pertinent to our inquiry are other criticisms made, justly or unjustly, by Bellamy's political opponents on the Left and by the historians of utopia. Unlike the outspokenly procapitalist criticisms, which long ago vanished into the mire whence they came, these latter have helped shape the attitude toward Bellamy that prevails today.

One of the earlier leftist critics was the English painter/poet William Morris, who reviewed *Looking Backward* in the socialist journal *Commonweal* in January 1889.[5] It is not easy to understand how Morris could have so completely misinterpreted the book – how he could so abysmally have failed even to recognize the passion and integrity of Bellamy's motives. We know that he was disturbed by the book's popularity; perhaps Upton Sinclair was correct in contending that Morris was prejudiced against it for the simple reason that it was written by an American.[6]

In any case, Morris's refusal to see in *Looking Backward* anything more than a "cockney paradise" does not show the author of *Art and Socialism* at his best. Indeed, another of his remarks on Bellamy – "If they brigaded *me* into a regiment of workers, I'd just lie on my back and kick" – displays rather the "rich artist-enthusiast" and "sentimental socialist" described by old Engels. Morris's most ardent defender in our time, E. P. Thompson, has had to admit that the great Pre-Raphaelite's "opposition to *Looking Backward* led him to willful exaggeration, more than once."[7]

Changed conditions and the passage of time have blunted the edges of Morris's ill considered polemic against Bellamy, just as they have blunted the edges of Engels's hasty gibes at Morris. Today, as we struggle to find our way out of a vastly more horrible maze than any of them could have conceived, we find that all of them help to light our way. To say that they had their faults is the merest truism – hardly poignant because we have faults of our own. What matters is that the going is easier, thanks to them.

Notes

1. All quotations from Bellamy, unless otherwise specified, are from *Looking Backward* (Boston, 1888), *Equality* (New York, 1897), and *Edward Bellamy Speaks Again!* (Kansas City, 1937). "The Religion of Solidarity" is included in Edward Bellamy, *Selected Writings on Religion and Society*, edited by Joseph Schiffman (New York, 1955).

2. Sylvia E. Bowman's *Edward Bellamy Abroad* (New York, 1962) traces Bellamy's influence in 28 countries. The bibliography lists 80 translations of *Looking Backward* into 23 languages.

3. The best sources remain Arthur E. Morgan, *Edward Bellamy* (New York, 1944), and Howard H. Quint, *The Forging of American Socialism* (Indianapolis, 1964).

4. See, for example, the long review of *Looking Backward* in *Industrial Solidarity* (Nov. 17, 1926).

5. A long excerpt from Morris's review is included in A. L. Morton, *The English Utopia* (London, 1952). In *The New Nation* (Feb. 14, 1891), Bellamy reviewed *News from Nowhere*, a book "exceedingly well worth reading" by "one of the greatest of living poets"; he is mildly critical only because "as to the industrial system . . . Mr. Morris is provokingly silent."

6. Upton Sinclair, *Mammonart: An Essay in Economic Interpretation* (Pasadena, 1925), 238.

7. E. P. Thompson, *William Morris: Romantic to Revolutionary* (London, 1977), 693.

The Significance of Yiddish Socialism

Paul Buhle

The Yiddish-speaking community from the 1890s to the 1920s was infused with socialist dedication and mass-cultural creativity as no other community on American shores has ever been. Its attainments, its difficulties, and its significance have nevertheless escaped the attention of everyone but the devotees of *Yiddishkayt*. For decades a little band of the faithful kept the memories alive, despite the indifference of most radical historians and culture critics. I. B. Singer's Nobel Prize and Irving Howe's *World of Our Fathers* have opened up the discussion. But only partway. At this late date, the brief merger of popular culture and Left culture reaches us through apoliticized nostalgia for vanished neighborhoods and for a people eager to make revolution in an unrevolutionary land. The truth is more complex, and more important.

Here was, indeed, a socialist culture that was worthy of comparison with any in the contemporary world. It existed not (as did the powerful Finnish-American radical culture) at the geographical margins, in far-removed mining camps and rural villages, but in the heart of the metropolis, Greater New York. It found the mediation with American popular life, therefore, crucial, sometimes tragically so, and always a matter for confrontation. No movement, no minority society could possibly survive the pervasive spread of "Americanization" intact – public schools, sports, the economic opportunities for those who stepped out of the ghetto. But it could fight for its own identity, perpetuation, and contribution to a society democratic enough for a plurality of cultures. That society, wise Yiddishists knew, had to be a socialist one. Within the existing order, it could make socialism not only a political goal but a way of life, an advanced look at the potential cooperation and collective joy ahead.

The literature of *Yiddishkayt* offers an extraordinary insight into Yiddish culture. The entire development of Yiddish as a modern literary language had to be compressed into a little more than a half-century between outmigration from the *shtetl* and the end of the heroic era – assimilation and the Holocaust. The tongue of an impoverished people with no professional litterateurs, Yiddish became a supreme instrument for raising the cultural level of the masses, for secularization and modernization. When its readers plunged into urban life, Yiddish became a language of leisure-entertainment, popular culture, as well. And yet, through all this, it retained roots in the ancient traditions of Jews; its various functions always somehow connected with the messianic promise of deliverance from oppression. It could no more shed the popular and millenarian elements than it could destroy its own identity.

The historic isolation of the Jews in the eastern European commercial towns and villages must be seen as an integral part of the process by which western Europe "underdeveloped" the east into a backward reservoir of agricultural and human resources. With their distinct background and culture, Jews adapted ambivalently. Unable and unwilling to assimilate, they developed a rich community life among themselves and increasingly (albeit often at a geographical distance) came in touch with metropolitan gentile culture. Yiddish derived from Middle-High German, with traces of Hebrew, Slavic, and whatever languages prevailed around them.

Paul Buhle

Considered vulgar, unfit for the religious use reserved for Hebrew, Yiddish remained the vernacular of street talk and of the *T'sena U'rena*, the "women's bible," for a long time the major popular text in the language.

Jewish followers of the Enlightenment considered Yiddish to be jargon, a stigma of backwardness. Yet they found the language their only means for reaching the Jewish masses with a rationalist message. Thus evolved the remarkable conception that Yiddish, suited for malapropism and satire, would perform its negative mission and then eliminate itself owing to its "aesthetic of ugliness." The vulgarian, the clown, the embracer of mass life instead proved to be the ideal language of socialism.

In its early years, modern Yiddish writing took on a folkish quality and the quasi-realistic tone that it maintained throughout most of its history. Mendele Mokher Sforim ("Mendele the Bookseller," a pseudonym, as are the majority of Yiddish authors' names) and Sholom Aleichem (a.k.a. Sh. Rabinovitsch) captured public attention in Russia of the 1880s–1890s by penning literary sketches that perfectly expressed the continuities and tensions of *shtetl* life. These tales were hardly one step removed from the semispontaneous, improvised storytelling familiar to folk life in all cultures. Yet they possessed the sophistication of the nineteenth-century European intellect, as if Dickens or Mark Twain (often called the American Sholom Aleichem) had entered a culture just when the culture entered history. The two Yiddish authors held a constant dialogue with their listeners, laughing about their sufferings as fellow members of persecuted ranks, cajoling them about the unnecessary cruelties of their lives, holding up their potential accomplishments against the narrowness of their current state. Here the detached observer might have seen a potentially mighty literature in its formative stage. Authors able to reach into and out of the vernacular–delivering heavy spiritual messages without either diluting the immediacy of everyday language or compromising the sophistication of their developing craft–could do great things. Yiddish writers were swept along by the contemporary European realism and naturalism. Yet their writing contained an element of fancy, as if the social experience of author and audience could not permit a complete commitment to the appearances of reality.

Anarcho-Zionist critic Baruch Rivkin later explained the secret. Yiddish had become the literary substitute for the geographic-national identity denied Jews, not as much a quest for some real territory as a postexilic yearning turned spiritual and political. Yiddish offered a linguistic world in which the mixture of material poverty, homelessness, and messianism (whether conservative-religious or radical) could be reconciled. The reconciliation might never come, the prophetic vision never be fulfilled: from any reasonable point of view, the odds were overwhelmingly against it. This irony, felt keenly by Yiddish radicals, symptomized a sense of the tragic and the tragicomic, which the language also brought to socialism.

The vast migration of eastern European Jews to America inspired hope and disillusionment in equal portions. Confined to overcrowded ghettos, the garment trade, and the lower echelons of business, they suffered high mortality rates, tuberculosis (the "proletarian disease"), suicides, and family disorders. The community's activist intellectuals and rising labor militants tilted toward socialism. A socialist press flourished alongside a popular, radical theater. In the crowds of suffering, poorly educated immigrants, socialist culture had a ready audience, but one that demanded its edification in easy-to-swallow doses.

The effusion that followed may be best contrasted with the preexisting radical culture. When eastern European Jews began to organize unions, constitute mutual benefit societies, and join radical parties, they learned their *political* lessons from the precisely organized German-American socialists. But whereas Germans arrived in the U.S. a generation earlier with a ready-made cultural perspective set in the European framework, the Jews reformulated their culture in the heat of immigrant life. A major Yiddish literary flowering considered impossible in 1885 became a fact ten years later. Edward King's contemporary novel *Joseph Zalmonah* describes a unique millennial character, a people's poet who offers songs to a mass audience of workers in the midst of a desperate strike. Hungry and ragged, the workers are stirred to new sacrifices. Every socialist and anarchist newspaper editor could tell a similar story from real life. Contributions by now-famous ghetto writers helped launch the papers, called the workers to consciousness, and brought new inspiration in times of crisis. For a historic moment in the 1890s, such writers had all but recapitulated the ancient functions of poetry with the substitutions of labor (or socialist) victory for clan triumph and the mysterious force of the people for that of God.

The writers' very success stirred the first rebellion against suffocating political orthodoxy—foreshadowing all those uprisings by leftist writers against their political masters in following generations. Whereas struggles over style and autonomy of literature had been practically unknown among the German-American socialists, the assertion of artistic autonomy and the formation of extraparty journals and magazines punctuated the Jewish 1890s. Morris Winchevsky, the *zeyde* (grandfather) of socialist writers, editor of the first Yiddish socialist newspaper in London during the 1880s, had drawn from German poets the rich sense of continental workers' culture as well as that of paradox in the socialist writer's role. His own Boston newspaper, *Emes* (truth), declared, "The party is more important than our newspaper, but socialism is more important than the party, and the truth is more important than everything else." This could only be political heresy. Winchevsky's stubborn independent-mindedness initiated a Jewish cultural revolt against the narrow and sectarian leadership of the existing socialist movement.

The poet's action helped set the stage for the merging of immigrants and native-born Americans in the new, consolidated Socialist party of Eugene Debs. The two sides recognized in each other the folkish qualities that eventually rooted the movement in both Oklahoma and the Lower East Side. In this golden hour, the cultural pluralism that has been American radicalism's greatest innovation embraced wide divergencies in a single cause. The movement did not grow wide enough or deep enough to accomplish its ideal, however. War, repression, mutual misunderstandings, and, above all, the overpowering strength of the industrial system brought it down. But the testimony of several hundred local socialist newspapers in more than a dozen languages preserves the truth of the successful adaptation. So does the parallel story of the Industrial Workers of the World, whose militants perceived what Yiddishists had seen first, the logic of the mass worker steered home by the all-embracing vision of a new society within the old.

Winchevsky's rebellion also inspired the formation of a remarkable daily socialist press. The *Forverts* (*Jewish Daily Forward*), directed by Abe Cahan for a half a century, outdistanced its rivals in circulation and influence across world Jewry. It did so in part by taking up the cause of socialism and of labor. But it did so mainly by stealing the thunder of the metropolitan tabloid. Like a socialistic *National Enquirer* or *USA Today*, it smelled of sensationalism, the immersion in daily life, which the twentieth-century reader expects from a daily paper.

Cahan had the genius to see newspapers as the only reading matter the great mass of proletarians would ever read. He pioneered the single-column short story, just the right length for the semiliterate worker to read on a subway bound for his or her job. Cahan could crusade for a strike or a socialist election campaign, but he could also publish gruesome accounts of murder. He could have reporters investigate the quirks and ironies of the neighborhoods. He could also seek to control the economic and cultural life of the Jews personally, abusing those writers, theatrical producers, and union leaders who declined his patronage or disputed his personal taste.

Socialism could not come quickly enough for the Yiddish world. Cahan had absorbed the poison of American mass culture, along with its genius for adaptation in design and in distribution of new goods. His novel, *The Rise of David Levinsky*, draws the semi-autobiographical archetype of the prospering immigrant manufacturer who suffers from the realization that American prosperity has tainted his soul. In real life, Cahan also tainted American socialism and the Jewish labor movement. The faults Cahan symbolized and, indeed, embodied did much to inspire a mirror opposite, Jewish-American bolshevism.

In that light, the rise of Jewish communism can be seen as a fundamentalist revolt against the inevitabilities of passive assimilation. Cahan had from the beginning proclaimed that Yiddish was merely a transitional language–destined for elimination. Young radicals of the 1910s, veterans of anti-Semitic pogroms in their homeland and keenly aware of anti-Jewish attitudes in the U.S., rejected Cahanism by embracing *Yiddishkayt*. Through a historical coincidence, the Russian Revolution spoke simultaneously to Russian homeland nostalgia and to Jewish messianism, to the rejection of American culture as it existed and to the determination to find an honorable destiny for Jewish immigrant idealism.

The failure of world revolution soon narrowed the real choices. Yiddish-speaking communists fought, with real but limited success, the political overlords who set their agenda. When they finally revolted, they had become elderly men and women, gathered around their few surviving institutions. For decades they had been a disproportionate force in maintaining the language and the culture. History, and their own compromises, had doomed them. It was too late for Yiddish culture to be a popular culture or for the Jewish Left to escape the consequences of its long-held loyalties.

Now Yiddish falters, although it refuses to die. (Singer has said, intelligently, that the language has been in trouble for centuries and is destined to remain in trouble for centuries.) It retains a strange, otherworldly quality. The young who grow up with the language are nearly all Hasids, conservative moralists whose messianism has, ironically, been corrupted by a combination of American middle-class materialism and extreme ethnocentrism but who, in their way, refuse as surely as did the old Jewish anarchists and communists to accept the world before their eyes as real and permanent. Once, several generations ago, some of these Hasids turned their inner fire to radicalism and, like the mystic novelist David Ignatov, created a vision worthy of today's Liberation Theology. Some of the youngsters educated in Hasidism will likely do so again. Others today, secular Yiddishists around the revival *Klezmir* bands and the National Yiddish Book Center, understand the nonrational nature and the popular-culture component of any future for the language. In their work lies great promise.

The last of the oldtimers who remember a different *Yiddish-*

kayt pass from the scene with increasing swiftness. A world is nearly gone. Yet a thousand unconscious gestures in comedy, a political commitment to peace and social transformation, and a lilting combination of irony and hope carry on the tradition to a still uncharted destiny.

Laughing Their Way: A Background to Women's Humor

Ann D. Gordon

When you see a person slip down on the ice, do not laugh at them. . . . It is more feminine on witnessing such a sight, to utter an involuntary scream.[1]

That tip comes from Eliza Leslie, who wrote the *Behavior Book, A Manual for Ladies* published in 1853. Martha Bruere and Mary Beard classified that book under "Ladies Laughter" in 1934. We are to understand either that ladies knew enough to laugh at the absurdity of their advice books or that to appreciate, let alone create, laughter in antebellum America required resistance to the rule of corsets and the tight grip of an escort's hand. The editors do not say that women's humor suffocated under nineteenth-century prescriptions for womanhood, but their selections imply it by drawing overwhelmingly from the first third of the twentieth century for an anthology that purports to survey a century of laughter. Surely women laughed out loud long before this century and lightened any number of chores and encounters with humor. Bruere and Beard kept their eyes on marketable humorous arts. Maybe the public spectacle of women's laughter *was* of recent invention, forged out of the awakening to freedom and the consciousness of a national community that characterized women's modernity. The editors, however, leave the reader with a suspicion that they prefer the humor of middle class, urban women whose angle on life is set by offices, parties, club meetings, shopping, books, and the *New Yorker*.

Martha Bruere, artist, author, sometime-socialist, and clubwoman, had written on women's work and social reform. No doubt she chose the 60 illustrations in *Laughing Their Way* – nearly all of them cartoons, more than half of which had appeared in the *New Yorker* – because they were the pinnacle of women's achievements as pictorial humorists. At the other extreme are the four nineteenth-century pictures of women expressed in the design of woven rugs and satire in cutout silhouettes. Their artists have observed domestic details with a bemused eye and employed their private media to reproduce them, but the works have little more audience than the artist's household. Access to publications, many of them devised by women, such as magazines of the suffragist and birth control campaigns, broadened not only the audience for women's humor but also the purposes of their laughter. Alice Beach Winter's drawing of a forlorn woman staring at a "Boy Wanted" sign, published in *The Masses*, took up public policies and indicated women's attitudes as they might be if women fully recognized their predicament. Helen E. Hokinson's clubwomen, a *New Yorker* staple for many years, dominate the selections. Her overstuffed matrons, tossing fur stoles and presiding over meetings and men, discuss municipal reform or "Bronxville and the League of Nations" and remark, upon meeting a budding social worker, "How brave!" Neither the characters nor the artist feel passion for causes or principles. The specific angle of woman's vision that is celebrated here features rarified banter between artists who ridicule the hollow shell of women's clubs in the 1930s and the club women who enjoy the joke – and the notoriety.

Mary Beard had turned from suffrage and labor agitation to a unique brand of scholarship by which she hoped to alter women's consciousness of their past, particularly to give name and substance to the force that women had always exerted in history. "An agency in creative enterprise," humor helped women to shape the nation's progress. It carries a heavy load throughout the book, for humor must provide keys not only to women's culture but also to the role of humor in civilization. Three stories, grouped as "Human Interest Stories," came about because middle-class women encountered the lower orders through social work and teaching and set down their impressions of social differences complete with immigrant dialects. The plots are easily summarized: college graduate takes Italian child to the country for fresh air; WASP schoolteacher meets feuding Russian immigrants; neighbor of Louisville settlement house, "Mrs. Wiggs of the Cabbage Patch," aspires to be respectable. They won't split your sides, but they will teach you, according to Beard, about women who laughed under the pressure of class conflict in cities, "preparing the way perhaps for a likeness-of-kind ideology—root of all amicable associations." Even though the middle-class women in these stories have the good grace to laugh at their own confusion over the unexpected sophistication of their needy clients, Beard's optimism about social harmony would be a bit more convincing if she included some good jokes on social workers too.

Whose minds worked along the calculated path that Bruere and Beard trace? Their preconceptions about what women's consciousness could be—their goals for women and civilization—steered them away from inventiveness that failed to take formal society seriously. Though she was a pioneer in social history, Beard overlooked, for example, the "surveys" of humor being compiled by folklorists and, instead, tracked down fine-honed wit, yet she presumed to answer questions about how women amused themselves and what they laughed at. Two of the three strands of women's humor included in B. A. Botkin's *Treasury of American Folklore* shatter logic. Neither civilization nor woman's contribution to it—as judged by Beard and Bruere—could be readily appreciated on the basis of Little Audrey jokes as told by Texas teenagers in the 1930s and collected by Cornelia Chambers.

One day Little Audrey and her mother were driving along when all of a sudden the car door flew open and Little Audrey's mother fell out. Little Audrey just laughed and laughed, 'cause she knew all the time that her mother had on her light fall suit.

And many more jokes in the same vein kept women laughing their way. "Borrowing trouble" tales existed in most European countries and many American states in the nineteenth century, testifying to their appeal to popular imagination. Though their details differed, the version reported from Massachusetts by Fanny D. Bergen in 1898 exemplifies the form.

A girl sat on a river bank crying. On being asked the cause of her grief, she replied, "Oh, I was thinking if I had a darter and my darter had a darter and she should fall into the warter, how dreadful it would be."

Mary Beard is determined to show us women who are fully engaged with society, whether by changing it or mastering its commerce of humor. And because reason, even if applied to absurdity and eccentricity, is their most powerful weapon for locking up the demons of antifemale attitudes, Beard stresses only its ideal manifestations.

At the forefront of nineteenth-century humor stood Samantha Allen, the creation of Marietta Holley and one of the great talkers in American culture. Samantha takes on everybody and everything, sniffing at the types who congregate at Saratoga Springs, marveling at her husband's obstinacy, and thinking about the "great subject of wimmen's rites." Beard notes that the author has an ax to grind, but she cannot help appropriating the historical rightness of Samantha's wit for 1874. Samantha has been talking to Betsey Bobbet, "a neighborin' female of ours," about contentment.

Betsey haint married and she don't seem contented. She is awful opposed to wimmen's rights; she thinks it is wimmen's only spear to marry . . . which makes it hard and wearin' on the single men around here. For take the men that are most opposed to wimmen's havin' a right, and talk the most about its bein' her duty to cling to a man like a vine to a tree, they don't want Betsey to cling to them, they won't let her cling to 'em . . . [S]ays I to 'em "Which had you ruther do, let Betsey Bobbet cling to you or let her vote?" and they would every one of 'em quail before that question. They would drop their heads before my keen grey eyes and move off the subject. But Betsey don't get discouraged. Every time I see her she says in a hopeful, wishful tone that "the deepest of men of minds in the country agree with her in thinkin' that it is wimmen's duty to marry and not to vote."

Holley's popular stories contain social commentary rooted in historically specific neighborhoods where gossip flourished and notable characters like Samantha and Betsey thrived. Although Samantha has a beef against a community that excludes women from politics on such shaky bases, her humor takes for granted the neighborliness of her life – reinforces and builds it, Beard would say – and the essential connection between what her neighbors think and what sort of society they will maintain.

The urban wits, whose classy and polished writing makes up the bulk of *Laughing Their Way*, celebrate a disengaged personality with a heightened sense of life's absurdity but no commitment to history, except in the rare instances where a fight over the rights of women captures their attention. Cracked hostesses, suburban tennis games, bureaucracy at city hall and the department store, these are the capers of the middle classes. Perhaps their audiences are no smaller than Samantha's, but the constraints on one's ability to share the joke are no longer agreement or disagreement but material conditions. At their best, as in Dorothy Parker's skit "The Garter," tales reach out to laugh at emotional states of such intense isolation and accuracy that the experience is simply human, albeit rendered with female details. Parker's "Garter" has just snapped on the leg of a woman who is seated at a party, leaving the woman preoccupied by the impossibility of ever rising from her chair without severe humiliation because her stocking will slip to the floor. No social gambit seems adequate in her acute anxiety. The fact that I've never worn such a garter does not lessen my share in the woman's dilemma because her monologue is so true to women's experience – to, say, knowing that I have just bled through my pants and the likelihood exists that when I stand up my pants will be obviously wet if not red, and that a puddle of blood will remain on the chair. There I might sit until hell freezes over and my wedding's gone by.

By pursuing the humorists who had the confidence to tell woman's story as she knows it to be, by insisting that women maintained a humorous and distinctive angle on life, and by circulating samples of the best work, Mary Beard laid a cornerstone for more raucous, physiological, and mass-produced humor by women in our generation, even if she failed to find a social history of women's laughter.

Notes

1. *Laughing Their Way: Women's Humor in America*, edited by Martha Bensley Bruere and Mary Ritter Beard (New York, 1934).

The Politics of Boys' Sports Novels

James P. O'Brien

I was visiting a small-town library in the Berkshires when my eye was caught by a shelf full of books that were free for the asking because nobody ever borrowed them. To my astonishment there were five books by the man who was the king of sports fiction writers in his day, the leading literary figure of my childhood, John R. Tunis. This chance discovery made an instant change in my reading habits. Over the next year I read close to 40 sports novels, continually telling myself that more research was needed on this interesting topic. Eventually the supply dried up (you can't find many of them in libraries, hardly any in bookstores, and the ones my sister sent for my birthday were pretty lousy), so I stopped.

The politics of boys' sports novels are not what you might think. If asked about this literary genre, the average leftist, aside from calling them stupid, will say that they teach snobbery, conformity, patriotism, the glory of winning, and acceptance of authority. But what I remember from childhood, and what my readings of a few years ago confirm, is something very different.

The sports novels can be arranged in a kind of gradient, starting with those that have the least character development and the fewest social implications. (Usually these authors can't write their way out of a paper bag; even their play-by-play narration is boring).

But here at the bottom of the barrel there are certain themes that deserve a close look. Winning (be it the league championship, the state tournament, or the "big game") is a reward not just for superior athletic ability but for good character as well. There is a kind of ethos that is assumed in all the boys' sports novels, whose main ingredients are fair play, gracious winning (or losing), and unselfishness. The last one is probably the most important: time and again an author asks his protagonist to submerge his own vanity for the good of the team. And always, virtue is compensated. The world of sports fiction is one in which right makes might, rather than vice-versa.

So far, nothing has been said to set these books apart from other juvenile fiction or even from most pre-1970 movies or television shows. Just as the "good guys" win Western shoot-outs, they win football and baseball games: the alternative—bad guys winning—is too horrible to contemplate. Even here, however, when we take only the bare-bones sports novels devoid of any creative spark, I feel that they transmit a certain kind of idealism. The moral lessons they convey are presented without the right-wing baggage of so many other cultural vehicles. The heroes are not cowboys crushing stereotyped Indians, they are not soldiers expanding or defending an empire, and they are not cops. The books teach ideals more or less in the abstract, divorced from any specific attachment to God, country, or the white race. This is a negative virtue but a virtue nonetheless.

So far we have been talking about the most obvious potboilers, the sports novels that are only about sports. A lot of books I read, though, had a social significance that went beyond the sports ethos; the authors were clearly interested in incorporating democratic and egalitarian lessons in their stories. Here are some examples:

Donald Hamilton Haines's *Triple Threat* (1933), in which a star football player at a boarding school turns away from the snobbish "gilded youth" of the school and befriends the poor Irish editor of the school newspaper.

John R. Tunis's *Iron Duke* (1938), in which the track team's champion miler, rebuffed by Harvard's upper-class clique until he wins first place in the Intercollegiates, snubs them in return by turning down membership in the student honorary society they control.

Tunis's *All-American* (1942), in which the protagonist actually transfers from his snobbish prep school to the local public high school; the book climaxes when he joins the star Irish player and the star Jewish player in fighting to have the school reject an invitation to play an intersectional football game in Miami to which the team's black player could not be invited.

Tunis's *A City for Lincoln* (1945), in which a small-town basketball coach, after winning the state championship, starts a youth program in town, runs afoul of the local Republican establishment, and then runs for mayor on a platform of municipal ownership of public utilities—my favorite childhood book prior to *Mutiny on the Bounty*, even though I was a Republican myself and didn't know what public utilities were.

Clair Bee's *Hoop Crazy* (1950), in which one of the themes is a high school basketball team's refusal to give an inch in demanding equal treatment for its black player when they play in a segregated city at the southern tip of their border state.

Gene Olson's *Fullback Fury* (1964), in which a high school football coach and his star player are attacked by the town's conservative newspaper owner, whose animus is rooted in his hatred for the town's Chicano population.

Olson's *The Ballhawks'* (1960), in which an aroused small-town community stands up to its leading businessman, who wants the basketball coach fired for putting a Chinese boy and the son of a ne'er-do-well on the starting team.

If there are two quasi-political themes common to the sports novels (not just the ones described above but a lot of others in which the politics are more submerged), they are a hatred of snobbery and a belief in racial and ethnic equality. Antisnobbery, of course, is not to be confused with proletarian class consciousness: in most books it simply means that a player from a wealthy family has to be straightened out and made to realize that it's the team as a whole that's important.

The theme of racial and ethnic equality also has its variations. Sometimes it can be a kind of crude assimilationism: admittance to "the team" is accompanied by a pressure toward homogenization. Sometimes also, a team's diversity is simply presented in the book without being made an issue. Still and all, it is startling, especially in books written in the 1950s, how often race *is* made an issue, how many of the books make an explicit assertion of the right of everyone to play sports based on ability alone. Some examples have been given above, and there are others, such as Duane Decker's *Hit and Run* (1949) in which the author inserts a black player (the first in his league) whose good character serves as an example to the book's protagonist. Or a semifictional book on a National League pennant race that goes out of its way to highlight the Dodgers' black players. Always, in all these books, the protagonist is white and specifically a WASP: aside from Chip Hilton and Bronc Burnett they have names like Jim Allison, Don Henderson, Ron Perry, Bob White, Chip Fiske, Greg Carson, Ky Butler, et cetera. The only partial exception I found was in Gene Olson's *Fullback Fury*, mentioned earlier, in which Coach Gus Harvath is on center stage: but he shares it with the fullback, Johnny Roland.

I don't have a very good notion about who reads these books, since most of my friends deny it vigorously. I have a sense the readership was on the fringes where I was: boys who liked sports a lot and played all the time in the schoolyard or vacant lots but weren't good enough to play in organized leagues. The difference between pickup games and organized sports came across to me once in junior high school, in an intramural touch football game. Billy Gray was putting on one of his usual, dazzling displays of broken field running. Here was a boy who, except for being homely, was straight off the pages of one of the sports novels: modest, sincere, profoundly democratic, completely honest. On one play that still stands out for me 25 years later, he broke loose for a long run, leaving all the opposing players except one far behind, along with the referee. It looked as though the safety may have tagged him before he went over the goal line. The following shouted dialogue then took place:

Referee: Did he get you, Billy?

Billy Gray: You have to decide.

Since the referee didn't actually see the play, he ruled it a touchdown.

In a pickup game with no referee, there's no question but that Billy Gray would have stopped and put the ball down as soon as he was tagged. But this was organized competition, and he felt no such obligation. This episode writ large is what I suspect happened to boys' sports novels in the past decade, and why they aren't read anymore. (I did see *some* sports fiction in a local bookstore recently, but it had large type and pictures, with only about a hundred pages instead of the 200 we used to get, and obviously was for a younger audience.) To put it simply, sports are more transparent now: the rough play, cheating, and cynicism that are obvious on the telecasts make the character-building novels ring hollow. Nonfiction sports-heroes books still sell as well as ever, but the Chip Hilton and Bronc Burnett characters are no longer believable. For me, it's a shame. *I* believed them; and looking back, I think they helped to build a picture of life as it should be. That image led to disillusionment and radicalization in the early 1960s when American society turned out to be something different.

Nursing Illusions: Nurses in Popular Literature

Barbara Melosh

From the Civil War's "Angel of the Battlefield" to Ken Kesey's "Big Nurse," nurses have appeared in popular culture in many guises. Nurses are canonized as self-sacrificing handmaidens of health, whereas they demonstrate more secular skills in pornographic books and movies; the sturdy American girl vies with the castrating bitch. Not content to leave their public image to the vagaries of such fickle followers, nurses have created their own literature. A surprising number of short stories and novels by nurses unfold a more consistent ideal nurse, one that provides a model of proper professional relationships and that subtly instructs the potential client about the proper patient's behavior.

This essay takes a look at an eclectic sample of nurses in American fiction from around 1920 to 1950, a period that saw tremendous expansion of medical science and technology, consolidation of the hospital industry, and development of new funding structures that gave government and insurance companies a powerful role in health care. The nurse's work changed from private duty in the home to staff work in hospitals. Nursing leaders sought more uniform educational standards, and lobbied for state registration of nurses to regulate entry into the occupation. Meanwhile, the burgeoning of medical knowledge and authority redefined the social experiences of sickness and health. Public health offered its own definitions and cure for poverty, and the broadening purview of medicine brought more middle-class people to the office and the hospital.

Nurses appear in fiction in the service of a range of intentions, from conveying advice to purveying pornography. The stories by nurses come from and help create their developing professional ideology. Consciously didactic, they dramatize nursing ideals to edify the public and to inspire their colleagues. Professional journals, novels for adolescents, and health journals for laypeople are the outlets for these highly respectable homilies. The popular fiction uses nurse characters more variously, drawing on them to evoke issues of work, death, dependence, sexuality, and womanhood. Most of the stories discussed here were first published in wide-circulation magazines, and many have at least pretensions to "high literature." Beyond this selection, popular fiction reaches another kind of audience. A common form is the pulp novel seldom found in public libraries, much less in academic collections. The Salvation Army and local garage sales are the archives for this kind of research material – short, simply written, cheaply printed novels sold on newsstands, often in a series. Circulation figures for such works are not available, and comprehensive bibliographies simply do not exist. But the volume and persistence of this kind of nursing fiction attest to its enduring audience appeal.

All these different fictional forms draw upon aspects of the same historical situation: the development of health care and the growth of nursing within it. Although only a few of the popular stories deal directly with the nurse's place in health care, they refer to it nonetheless; their meaning and appeal depend on and imply common understandings of available images of nurses. Both the popular and the professional viewpoint speak to the underlying questions about the nurse as a professional woman and to larger cultural assumptions about health and medical care.

The nurse's ambiguous status in medicine and in the dominant culture makes nursing a significant focus for understanding cultural

ideology of health. Nurses simultaneously represent and defy expectations for women. The nurse is traditionally halfway between
patient and physician: interpreter of abstruse medicine, surrogate
mother with both its nurturing and its disciplinary implications. Associations with mothering, deference to male doctors, and sentimental images of selfless service all evoke traditional conceptions
of women's roles. But at the same time, the technical skill of nurses,
their association with the esoteric knowledge of medicine, and their
physical access to male and female patients make their roles anomalous. The stories by laypersons illustrate the cultural unease about
women in this role, and these cultural contradictions make nurses
the locus for expression of ambivalence about and resistance to
medicine.

This intermediate status is a shaping force in nursing history
underlying the development of professional ideology. Early articulation of nursing ideology mediates a fomenting conflict: late nineteenth-century physicians had little more training than nurses and
feared encroachment on their own newly established professional
prerogatives. By specifying the separate spheres of the doctor and
the nurse, nursing ideology sought to ease these tensions and to
clarify the legitimate role of the nurse as a professional colleague
of the doctor. Over the decades, this stance continued to assert a
certain equality, masking differences in power, class, and sexual
status even as it spelled out the proper social relationships within
an increasingly stratified medical hierarchy.

How does such a contradiction function in practice? At times,
nurses have used professional ideology to support the hierarchical
system of health care and to defend their own position in it. But
they have also used the dictums of professional ideology strategi-
cally to resist and innovate in the medical hierarchy.

At times they have overtly resisted the hierarchical decisions
of medicine; perhaps more often, they undercut or subtly modify
the doctor's influence by indirect means. They often act as patient
advocates, supporting the special needs and rights of patients
against medical and institutional impersonality. Professional ideology in nursing helped to foster women's identities as workers as
well. Although it seldom addresses the particular problems of

women on the job, it motivates women to consider themselves as workers with special skills, contributing members of a public life often implicitly reserved for men. And nurses offered a broader vision of medicine's role in society. In opposition to doctors' narrow defense of the entrepreneurial relationship of individual physician and private patient, nurses argued early for a broader social distribution of health care.

Nurses' fiction reveals the influence of professional ideology. From these stories emerges a clearly didactic model for a woman professional. Her characteristics come from a traditional conception of female nature, reinterpreted as part of a public role. Moreover, nurses saw themselves as part of a health movement: they were conscious of the social meaning of their work. Much of the fiction focuses on public health nursing. It is sometimes directed to nurses themselves: a few stories are fictionalized case histories published in *Public Health Nursing,* the official organ of the National Organization for Public Health Nursing. Another prime audience seems to be young girls or women who might aspire to be nurses. Interestingly, these often debunk the standard romantic notions of the nurse as an angel of mercy, emphasizing instead a more modern vision of the personal satisfactions of competence and service. I also detect an effort to address those middle-class people who were increasingly the consumers of health care. The short stories in *Hygeia,* now *Today's Health,* interpret professional methods and goals to the layperson, and they also provide models for the behavior of properly cooperative and appreciative patients.

A school nurse in "Tonsils and Tact" illustrates the ideal approach of the public health nurse. Gaining the confidence of an Italian family, the nurse "showed no spirit of officiousness. . . . Like a ray of sunshine she came, and the place began to bloom. . . . She radiated good health. . . . She treated Mrs. Annuzzo as a personal friend."[1] This description echoes the public health manuals, which urged nurses to work by indirection and tact, to teach by their own example of glowing health, and to establish personal relationships with family members as a basis for winning future cooperation in health programs.

The fictionalized case history provides even more direct

prescriptions. This strange form of fiction comes from a contest run by *Public Health Nursing*, and the four prizewinning stories are strikingly uniform. They sound very much like the anecdotes in the public health manuals recounted from selected real life cases to illustrate nursing pointers. In all these stories, tactful intervention wins the day for the nurses and the forces of progress. One example conveys the overall message. In "Neblett's Landing,"[2] a young, capable nurse rides over rugged roads in rural Mississippi to reach a suspected case of meningitis. Once there, she hears from a neighborhood woman that the man has already been hospitalized. Never one to waste a trip, the alert nurse turns her skills to the material at hand. She notices that her informant is tired-looking and pregnant, and she engages her in a friendly conversation. Before her unsuspecting victim can resist, the nurse has gently instructed her on prenatal care, collected a urine specimen, and arranged·to immunize a small child who lurks underfoot.

The form of these fictionalized case histories reinforces the message: the narration is from the nurse's observing viewpoint, but she is nearly invisible as a character. The action unfolds through the patient or family while the nurse behind the scenes actually shapes the action. The patients seem to speak for themselves, but somehow, by the end, they always say what the nurse wants to hear.

These dramatizations also reveal the public health emphasis on "case-finding" and document the changing definitions of health care. The emphasis is environmental, preventive, and positive — health is no longer merely the absence of debilitating disease but comes to represent a broader vision of the good life. Maternity and baby care are comprehensive examples: public health pushed medically monitored childbirth, and postnatal programs struggled to replace traditional methods with nursing and medical regimens for child care. Nurses also argued for new surgical procedures. A few stories reveal the contemporary medical enthusiasm for tonsillectomies, and one even deals with securing plastic surgery for a young girl with burn scars.[3] Finally, public health nurses intervene in a range of family and social concerns: unemployment, generational conflict, and immigrant assimilation are all considered to be part of the province of health. Mental and emotional "hygiene" work their way into the public health manuals.

The darker side of this widening view of medical care is its intimation of social control by professionals who define health and control information. At times the didactic fiction indicates the client's subordinate role in this health endeavor, the emergence of the "good" patient as passive and trusting. Sue Barton's Harlem supervisor assures her, "You'll love working with colored people. . . . They're so willing to cooperate and so eager to learn!"[4] Three stories in *Hygeia* take a more pointed and aggressive position on patient behavior. In "The County Hires a Nurse,"[5] the author caricatures a black washerwoman. who finally sees the light and abandons her opposition to the county nurse. Questioned mischievously by her white lady employer, she praises the clever county nurse lavishly. Exaggerated dialect and cartoon illustrations of blacks with wide white eyes, huge lips, distorted postures, and ragged clothes reinforce the amused superiority of the narration. This story discreetly warns the middle-class consumer: resistance to medicine is associated with ignorance and social inferiority.

Two stories hit closer to the target: one deals with a poor white family and the other with an urban working-class family. Interestingly, these are the only two stories I have found that deal with native-born whites. In "Medicine, Moonshine, and the McFlannels,"[6] a broad humor mocks the ignorance and shiftlessness of Texas rural poor whites. Two public health nurses guide the family through a number of medical services when their daughter swallows a carpet tack. The McFlannels straggle along begrudgingly, complaining loudly about medical meddling and doctor profiteering. The doctors and nurses view them with long-suffering humor, knowing that the chronically indigent family will never pay them anyway. "Was It the Teacher's Fault?"[7] poses the most direct warning about the resistance to medical management. When the daughter of a white factory worker begins to fail in school, the teacher and public health nurse suggest that she needs a tonsillectomy. The parents reject this advice, accusing the teacher of grading their daughter unfairly. When the girl gets a bad ear infection, their private doctor confirms the diagnosis of tonsillitis. The delay has resulted in a more serious illness, and, to make a bad situation worse, the father has just been laid off. The nurse and the teacher shake their heads; if only the family had listened. . . . The chastened parents apologize profusely, and the teacher lends them money for the operation. In the end, all parties resolve that there will be closer cooperation between school, home, and local health department.

These disagreeable homilies on patient compliance reveal the social control that public health sometimes imposed. This is undeniably an effect of public health in America and a thread that runs through the nursing manuals and fiction. Although nurses did not usually control the funding or administration of public health beyond the agency, they did participate in this control to the extent that they identified with medicine's elitism and hierarchical organization and relayed it to their patients.

Still, with all its limitations, the public health method leaned toward a more democratic interpretation of the emerging medical model of patient-professional relationships. Most of the stories indicate respect and affection for the nurses' clients, whether sturdy rural sorts or urban immigrants. They portray immigrant neighborhoods as colorful and alive; as Sue Barton exclaims on her first visit to the 1930s' Lower East Side, "Why! It's like living in an electric current! And I thought the slums would be dreary!"[8] This sentimental affection for immigrant life is often tinged with condescension, yet it does acknowledge other cultural traditions. Public health manuals advised nurses to adapt their methods to existing practice and belief when possible and not to assume blindly that they knew best. Manuals counseled respect for the patient's own definition of the service relationship. "We are attempting to find out what it is that the patient wants from the nurse and what, because of his individual capabilities and situation, he will be able to use. It is *his* situation—*his* life.[9]

Most important, public health continually stressed education and self-care. The good public health nurse did as little actual nursing as possible; her real role was to help her clients nurse themselves and one another. In the larger context, this looks suspiciously like a strategy to spread medical care thinner among those who can't pay for it and to substitute lower paid nurses for private doctors. Still, from the viewpoint of the late twentieth century's overcontrolled, overmedicated, and underinformed layperson, this approach seems refreshingly pragmatic and demystifying.

Although prominent in the fiction, public health never dominated the nursing field. In 1928, one survey estimated that 19% of nurses worked in public health.[10] During the Depression, some state and federal programs funded public health work, but it occupied a shrinking percentage of all nursing work. Just before American involvement in World War II, public health nurses numbered only 24,000 compared to over 100,000 hospital nurses and almost as many private-duty nurses.[11]

Although the public health nurse was never typical, the fiction appropriately selects her to represent professional ideology. First, public health nurses saw themselves as leaders, early pioneers looking to a future of comprehensive social medicine. The nurses in public health had more education and enjoyed the highest status inside the profession. Second, the work situation of the public health nurse favored the fullest expression of professional ideology. Most public health agencies were administered by women, older nurses with experience and acumen. Although the agencies had to work out relationships with local doctors, doctors rarely had a direct role in defining the immediate work situation. In contrast to private duty, where the nurse worked under the doctor's monitoring and where her future employment often depended on catering to his whims, or to the hospital, where doctors hovered over the nursing staff, the public health nurse worked independently and was directly responsible to a nursing organization. Finally, the clientele of the public health nurse probably supported her claim to professional authority more than the middle- and upper-class clients of private-duty nurses or the increasingly middle-class patients in the hospital. One California public health nurse said, "There is greater satisfaction in doing for these poor unfortunates than in catering to patients who have lived lives of pampered luxury."[12] A Kansas nurse echoed the sentiment: "You meet a class of people who need your care and advice. . . . One is more appreciated."[13] The public health patient apparently was more likely to admit that the nurse had special skills and to regard her as a professional rather than as a domestic servant.

If all these advantages made the public nurse more like the professional ideal, they also set her apart from the larger body of nurses. All the popular stories deal with private-duty or hospital nurses, and their portrayals mark the distance between the nurses in those settings and the public health nurses. If the nurses' fiction reveals the positive social potential of professional ideology, the popular fiction outlines the social and cultural limitations that constrained nurses. Sometimes directly, sometimes unintentionally, they unfold the grimmer side of nursing: long hours, hard work, poor pay, loneliness, and social isolation. Most of these authors are unsympathetic to nurses, either taking their roles lightly or projecting other fears associated with medicine onto their portrayals of nurses. But this very distance allows them to observe and express aspects of nursing that the professional fiction suppressed.

Most of the popular stories show conflict between the nurse as a professional and the nurse as a woman: the didactic stories' happy amalgam of the healthy, pretty American girl and the resourceful nurse is nowhere to be found. The professional women in these stories are usually distressingly unprofessional, "cute" nurses. And popular imagination seemed obsessed by the less admirable specimens of the profession, from the merely dull or incompetent to the downright unsavory. Nurses' fiction was inspirational and motivational; popular fiction was the patient's revenge.

Only three popular fiction stories parallel the elements of professional ideology set out in the didactic stories. Through the viewpoint of a young nurse, F. Scott Fitzgerald's "An Alcoholic Case"[14] portrays the self-destructiveness of an alcoholic man. The nurse's commitment to service and her determination to intervene contrast powerfully with the alcoholic's single-minded struggle for the bottle. Her final frustration with the case signals his inexorable ruin. In "The Shadowy Third,"[15] Ellen Glasgow unfolds a tale of a "nervous case" and a ghost child; the nurse's sympathy with her charge enables her to share the woman's supernatural vision of the dead child. "Who Lived and Died Believing"[16] also focuses on the nursing of a psychiatric case. Nancy Hale affirms the nurse's emotional involvement with her difficult female patient, who slowly improves.

Sympathy, service, and the will to intervene all characterize nurses in both popular fiction and didactic stories. But all the layperson's portraits of nurses are tempered with realism about the hazards of such commitment. In all three stories, another character advises the young nurse against over-involvement. The supervisor in Fitzgerald's story monitors her young charge and warns against the discouragement of caring for alcoholics. Glasgow's character discusses her empathy with patients with the older nurse who heads the registry, who tells her, "When you are drained of every bit of sympathy and enthusiasm, and have got nothing in return for it, not even thanks, you will understand why I try to keep you from wasting yourself."[17] In Hale's story, the protagonist's boyfriend, a cynical intern, counsels her to forget her case after her hours on duty. More than professional literature, which facilely counsels sympathy but objectivity, these stories strike the core of an involved nurse and her experience.

Significantly, sexual conflict appears in all three stories. The didactic stories evade the question: their personable, warm nurses are never glimpsed outside the work situation. In these popular stories, the nurses have the same youthful appeal and the same seriousness about their work, but that work disrupts their private life and their relationships with men. In Fitzgerald's story, nurses at the registry form a weary alliance against the advances of "fresh" patients, and their case loads leave them little time for social life. Glasgow's protagonist is attracted to her patient's husband, a doctor, but as the story develops we discover that his charming surface masks the ultimate depravity, for he has killed his own small daughter. The psychotic woman of Hale's story is insane because of a faithless husband; while her nurse muses on the unfairness of love, her lover, the intern, breaks off with her because she is so absorbed in the case. Once again, nurse and female patient ally themselves against male sexuality.

The fictional solutions may seem drastic and negative, but they serve to dramatize the anomaly of a woman professional: the demands for involvement with work clash with the cultural expectations for women's emotional lives. Where nurses *are* romantically involved, their work interests are explicitly secondary. Two saccharine stories illustrate the genre. "Nurse's Choice"[18]informs us gaily that "having to choose between two personable doctors is what nurses dream about." Interestingly, the nurse's decision affirms separate codes of personal and professional behavior. When this usually cool surgical nurse develops a hot appendix, her two vying lovers meet in the operating room. The younger resident, unhinged by love, cannot operate; the prestigious older surgeon takes the knife from his faltering hand and completes the surgery. This clinches the nurse's choice: she decides in favor of the resident, repelled by the older surgeon's detachment. His medical objectivity, the usual ironclad ideal, disqualifies him romantically. She reassures the resident about his professional failure: "I would have acted the same way if you had been on the table," and makes the final diagnosis, "It's just love, Joe."

This same condition afflicts the intern of Agnes Sligh Turnbull's "Dear Little Fool."[19] Young Doctor MacNaughton, the heartthrob of the student nurses, is friendly enough, but to the distress of all, he is preoccupied with his work. Soon his businesslike manner breaks down under the influence of a young redheaded student nurse dubbed "Little Carrot." Warmhearted and impulsive, she nurses by instinct, with a woman's sense of patients' emotional needs and a cheerful disregard for protocol and procedure. She has the natural sympathy recommended in professional ideology but lacks the discipline, respect for theory, and career commitment of the professional nurse. The discipline of hospital life thwarts the womanly sympathies that attracted her to nursing, and, at the end of the story, she eagerly accepts a more appropriate offer. In the romantic setting of night duty on the ward, the smitten intern proposes. "I wonder . . . if you've ever thought about any other career but nursing. What I mean is, your first year's up next month, and at that time – well, there's another job waiting that I've had in mind for you for a good while. . . . This would be one for life."

These stories evidence the personal conflicts that nurses confront, but their perspective is that of the layperson's, the consumer of health care. As such, they reveal the changes in the consumer's

Barbara Melosh

role and, from the consumer's viewpoint, imply a health system that diverges sharply from the public health nurses' ideal visions.

By the late 1930s, hospital services had expanded tremendously, mostly because of new insurance funding, and its functions and clientele had changed. The middle-class readers of these stories were using the hospital more. Insurance coverage meant that more diagnostic tests were performed in the hospital. The ongoing redefinition of childbirth also accounted for heavier use of hospitals; increasingly, the respectable middle class chose the hospital rather than the home. In this context, I suspect that these lighter romances represent an effort to render the hospital more familiar, to overcome an underlying fear of a burgeoning and mystified medical technology, and to combat the estrangement and loss of control that patients experience in a hospital setting. Against these disquieting possibilities, the stories show doctors and nurses as participants in a hospital that looks very much like a small town, complete with gossip, intrigues, and romance. They are an attempt to humanize a threatening and distant world, to make the hospital into a friendly place, to show that doctors and nurses are not technological demigods but just folks subject to the same foibles as everyone else. Heterosexual romance is the dialectical counterpart to the medical and nursing prescription of objectivity and emotional control.

Whatever the palliative effect of such whimsey, it failed to confront the issues of a widening professional authority and concomitant loss of control for laypersons. Ring Lardner's famous "Zone of Quiet"[20] illustrates this tension. A beleaguered male patient suffers the monologues of a comically garrulous nurse. Gossipy, dumb, and incompetent, she reports for duty yawning after nights of dancing and drinking and wears out her patients with vapid stories. The deft humor of this story has its source in the undercurrent of fear associated with the hospital setting. To laugh at a flapper in uniform has a powerful demystifying effect: the nurse is like any other young woman, only more so. At the same time, the humor works by evoking an incongruous reversal of class and gender prerogatives: we observe a cool, intelligent, cultured man at the mercy of a gum-chewing, English-abusing woman.

But although the layperson does not want to feel controlled by his or her inferiors in the hospital, there is cold comfort in the opposite suggestion—that one is sick and helpless in the hands of incompetents. Lardner plays on this possibility when the nurse tells her dismayed patient that her first five patients have died and wonders out loud if he will break her losing streak. Yet he keeps the threat from predominating and overwhelming the humor: his character is a graduate nurse who has not yet passed her state boards. This plot device allows the reader to acknowledge the threatening aspects of the hospital situation by accepting the humor based on them, yet simultaneously defuses the possibility it suggests by making the character not really a nurse.

Nurses entrenched in their jobs are also entrenched in personal peculiarities. Sometimes a misfit character is admiringly portrayed: celibacy and social isolation produce selfless devotion to duty. A sentimental *Saturday Evening Post* story, Arthur Gordon's "Old Ironpuss,"[21] shows a crusty older nurse whose harsh facade hides the predictable heart of gold. Although she is a sympathetic character, she is not an appealing model: her courage and strength are linked explicitly to her isolation, eccentricity, and asexuality.

Other misfits are not heroes but only outcasts. Dorothy Parker's "Horsie"[22] shows the loneliness of private duty in a humorous story about a spinsterish nurse. Taking care of a spoiled young matron who has just had a baby, she tries pathetically to fit into the household, while the husband and wife laugh behind her back at her social ineptitude. Finally she goes back home to her sick mother, leaving them to their superficial and comfortable life. The powerful contrast of the middle-aged, single, drab nurse with the carelessly wealthy young couple points strikingly to class differences. Having a live-in nurse after childbirth is a symbol of status and leisure: nursing is merely a specialization of domestic service.

Another sort of service is rendered by that notorious misfit, the nurse as sexual pervert. T. K. Brown's "A Drink of Water"[23] is one of the more bizarre examples of the theme of decadent sexuality that often develops around nurse characters. Written in 1958, the story revolves around a wounded soldier. Fred MacCann has lost both arms and legs and is blind as well, in what some skeptics might consider an excess of authorial zeal. Fred spends a lot of time brooding over this situation until diverted by the attentions of a gentle nurse. Although she is not very bright, she is good at anticipating his needs – in short, she is the ideal woman. Eventually, to his amazement and gratitude, she approaches him sexually. They embark on a torrid affair, despite certain obstacles imposed by hospital authorities who take a dim view of this budding relationship. But one night during a drunken orgy in his hospital room, Fred discovers the horrible truth. As she breathes heavily into his ear and calls him her "man-thing," he bitterly realizes that to her he is only a "phallus on a pedestal of flesh." His beloved has always hated men, and she can love him only because of his mutilation. In despair, he kills himself, an act requiring no little ingenuity under the circumstances. (First he is stumped, but he gropes his way to a solution.)

This peculiar story makes some fascinating comments on the nurse-patient relationship. The overdrawn injuries of the patient dramatize the patient's utter dependence in this hospital situation, and the nurse's exploitation of this dependence underscores the patient's vulnerability. Moreover, the story implies that the woman's need to control is what makes her a nurse: her gentle efficiency and deference to the patient's comfort mask a perverted dominance. Significantly, her corruption is an excess of an otherwise valued feminine trait, the desire to nurture. Ironically, Fred takes the sexual relationship as an affirmation of his adult status – as egalitarian love; actually it is the ultimate objectification, for the nurse sees him only as a phallus that she can control because of his physical dependence. This plot speaks strikingly to fears about the hospital, medical impersonality, the nurse's physical access to the patient, and her control over the immediate environment.

These fictional worlds can tell us much about the perceived opportunities and threats of an expanding culture of expertise. For nurses, the growth of medical institutions and authority represented an opportunity, and they sought to carve out a place for themselves in that new world. Laypersons responded with more ambivalence as new technological resources redefined the experiences of sickness and health. At the same time, both groups faced the expanding hospital empire within a world that was also redefining the possibilities and limitations of gender. In the didactic fiction, nurses constructed a professional identity that subsumed the cultural contradictions of work and womanhood. In the popular fiction, laypersons emphasized those same contradictions to express unease about the widening of professional authority and the changing place of women. Taken together, these stories offer a glimpse of a complex cultural dialectic about work, gender, and professional authority.

Notes

1. Paul Stevens, "Tonsils and Tact," *Hygeia* 13.1 (Mar. 1935): 256–58.
2. Pattie R. Sanders, "Neblett's Landing," *Public Health Nursing* 29 (June 1937): 387–88.
3. Lucretia Penny, "They Name Her Demetria," *Hygeia*, 18.1 (Feb. 1940): 134–37, 174.
4. Helen Dore Boylston, *Sue Barton, Visiting Nurse* (Boston, 1938), 133.
5. Lucretia Penny, "The County Hires a Nurse," *Hygeia* 9 (Aug. 1931): 712–14.
6. Mary Holdsworth Butt, "Medicine, Moonshine, and the McFlannels," *Hygeia* 17 (Jan. 1939): 22–25.
7. Esther A. Canter, "Was It the Teacher's Fault?" *Hygeia* 9 (Sept. 1931): 844–45.
8. Boylston, *Sue Barton*, 38–39.
9. Ruth Gilbert, The Public Health Nurse and Her Patient (New York, 1940), 162.
10. May Ayres Burgess, *Nurses, Patients, and Pocketbooks* (New York, 1928), 249–50. A wonderful source, this is a survey sparked by the problem of nurses' widespread unemployment in the twenties. The data comes from the findings of the Committee on the Grading of Nursing Schools, mostly from detailed questionnaires that were sent to nurses, doctors, and patients.
11. Mary M. Roberts, *American Nursing: History and Interpretation* (New York, 1954), 428. A good history by a nurse and former editor of the *American Journal of Nursing*.
12. Burgess, *Nurses, Patients, and Pocketbooks*, 269–70.
13. Ibid., 270.
14. F. Scott Fitzgerald, "An Alcoholic Cast," *The Bodley-Head Scott Fitzgerald*, edited by Malcolm Cowley (London, 1963), 314–22. The story was written in 1937.
15. Ellen Glasgow, "The Shadowy Third," *The Shadowy Third* (New York, 1923) 1–43.
16. Nancy Hale, "Who Lived and Died Believing," *The Best American Short Stories, 1943* (Boston, 1943), 144–65.

17. Glasgow, "The Shadowy Third," 5.

18. Frederick Hazlitt Brennan, "Nurse's Choice," *Collier's* 100 (Dec. 11, 1937): 17.

19. Agnes Sligh Turnbull, "Dear Little Fool," *Saturday Evening Post*, 221:24 (June 25, 1949): 64–75.

20. Ring Lardner, "Zone of Quiet," *The Love Nest and Other Stories* (New York, 1926); 57–59.

21. Arthur Gordon, "Old Ironpuss," *Saturday Evening Post* 223:35 (May 12, 1951): 149–53.

22. Dorothy Parker, "Horsie," *After Such Pleasures*, (New York, Viking, 1933), 3–34.

23. T. K. Brown, "A Drink of Water," *Prize Stories, 1958: The O. Henry Awards* (New York, 1958), 179–201. First published in *Esquire*.

People's Music

Penelope Rosemont *Sun Dance of the Kite-Birds* (ink, 1978)

In Pursuit of
Polka Happiness

Angela Keil and Charles Keil

The strongest musical styles of the twentieth century have
come from the formation of the working class in various countries:
Afro-American blues, jazz, rhythm and blues, gospel; white American country and western; Trinidadian calypso; Jamaican reggae;
Greek laika or rebetika; Argentine tango; Brazilian samba and
bossa; Cuban and Puerto Rican latin; Polish-American polka. In
each of these styles, class factors (especially the relative importance of lumpen life styles and values) and various ethnic traditions
blend differently, but each synthesis has the power to evoke strong
responses across class and ethnic lines so that the effort to com-
modify these styles is usually unrelenting soon after their birth.

Our perception of the polka has been shaped by Charles Keil's
studies of Afro-American blues, Yoruba studies of Afro-American
blues (1962–65) and Yoruba juju (1965–67), Angela Keil's work
(1976–82) on the life of Marcos Vamvakaris, father of Greek laika or
bouzouki music, and by a continuing interest in a number of the
other styles previously mentioned. These studies show that the
former peasants who became the working class not only survive

and build the industrial networks, and so forth, but also create distinctive cultures.

A few generalizations about these three styles may help to suggest a framework for closer study. It is sometimes easy to forget that urbanization in this century is an unprecedented phenomenon. Since 1900 over two million Greeks have moved to Athens, almost one million Yoruba have moved to Ibadan, and one million blacks have moved to Chicago. All those people once lived on the land in a state of delicately balanced oppression, an oppression made tolerable by its very predictability, by respect and solidarity within and between families, by pride in locality, by sacred distrust of cities, and by less articulate values that have to do with their manual labor in natural surroundings. Through a combination of industrial processes that seemed inevitable until very recently, the peasantries of the capitalist world were forced off the land and pushed to the bottom of the cities, there to suffer a kind of predictable and, initially, almost total oppression. The catalog of slum problems is long and familiar but always worth reciting: unemployment, underemployment, degrading employment for men and women and children; new "freedoms" to consume and be consumed; a breakdown of traditional family and kinship patterns, adultery, illegitimacy, prostitution; malnutrition and diseases; dependence on alcohol and drugs; crowded housing and high incidence of crime; alienation, anomie, and other high-sounding names for despair.

Conservative peasant values serve in this environment only to make despair total, humor desperate, and song lyrics enduring for as long as the human spirit struggles to survive.

Afro-American blues took shape as a style very early in this century; it became recognizable just after World War I, but it did not reach a peak of popularity outside the Afro-American cultural context until the past decade. Though most scholarship has placed the origin of the blues in the rural south, it seems clearer all the time that style qua style crystalized in the cities, and the model was secondarily disseminated to the rural areas where more idiosyncratic versions of it developed. In the cities, the blues went through various stages and passed into the mainstream of American and world music as "rhythm and blues" or "soul music" – a blend of secular blues, sacred gospel, and black art music or jazz. Once a basic reference point only for black Americans migrating from country to city, it has become everyone's music. Musically, the urban jungles of Memphis and Chicago have not produced wild cries, turbulent rhythms, and complex structures but a unified style of great simplicity—the 12-bar blues: a four-bar call/response pattern repeated a second time for clarity and intensity and resolved in the final four bars; rudimentary underlying harmonic and rhythmic pattern; melodic patterns very uniform though subtly inflected; four/four meter.

Yoruba juju style emerged in the cities of Western Nigeria during the 1920s, the name juju an ironic reference to the coval church harmonies and the Salvation Army source of the initial instruments used—tambourine, cymbals, triangle. The practitioners of the style have always been semiliterate migrants to the big cities, not really good Christians, good Muslims, or good, traditional, Yoruba, another reason for the "juju" label. It has been only during the past 15 years that this style has emerged to dominate the Yoruba musical scene. The popular juju bands of today feature call/response singing and electric guitar counterpoint over a complex foundation provided by eight or nine drummers. This music from the slums of Ibadan and Lagos presents another tightly integrated style. Each of the eight or nine drummers plays a relatively simple rhythm in isolation, but combined, the nine drums create a controlled sound that has the texture of tightly woven cloth and the buzzing, blooming confusion of an African marketplace. They sing in the sweet church harmonies of a traditional culture torn apart, of the good old values people should live by. Leader and chorus, guitar and percussion, always balance perfectly, and gentle dance movements are built upon a dignified shuffle.

Greek "rebetika" or "laika" style is more familiarly known as bouzouki music, as in "Never on Sunday," or "Zorba," and the Olympic Airways television commercials. This style was also created by peasants, refugees, and migrants to the ports and slums of urban Greece during the period immediately following World War I. And again, 40 years of stylistic evolution had taken place before the music achieved wide popularity throughout Greece and some acceptance outside as well. From the hashish dens, jails, brothels, and army barracks of Piraeus and Athens comes the Zembekiko, the fundamental dance meter of laika style, slow measured, stately, 18 very carefully accented eighth notes to the bar. The bouzouki players are always in perfect unison, the singing is precise, the dancing a precious balancing of the bodily scales. The total effect is Apollonian in the extreme.

Perhaps for the lack of immediate continuing pressures from other cultures, Greek urban music is the least changed in its most recent evolutions. There has been a gradual smoothing out of rough edges, more European harmonies, some melodic borrowings from Indian film music, and perhaps an overall loss of vitality despite a relatively recent revival of interest in the 1930s, composer-singers.

In stark comparison, juju has accomplished a drastic return to its origins. Beginning as an Afro-Western synthesis with melody instruments like guitar, mandolin, piano, and even violins predominant in the earlier recordings, juju has dropped the Western instruments leaving only the guitar; the Salvation Army-borrowed tambourine, triangle, and cymbals were put aside while more drums were added decade by decade until the components of the traditional Yoruba drum family were reunited. Once, all songs were performed in standard Yoruba, but now each band sings in a regional dialect, often using idioms incomprehensible to Yoruba from other regions. The push back to localized roots continues with the bandleaders, who seek out the proverbs and rhythmic patterns unique to their district or town of origin. Even high-life, once a pan-Nigerian or pan-West African style, was reacculturated during the 1960s. Pidgin English and standard instrumentation have been cast aside by the most popular bands whose words and music are distinctively Ibo, Yoruba, Kalabari, Bini, et cetera.

Afro-American music has an extraordinarily complex development because of the accelerated pace of cultural homogenization, provoking musicians to repeatedly attempt to reassert the autonomy of their audiences. Every white theft of a black style—dixieland, swing, rhythm and blues—has forced black Americans to delve deeper into their own resources to shape a new style they can call their own. Waves of black church music have been absorbed by

American popular song, and Afro-American innovators are looking to the Caribbean and Africa itself for nourishment.

The Residual Is the Emergent

The most interesting fact about Polish-American polka style in relation to blues, laika, and juju is that it has never been researched; bourgeois (and radical) scholarship has shown no interest. It is still a proletarian style at roughly the point where blues, juju, and laika were in the early 1950s. At this stage of our observation, the polka style can be better described than analyzed in a parallel manner.

We can begin, however, with some features that the Polish-American polka music shares with the other styles described:

1. The creativity of the relatively new urban dweller is especially obvious in the presence of a new musical style, something that can be created only by generations of intense and shared experience and is confirmed by corresponding styles of dance, dress, and speech, the aural and bodily crafts or "a-b-c's" of proletarian culture.

2. The creation of these styles is a living continuation, an active development and constant reworking of peasant traditions. This process has nothing in common with and is really opposed to the bourgeois passion to preserve or recreate or create "folk" culture and "folk" lore.

3. But the new style is based not only on reworking older forms but also on incorporating contemporary elements and forces like electricity. Again, this process has no concern for the "authenticity" or "purity" of the kind that provides almost a raison d'être for the bourgeois connoisseur. Instead, it seems to resemble the joyful and catholic interest in food of the robust organism whose digestive process absorbs all that is of use and swiftly eliminates everything that is not.

4. These styles both confront and retreat from urban social reality and the conditions of life defined by wage labor. The lyrics speak occasionally of the slums and brutal working conditions and, more often, celebrate the avenues of escape—drink, travel, "good

times." Most lyrics, however, focus on the struggle to make a life, to strengthen love, family, and friendship ties while under the attack of an all-usurping commodity economy.

5. The proletariat achieves its styles through the preservation of the communal forms of social creation and the ingrained methods and skills and sensibilities of the oral tradition. It is important for those of us who have learned to associate art and certainly great art with great individual artists to keep in mind that this is a rather recent twist in history; the great traditions of knowledge and expression before the bourgeois period came out of cooperative social efforts that in turn depended on their embeddedness in the life processes of the community. In the final analysis, vitality of style depends upon the health of the community.

Polka music is alive and well in the Buffalo community because a group of less than a thousand Polish-American working people have a passion for it—as music, as a dance, as a party that goes full blast for all ages and both sexes, for family and friends, where time is suspended in a state of happiness. The rest of the Polish-American community dances the polka at weddings, at parish dances and lawn fetes, and may listen to it on the weekends on one of the four small local radio stations catering to special audiences. But it is the hard core of a dozen top bands, along with their families and fans, that supports the polka as their primary process of recreating themselves, who keep the music honed to perfection and bring it to the rest of the community.

The economic base for polka events is built by this hard core within the community. Big record companies, big radio and television networks are not interested in the polka. So bands make their own records and sell them from the bandstand; bandleaders become disc jockeys on local radio stations.

For a description of the always evolving style of the bands, one has to probe their little-understood history. Generally, we can see a movement from "Eastern style" to "Chicago" or "Honky" style. As recently as 15 years ago, all the bands in the Buffalo area played the "Eastern" style. It was just about the only Polish-American music to be heard on records 25 years ago, and the large bands on the East Coast reigned supreme. The legendary promoter "Big Ziggy"

Zywicki brought them all to Buffalo's ballrooms where they mixed polkas, obereks, waltzes, and good swing to the delight of packed houses. It was a golden era and one of fine musicianship. Most everyone read music, arrangements were very tricky, tempos were very brisk, and bands were admired for the crisp articulation in the saxophone section, impossible clarinet duets, perfect unison from the triple-tonguing trumpet players.

The last great Eastern band—the Connecticut Twins, Jas and Stas—perfected the style, reduced the size of the band from ten or 12 pieces to six by introducing amplification, and provided the model for many Buffalo bands in the 1950s. But by then, Li'l Wally Jagiello from Chicago was knocking at Buffalo's door.

At first the Eastern establishment laughed at the slow tempo, the loose phrasing, the whining squeezebox concertina, the unembarrassed vocals "from the heart" and, above all, the one-man band aspect of the whole thing. For Li'l Wally was thumping the bass drum with his foot, squeezing the concertina, and singing simultaneously without a note of music in sight. How does a symphony musician feel when he hears his first bluesman from Mississippi?

Polka disc jockeys returned Wally's first records marked "defective," "too slow," or "go practice some more." But somehow, and no one we've talked to is very clear about the how and why of it, Li'l Wally Jagiello caught the ear of the people with hit after hit in a musical idiom that seems to have its roots deep in the Goral Mountains and small towns of Galicia Province in Poland.

Not that this is Polish music—you won't find either Chicago or Eastern style polkas in Poland anymore than you find blues and jazz in Africa. But the music developed by Wally, Eddie Zima, and many others along Division Street or "Polish Broadway" in Chicago during the 1940s does echo the village of nineteenth-century Poland in a way that the flash and perfection of Eastern style do not. In the hands of Chicago musicians like Marion Lush and Eddie Blazonszyk, the "Chicago" or "honky" or "dyno" style has proven itself dynamically responsive to the changing tastes and needs of Polish-American communities across the nation.

The massive shift from Eastern to Chicago style polkas began in Buffalo in the early 1960s and today 90% of the polkas you will hear in greater Buffalo are based in the Chicago tradition.

Whatever the style, every polka event is built by polka people. The wedding is perhaps the prototype: find and rent a hall, pick a caterer or recruit family and friends to cook; buy the food; hire bartenders; buy booze; pick the band or bands and pick a day when the bands you want are free; send out invitations (or put up posters, pass out slingers, sell tickets); and make sure that all the tasks of preparation are spread evenly and yet done well so that no one will be too unhappy or so that everyone can be equally happy on that happy day. The amount of time, energy, volunteer labor required to produce a parish dance or lawn fete or a booster club monthly "meeting" is considerable and the return on this investment is carefully measured by everyone in terms of the number of people who come and how good a time they have.

In fact, this calculation is as aesthetic as it is economic. Since the highest goal is happiness for the greatest number and not profit, anything that will contribute to keeping the cost of tickets low and the price of drinks down is a plus. Big summer events under a tent when the dozen better bands agree to donate their services or play for small fees are the high-point of the season, pointed to with pride by everyone, because so many people attend and pay so little for so much joy. This same value or evaluation is applied to all polka events.

A great many other values are linked to this ideal and are explicit or implicit in the many features of a polka fest that make it such a joy. For brevity's sake, we'll list some of these features:

All ages participate.

Everyone dances.

Although the spinning and stomping can become very intense and although the floor is full, people rarely bump into each other.

Coupling is not at a premium.

A new partner for every dance is the ideal.

Women dance with women a lot.

Some of the best musicians are also some of the best dancers; all the younger musicians enjoy dancing.

Many musicians can play two or three different instruments and a few can play all the instruments in the band.

All musicians hold jobs in addition to their polka work.

Songs for the band repertoire are often suggested by fans, and in most bands all members contribute to the composing and arranging process.

All bands have an "English book" with a mix of popular hits that emphasizes "country and western" or "soul" or " '50s rock" or "Glenn Miller songs" depending on the band.

Bands try to answer every request.

Almost every song is dedicated to someone or to whole families or "tables," "going out" either from the band or from one participant to another via the band.

Sexual teasing and joking and open flirting at polka dances have a "fun for the whole family" feeling.

There is wide tolerance for different styles of clothing, hair, demeanor.

Individual dancing styles and styles that pairs of people develop are very much appreciated.

Birthdays are always announced by the band and the song is sung. Anniversaries, weddings, engagements are noted. No one's life cycle is neglected.

Musicians are not stars or sex symbols but are expected to be "regular," part of the crowd, to play until they are exhausted.

Dancers are expected to dance to the point of exhaustion.

Everyone should drink a lot (eat some too) to get silly or happy but not to get drunk.

There should be "no fights."

Did everybody have a good time?

Looking for a Style: Male Images in Country Music of the 1970s

George Lipsitz

Decades establish their own mythical significance. What we refer to as the sixties usually encompasses 1967–72, and the music of that period that we choose to remember generally includes Janis Joplin and Jimi Hendrix while forgetting Sgt. Barry Sadler and Tommy James and the Shondells. As soon as the seventies arrived, the myth of the sixties became a paralyzing illusion directing our sights back to a paradise we thought we lost and away from the political and cultural opportunities being created in a new context.

Today, when we look at the hairstyles and dress of country music stars, when we listen to song lyrics that exclaim, "Take this job and shove it," and when we witness the major increase in women singers and songs concerning women's lives, we might be tempted to say that for country music the sixties happened in the seventies. Yet the truth is even more exciting and promising. The interplay of cultural forces in contemporary country music reflects a new reality in which some of the cultural deadends of the past have been transcended and a new culture is being created. This is not to say that a hundred years of black and white working people's music have properly culminated in Olivia Newton-John singing "Please Mr. Please" or that a new society will be built to the strains of "Dropkick Me Jesus Through the Goal Posts of Life"–but it is to assert that social critiques previously existing as the separate statements of various marginal groups are moving closer together and becoming more interchangeable in a way that gives voice to more universal aspirations.

One example of this trend can be seen in the changing concept of male roles and images of country music in this decade. As Bob Oermann and Mary Bufwack brilliantly demonstrate in their work on women and country music, which is included in this collection, this music has always been sensitive to the concerns of everyday life and has reflected and shaped women's attitudes and self-concepts from the beginning. As the women's movement has become more powerful and more widely understood, women in country music have incorporated elements of feminism into traditional, strong female role images leading to an ever stronger synthesis. Male self-images in country music have traditionally run the gamut from idealized declarations of love ("She could kiss the ground in the winter time, and make a flower grow," sings Johnny Paycheck in "Don't Take Her, She's All I Got") to bitter expressions of anger and betrayal directed against women ("Your Cheating Heart," etc.). In the past decade, male country music singers have responded to the women's movement, to the broader population listening to country music, and to their own discomfort with traditional male models by searching for a different male persona. Three diverse but complementary examples can be found in the recent work of Tom T. Hall, Bill Anderson, and David Allan Coe.

In the late sixties and early seventies, Hall emerged as the liberal conscience of country music. A shrewd observer of everyday life and an engaging storyteller, Hall's wry sermons on economic and social issues in songs like "Morning Dew," "One Hundred Children," "Strawberry Farms," and "America the Ugly" combined elements of evangelical Protestantism and rural populism into profound and relevant social commentary. "The Man Who Hated Freckles" and "Coot's Blues" attacked racism, and "Mama Bake a Pie" endures as one of the most bitter and effective country antiwar songs. Hall's own journalistic abilities played a large role in the credibility of his lyrics, but, above all, it was the social nature of his lyrics from the perspective of a man who didn't place himself outside the experience of others but who reflected their lives from within that made him such a brilliant commentator on the times.

Yet Hall's very success led to his demise as a creative artist. The man who worked as a gravedigger and gave us the amusing "Forty Dollars" as a result, who had nearly starved to death in Roanoke, Virginia, and turned that experience into "Ode to Half a Pound of Ground Round," could not survive the greatest hardship of them all – success. As a star, Hall became cut off from the constituency that provided the material for his songs and that told him that he was doing something worthwhile. Although he swore in "Uncle Curt" that success hadn't changed him, by the time he recorded "Joe, Don't Let Your Music Kill You" and "Last Hard Town," he was alerting his listeners to a movement away from socially relevant lyrics and into a closeted romanticism. Those songs detailed the assaults on his dignity and the draining character of life as an alienated artist. Lacking a supportive community, Hall could continue to stare into the abyss as Hank Williams had (with tragic personal results), or he could retreat from his art and sell records and lead a happy life closing his eyes to its pain. Simplistic ultraromantic nonsense like "I Love," "Somewhere over the Rainbow," and "It's All the Game" soon followed.

Hall's recognition of his own cynicism surfaced in "Faster Horses," a song which he begins by asserting that he is a poet whose soul is on fire but winds up concluding that hard experience has taught him that the only things that matter are faster horses, younger women, older whiskey, and more money. The crudeness of the formulation betrays a self-deprecating humor, but the bankruptcy of his position remains. His recording of "Your Man Loves You, Honey" was the nadir of his self-indulgence, responding to his wife's pleas to stop drinking and living irresponsibly by immersing himself in guilt and self-pity to simply mask his own refusal to change.

Yet, in a funny way, Hall's retreat from social issues reflected a certain part of the experience of his constituents. Persistent demands for social change threaten the isolated individual, and those without a supportive community have little reason to believe that social change will better their lot. For many men, demands from women to change their behavior without a tangible promise of it leading to a better life leads to a truculent self-indulgence that perverts the healthy desire to have a happy life into a misguided personalism that ignores everyone else's well-being.

Bill Anderson's career has followed a path diametrically opposite to Hall's. Except for occasional flashes of class-conscious wit (as in "Po Folks"), Anderson's music in the 1960s was melodramatic, ultraromantic, and swallowed virtually every cliché in Nashville culminating in the political/religious epic "Where Have All Our Heros Gone?"–possibly the worst country music record of all time. Yet in the early seventies, Anderson began to display a marvelous understanding of the relations between men and women and the complications therein.

In "Quits" and "Dis-Satisfied," Anderson explored the ways in which men and women view the same relationship from different perspectives. While Hall's commercial success alienated him from the life he talked about, it was precisely Anderson's understanding of the role of the media in purveying life-denying illusions and its subsequent effect on interpersonal relations that enabled him to write his two best songs, and possibly the two best ever written about male sexuality and fantasy images–"Everytime I Turn the Radio On" and "Between Lust and TV."

"Everytime I Turn the Radio On" ridiculed the idealized romantic myths in country music and presented the dilemma of a man attempting to reconcile those images with the reality of his own life. "Between Lust and TV" brilliantly attacked both the sterility of monogamous sexuality and the emptiness of objectified fantasy images of sex. Anderson pleads for sexual pleasure tied to human companionship and for liberation from the twin oppressions of *Playboy* fantasies and television. Together with "The Corners of My Life," these songs signal a changing male attitude about sexuality and a rebellion against traditional macho or self-pitying roles.

It is ironic that such a rebellion should also find expression in one of country music's most blatantly macho characters–David Al-

George Lipsitz

lan Coe—but country listeners are accustomed to ambiguity. The Statler Brothers aren't brothers and aren't named Statler; bluegrass and gospel quartets have five members; and sometimes leading performers record under pseudonyms to give voice to suppressed sides of their psyches, such as Hank Williams's "Luke the Drifter" and Sheb Wooley's "Ben Colder." But even to those used to ambiguity, David Allan Coe remains an enigma to friend and foe alike.

Although his two major hits have been humorous novelty songs ("You Never Even Called Me by My Name" and "Longhaired Redneck"), few people on earth are more serious than Coe. Musically he draws on the major sources of rural and working-class music (urban blues in "Penitentiary Blues," white folk music in "The Mysterious Rhinestone Cowboy," modern country music in "Once upon a Rhyme," rock and roll in "Longhaired Redneck," and country rock in "David Allan Coe Rides Again" and "Tatoo"). Yet Coe's diversity and complexity are not confined to his music; he is a compelling performer because his emotional, political, and intellectual contradictions reflect those of much of his audience and much of America.

As country music has always done, Coe's songs draw on the past for sanction to criticize the present. Feeling a deep allegiance to the rebellions, community, and individualism of the Southern past, he also acknowledges the need to "live for more than yesterday." In "Old Man Tell Me" and "I Still Sing the Old Songs," he draws upon the everyday life of Southern whites for the anger, violence, and lost opportunities that form the basis of his own rage and confusion. Yet in those songs and in "Willie, Waylon and Me" and "Rock and Roll Holiday," he also celebrates the longhaired present and the recent psychedelic past, looking to a mixture of hedonism and community as the promise of a freedom that can transcend the limits and self-hatreds of American tradition. Coe's anger about the present and his inability and unwillingness to identify with prevailing cultural values make him flaunt the ways in which he is different—to assert pride in what other people look down on. Yet at the same time, his desire for a life-oriented solution makes him guiltily disown the stifling and unsatisfying dogmas of the past that offer no solution to today's problems.

There are overtones of violence in Coe's lyrics, hints of racism, and a distance from women not entirely due to his prison experience. His eagerness for recognition sometimes leads him to vain posturing, like the time he told an interviewer that he was the only man in Nashville who hadn't sold out. Coe is not a role model for a new society, but he is an accurate reflection of our current contradictions and dilemmas – indicative of someone struggling for dignity and happiness and asking all the right questions. Coe may not tell us what we'd most like to hear, but he does expose what we need to overcome in others and ourselves without losing sight of his and our strengths. Coe represents the roughest edge of the "outlaw" and "longhaired redneck" phenomena in which behavior and dress that originated in the working class became adopted as a symbol of rebellion by middle-class youth, has now come back to the working-class more loaded and promising than ever. Coe's rough edges bring us full circle on male roles – men can't be the kind of people they need to be in isolation from social solutions, but those solutions can't come about unless men become different people. How men earn a living, the burdens of the past and future, and the commitments they make as political people speak directly to how men perceive their gender roles, but their hangups as men also inhibit and shape politics.

Hall, Anderson, and Coe represent the confusions as well as the possibilities facing men in a society where changing gender roles raise important questions about status, hierarchy, community, and freedom. Although none of them have challenged sexism as directly or as devastatingly as Shel Silverstein has in Tompall Glaser's "Put Another Log on the Fire" and Bobby Bare's "The Winner," sexism and gender expectations are at the root of their problems and dilemmas. Some of their responses may be disappointing, but at their best they echo the plea made in an early Tom T. Hall song: "I don't believe I'm where I'm going, not by many a mile/If you don't like me, help me to change, I'm still looking for a style" (Newkeys Music, 1970).

George Lipsitz

Where that search leads in country music will depend on where it leads everywhere else. We may be facing a tragic ending, but positive possibilities exist that exceed our fondest dreams of ten years ago. We only can hope that in another ten years we'll see them realized.

Women in Country Music

Mary Bufwack and Bob Oermann

The women who write and sing country music can be seen as "organic intellectuals" of the working class. They act as such in that they critically evaluate their working-class experience, are critical of present relationships, maintain strong self-approving images, and articulate aspirations for liberation and change. Their self-assertive songs come from their resistance to oppressive class and sexual experience. The personal rather than social orientation of these resistance songs is conditioned by the pressure of the commercial popular culture industry. On the other hand, country music retains political tendencies. Thus, we are not examining country music songs as totally manipulative, commercially produced illusions; but neither can they be seen as straightforward documents of American working-class life. Rather, they must be analyzed in a dialectical way as mediated cultural expressions of a class, exhibiting all the contradictory influences of social relationships in commercial capitalism.

The study of popular culture must be rooted in a careful analysis of the social relations and social environments of the people who make it, buy it, and identify with it. Most studies of country music take one of two approaches. The first approach describes it as corny, unsophisticated, ignorant, racist, right-wing, simplistic, maudlin, fundamentalist, red-neck, sentimental, and/or fascist. The second approach romanticizes it as people's music, as the bearer of noble folk traditions, as an exponent of down-to-earth grass-root honesty, as an expression of our longings for the freedom of a rural past, or as cultural rebellion against an industrialized mass society. Both approaches contain elements of truth, yet neither is adequate. The first fails to take into account the music's progressive social messages and its positive social function. The second ignores its contemporary content and continuing vitality. Neither speaks of how country music relates to a particular social group (the working class) in a continual and complex way.

Although not all members of the working class listen to country music, there is ample justification for viewing country music as a working-class phenomenon. First, the daily experiences and worldviews of working people are the subject matter of many country songs. Jobs such as truck driving, factory working, waitressing, railroad working, and housekeeping are not uncommon subjects in them. Second, the music's consumption is distinctly class related. A 1975 survey of 49 country music radio stations' listeners found that:

"Country music stations' listeners are nearly absent from professional occupations and are underrepresented among executives and managers. They are generally overrepresented among unskilled and service workers but are highly concentrated in the skilled and semi-skilled blue collar occupations."[1]

A 1973 poll taken at the Grand Ole Opry in Nashville indicated that 60% of the audience had not completed high school and that only 12.8% had had some college education.[2] An analysis of those attending a 1973 Tammy Wynette-George Jones concert in New York City revealed a preponderance of occupations in the "skilled, and semi-skilled bluecollar" job categories.[3] The class nature of this music's audience becomes clearest when the selections on juke-boxes in the neighborhood bars of working-class areas in any American city are examined, when the musical preferences in truck

stops and union halls are noted, and when the locations and atten-
dance patterns of country music nightclubs, dances, and concerts
are considered. Furthermore, the biographies of country music artists confirm the nearly universal working-class origins of its
writers, producers, and performers.

Working-class women are especially important participants in
country music culture. Female visitors to the Grand Ole Opry were
found in one study to outnumber men 57% to 43%.[4] Tammy
Wynette claims she has a survey that shows conclusively that her
listeners are predominantly women between 22 and 45 years old.[5]
Many radio station surveys have indicated that women are the primary consumers of this music, particularly during daytime broadcasting hours. Country music station KRAK in Sacramento states
that it has a larger share of the listening audience than that city's
two rock stations combined during the morning hours when teens
are in school and the listeners are "mostly housewives."[6] "Eighty
percent of country records are bought by women."[7] Our own survey
of the biographies of the 25 top country women singers indicates
that 84% come from working-class families. The current importance
of women in country music culture is by no means a recent event.

Country music grows directly out of a communal folk tradition that stretches back hundreds of years through rural American
life to an Anglo-Saxon folk music heritage. In this folk tradition,
women were as important as men in the roles of carriers, creators,
and performers of music. An examination in folklorists' collections
of the Appalachian ballads that have survived to the present day
reveals a rich vein of woman-oriented material: a body of songs
probably nurtured and shared for generations by women. In fact,
Alan Lomax asserts that most of the precommercial country
songs—these Appalachian ballads—are concerned with sexual
conflict as seen through female eyes.[8]

In addition to the many escape fantasies (like "The Gypsy
Rover" and "Black Jack Davey"), female ballads (like "Lady Isabel"
and "Barbara Allen"), and heartache songs (like "Careless Love,"
"All for the Love of a Man," and "Come All You Fair and Tender
Maidens"), there are a substantial number of female protest songs

in the folk tradition. Some espouse a fierce independence, a refusal to admit to male domination. These include "Who's Gonna Shoe Your Pretty Little Feet," which concludes, "I don't need no man"; "I Never Will Marry," which states, 'I never will marry, I'll be no man's wife," and "How Old Are You My Pretty Little Miss," whose heroine vows, "I'll marry you, but I won't do your washing or your cooking." In the famous folk song "Housewife's Lament," the repetitive drudgery of housework is viewed as totally self-defeating labor. One stanza of "The Wagoner's Lad" contains the protest: "Oh hard is the fortune of all womankind,/They're always controlled, they're always confined,/Controlled by their parents until they are wives,/Then slaves to their husbands the rest of their lives."[9]

Women in the work force also developed a number of protest songs in this precommercial folk country collection of songs. One of America's older labor protest songs is "The Lowell Factory Girl," whose North Carolina variant is called "No More Shall I Work in the Factory." "I Love My Union" and "All the Doo Da Day" have been found in women's mill worker journals, such as *The Factory Girl* and *The Factory Girl's Album*, which began appearing in the 1840s. The renowned "Rising Sun Blues" is sung from the perspective of a bitter, rueful prostitute.

Some male-oriented folk songs have female variants. "The Young Girl Cut Down in Her Prime," whose heroine dies of syphillis bemoaning her fate is one example of this. There is also a woman's version of "Greenback Dollar" with the lines: "I don't want your greenback dollar/I don't want your diamond ring,/All I want is a .38 special/To blow out your dirty brains."[10] Similarly, the murder conclusion to "Frankie and Johnny" ends with the lines, "This story has no moral; this story has no end; it only goes to show you there ain't no good in men."

The transition between the folk/country era and the commercial period of country music's history began in the early 1920s. Throughout the first decades of commercially recorded country music, a great deal of the material recorded by women continued to be songs from their folk tradition. One of the first recorded country string bands was Samantha Bumgarner and Eva Davis who performed the traditional "Fly Around My Pretty Little Miss" in 1924.

Theron Hale's daughters Mamie, Ruth, and Elizabeth played spirited jigs and rolls on early country music radio broadcasts from Nashville.

But it was not until the recording and subsequently phenomenal success of the Carter Family in 1927 that country music really came into its own as a commercial form. This woman-dominated group first caught Victor Records' talent scout's ear with the female protest song "Single Girl":[11] "Single girl . . . going dressed so fine;/Married girl . . . goes ragged all the time."[12]

In the 1930s, women country performers continued to contribute assertive female-oriented songs. Kentucky's Coon Creek Girls became the first totally self-contained all-female string band on the radio. Their leader, Lily May Ledford, composed the spunky "Banjo Pickin' Girl" partly in response to the difficult experiences the group had with male audiences and musicians on tours.[13] One of the first great women solo singers in country music, Cousin Emmy, performed such self-assertive woman-oriented songs as "Single Girl," "Ruby Are You Mad at Your Man," and the humorous "Cat's Got the Measles," with its repeated chorus, "Doggone any woman – who let a man be her boss."

During the Depression, field recorders for the Library of Congress Archive of American Folk Song discovered many strong, independent mountain women singers of quick-witted native intelligence from whom country music has always recruited its best female singers. Many of them used their music as a political tool. Aunt Molly Jackson sang union organizing songs such as "I Am a Union Woman" and "Join the CIO," and also commercially released songs such as "Kentucky Miner's Wife (Hungry Disgusted Blues)," and Sarah Ogan Gunning contributed "I Hate the Company Bosses," "I'm Going to Organize," and "I Am a Girl of Constant Sorrow" among others. During the same period, Ella May Wiggins wrote "Mill Mother's Lament," Cleda Holton wrote "Shirt Factory Blues," and Florence Reese wrote "Which Side Are You On," which became the most famous of all union organizing songs.[14]

The incompatibility of such explicitly political work-related material with commercial interests resulted in record companies encouraging those women singers who couched their protests in more personal and domestic terms. Thus, Gail Davis's "I'm a Female Thru and Thru" and "Tomboy," and Texas Ruby's "Shanty Street" and "Love Me Now" became the more typically indirect kinds of female self-assertion in commercial country music in the following decades.

The history of country music in the 1940s and 1950s is the history of a social group's transformation from a rural, agrarian lifestyle to an increasingly urbanized, proletarianized existence and the resulting disruption of its social relationships. During World War II there was a breakdown of emphasis on women's role in the family, and women became still more involved in the work force. This also involved a shift in identity as many women came to positively identify with wage-earning work and the independent social standing it gave. A reassertion of a subordinate domestic role after the war resulted in inevitable male-female conflicts. Both men's and women's country music lyrics came to focus increasingly on the problems of love, marriage, and family life during these years. A musical battle-of-the-sexes reigned, with women stars performing more and more material aggressively sung from a subjugated working-class woman's perspective.

"It Wasn't God Who Made Honky Tonk Angels," by Kitty Wells (1952), became the first massively popular woman's song of self-assertion in country music. This song claimed that every time one found a fallen woman of loose morals it "was because there . . . was a man to blame," insisting that women's problems were the result of male domination. Profiting from the success of this initial breakthrough, dozens of women singers of the 1950s and 1960s began recording this type of material. Connie Hall criticized men for their drinking in "The Bottle or Me," as did Wanda Jackson in "A Girl Don't Have to Drink to Have Fun." Bonnie Owens complained about her "Number-One Heel," and Liz Anderson told hers, "(You're) Excedrin Headache #99." Jan Howard released, "I Wish I Was a Single Girl Again," and in "Rock Me Back to Little Rock," she longed for a simpler time in her mother's hometown "where the men don't try to take advantage of every woman who smiles."

A common way of expressing dissatisfaction with roles and expectations was with the "answer song," which would reply to a man's song with a woman's perspective. After Jim Reeves's command, "He'll Have to Go," meaning that his girlfriend should dispose of his rival, Jeanne Black calmly replied, "He'll Have to Stay," explaining his thoughtless behavior that led her to find a new lover. Margie Bowes smartly turned the tables on Johnny Cash's macho "Understand Your Man" with the retort, "Understand Your Gal." Webb Pierce's "Back Street Affair" was answered by Kitty Wells's bitter "(I'm) Paying for That Back Street Affair."

Whereas Skeeter Davis privately sang, "It's Hard to Be a Woman," others used confrontation tactics to get the point across. This was often done in the context of duets, which in country music are often dialogues between a man and a woman that reveal their different points of view. They have also tended to be small singing slices of working-class life. Jonie warned Johnny Nosby, "Don't Call Me from a Honky-Tonk." Jean Shepherd and Ray Pillow humorously argued about divorce in "I'll Take the Dog." Ernest Tubb and Loretta Lynn further explored marital problems in "Mr. and Mrs. Used-to-Be" and "Who's Gonna Take the Garbage Out?" Tammy Wynette and George Jones celebrated their membership in the working class with "(We're Not) the Jet Set," and sang about divorce in "Golden Ring." Jones and Melba Montgomery enacted the familiar scene of a domestic quarrel following a party in "Party Pickin' " and sang of a hillbilly couple on welfare in "Livin' On Easy Street."

Norma Jean continued the tradition of working women's songs with her "Heaven Help the Working Girl (In a World That's Run by Men)" and in "Truck Drivin' Woman." Billie Jo Spears complained about the degradation of her secretarial job and quit it in "Mr. Walker It's All Over (I Don't Like the New York Secretary's Life)." Country music traditionalists such as Hedy West ("Cotton Mill Girls"), Anne Romaine ("Indiana Factory Job"), and Hazel Dickens ("Black Lung") also contributed songs to this genre.

Paramount among today's female "organic intellectuals" of country music is Loretta Lynn. She has maintained country music's long tradition of interpreting and dealing with the everyday life experiences of working-class women. Kentucky-born Loretta Lynn goes even further than her immediate predecessors (and most of her contemporaries) in promoting a positive, self-affirming image for them. Her compositions stress a refusal to be stepped on by either her man or society at large. She warned her man, "Your Squaw Is on the Warpath (Tonight)," and told him, "Don't Come Home a-Drinkin' (With Lovin' on Your Mind)." In defense of her working-class background, she has asserted that she is proud to be a "Coal Miner's Daughter."

Recent songs have been still more assertive and ideologically specific, addressing themselves especially to women's issues. "Rated X" condemns men who look upon divorced women as used property and easy lays. In her biggest-selling single, "The Pill," she celebrates the freedom that birth control has given women. "Hey Loretta" serves notice that she will no longer be exploited by her husband. In it she sings, "The woman's liberation, Honey, is gonna start right now." Although she has had little formal education, the earthy wisdom, spunk, and sensitivity of Lynn's tremendously popular songs have made her an articulate spokeswoman for abused working-class women. Her sassy point of view has a genuinely liberating effect on her audience.

Country music women's songs of self-assertion are often affirmations of passive values as well as active ones. In defining their attitudes toward their womanhood, the country music stars and audience are influenced not only by the proud folk tradition of rural and working-class life but by middle-class norms and values dominant in mass media as well. So it is that the decidedly self-assertive material performed by Tammy Wynette exists as a celebration of an essentially conservative bourgeois ideology. On record after record she suffers through bad relationships with men, maintaining all the while that it is a woman's lot in life to give and understand and expect nothing in return. In Wynette's works, the woman, although victimized and hurt, is enobled by suffering. Many of her songs are veritable textbooks of female masochism. Examples of this ideology are "Stand by Your Man," "I'll See Him Through," "My Man," and "Love's the Answer."

The nobility and pride inherent in these acceptance-of-abuse songs, however, is dependent on the woman's conscious understanding and manipulation of the situation in which she finds her-

self. Wynette's songs about role-playing isolate this dialectical nature of her attitude, since they take an articulate and clear-eyed
view of the inequalities in male-female relationships – indicating the
woman's superior intellectual grasp of that reality – yet they advocate the acceptance of inferior status. Her role-playing hits have included "Your Good Girl's Gonna Go Bad," "A Mother," and "Good
Lovin'." Thus, Tammy Wynette explicitly articulates and explains
the dilemmas of her audience but maintains an essentially counter-
revolutionary outlook.

Few country women singers function more clearly as commu-
nicators of working-class attitudes than does Dolly Parton. Again
and again her songs emphasize her working-class background. In
fact, one can begin to speak of an embryonic class consciousness in
this artist's works. There is an implicit social criticism in such songs
as "In the Good Old Days (When Times Were Bad)," a painful recol-
lection of Parton's past filled with images of hard work, hunger,
rats, cold winters, and material deprivation. Her recording of "In
the Ghetto" is an encapsulation of the cycle of poverty, crime, and
death in the inner city that ends with a plea for understanding and
a "helping hand." "Chicken Every Sunday" asserted that poverty is
nothing to be ashamed of. In it she contrasts some of the positive
values that coincided with shared rural poverty against the negative attributes of rich people. Of the former she sings, "If that's the
lower class then I'm glad that's what I am," and of the latter she asserts, "Just because they've got money and a big fine house, why we
won't take no sass offa them." "Coat of Many Colors," "The Better
Part of Life," and "Daddy's Working Boots" recapitulate this poor-
but-proud attitude.

Like Loretta Lynn, Parton has the "organic intellectual's"
ability to creatively express the problems and aspirations of her
working-class-woman constituency. Her first hit was a self-
assertive song called "Dumb Blonde" that indicated she was nothing
of the kind. "Just Because I'm a Woman" decried the sexual double
standard. "(I'll Be Movin' On) When Possession Gets Too Strong" is
another of her self-assertive woman songs. "Daddy Come and Get
Me" describes the way mental illness is used by men against
women. The allegations made by the institutionalized protagonist

of this song were substantiated in Phyllis Chesler's *Women and Madness* published two years later. In songs that both defend the social honor of the poor and uphold women's dignity, Dolly Parton repeatedly gets at social truths through the medium of country music.

We have chosen Loretta Lynn, Tammy Wynette, and Dolly Parton as the 1970s representatives of working-class women's attitudes revealed in country music because, according to *Billboard Magazine*'s year-end charts of this decade, they are the most consistently popular female stars.[15] But many others also fill the bill as "organic intellectuals." These three are only the tip of an ever-growing iceberg.

Country music women are participating both in the increasing proletarianization and, as revealed in their songs, in the self-aware process of consciousness-raising. They are, also, however, especially vulnerable to the restrictive tendencies in this commercial form. Because so much of their subject matter deals with women's issues which easily translate into political issues, they must tread a thin line.

In today's country music, private experience continues to become public expression but not necessarily political action. The commercial need for a mass audience results in a cultural form that maintains a class identity without class organization. By themselves the cultural products cannot stimulate political action or organization, but they can raise consciousness and sometimes offer an alternative to the dominant bourgeois ideology. If their popular cultural forms are analyzed, the consciousness of working-class women is revealed as comparable to, and often more progressive or insightful than, any other group of American women.

Notes

1. Richard A. Peterson and Paul DiMaggio, "From Region to Class, the Changing Locus of Country Music: A Test of the Manifestation Hypothesis," *Social Forces* (Mar. 1975); 503.

2. Bill Williams, "Grand Ole Opry," *Billboard*, sec. 2, "World of Country Music," (Oct. 1973).

3. Peterson and DiMaggio, "From Region to Class," 503.

4. Williams, "Grand Ole Opry," 25.

5. Melvin Shestack, *The Country Music Encyclopedia* (New York, 1974), 319.

6. Paul Hemphill, *The Nashville Sound: Bright Lights and Country Music* (New York, 1971), 11.

7. Joan Dew, "Country Music's New Women," *Redbook* (Jan. 1975): 73.

8. Alan Lomax, *The Folk Songs of North American* (New Jersey, 1975), xxi.

9. As quoted by Dorothy A. Horstman, in "Loretta Lynn," *Stars of Country Music*, edited by Bill C. Malone and Judith McCulloh (Illinois, 1975), 309. Horstman cites a version of Buell Kazee on Folkways Record FA-2951, "American Folk Music, Vol. 1, Ballads."

10. As quoted by Alan Lomax in *Folk Songs of North America*, 282. The song has a great many variants.

11. John Atkins, "The Carter Family," *Stars of Country Music*, 97.

12. As quoted by Steven D. Price in *Take Me Home: The Rise of Country Western Music* (New York., 1974), 29–30. An almost identical version can be heard on the Carter Family album "The Original Carter Family From 1936 Radio Transcripts" (Old Homestead Record OH-90045).

13. Interview with Lily May Ledford in *Sing Out*, no. 2 (July/Aug. 1976): 4–5, 8.

14. John Greenway, *American Folk Songs of Protest* (Philadelphia, 1953), 142–252.

15. *Billboard*'s year-end charts, in the final issue of each year from 1970 to 1976, included Lynn, Wynette, and Parton among the top 50 country vocalists. In addition, they were each recognized as an "Entertainer of the Year" by the Country Music Association during the 1970s.

Janis Joplin
Was No Rose

Ann D. Gordon

A decade ago I wanted to write an article about Janis Joplin. Remnants of abortive starts are still filed hopefully under "rock and roll," four cross-country moves of the file cabinets later. *The Rose* has jolted me into reconsidering these old notes. What intrigued me about Joplin then, as now, was her essential fitness for the particular moment in women's politics. *The Rose* would have us dismiss Joplin as a sick woman. I remember a gutsy woman exploring whatever potential for resistance could be found in rock music and the associated stardom. Her driving ambition, not just to advance herself but, more important, to shatter repressive images of womanhood, is made pitiful by the filmmakers. By implication, the woman's movement of that era is made equally pitiful. Just when I have a hankering to launch the eighties with a revival of Joplin's sassy responses to ridiculous conditions and her outrageous disregard for double standards, a movie assaults my sense of history and reduces Joplin to drivel.

In each of the attempts I made to write an essay on Joplin, I included a tale of watching Janis Joplin on Dick Cavett Show reruns, the summer of 1970 or 1971, in Madison, Wisconsin. After meetings of the teaching assistants' union, we went to Sam's Hialeah Club, where on our usual Sunday night we had the place to ourselves, save for a few of Sam's buddies, who still stopped in long after the surrounding neighborhood had been destroyed. On other nights of the week, the Hialeah filled up with young men whose solitude was so complete that a woman could stand among them and feel invisible.

Although I never attended a Joplin concert, I venture that her Cavett performance was vintage Joplin. Her song ended and she bounded across the set to take her place with Cavett, shattering the waiting room tone of his interviews which regularly suppressed vitality in his female guests. Landing in the chair, she smiled at the audience's cheers, slapped Cavett's raised foot, and shouted: "I can tell what a stud you are by the shoes you wear!" Off balance and blushing, Cavett struggled to regain his advantage as host, seeming to consider whether such a crude pass might add a notch to his pistol grip. The host asked the guest to explain her song. Unrelentingly she launched into a parable about the donkey carts that kept a carrot suspended just beyond the donkey's reach to lure him into forward motion. And that song, she concluded, is about men keeping that carrot in front of women, always promising a lot more than they can deliver.

In Sam's Hialeah, Joplin's presence on the television had drawn a crowd of men to one end of the bar, and I stood among these strangers. She pulled them from their solitude into a cheering, panting group. Laughing at her put-down of Cavett, they drew closer in anticipation of more, and the carrot parable delivered it. Lest I leave an impression of cool impartiality, I hasten to say that I roared with laughter and glowed, my feet ready for walking and my hips primed for strutting. As the show came to a close, the elation subsided for all of us. I headed back to the group I'd come in with, aware of the fact that none of them inspired a good strut.

Joplin not only put men down—a minor art form permitted such celebrities—but she cracked a masculine hold on rock and roll. After a brief interlude of self-mockery and boyish playfulness with the Beatles, rock music had grown into a nightmare of male sex privilege and power by 1970. Without female stars, the personal idiom of rock had become oppressively onesided. Innovative stage shows were not only sexy but they were violently so; audiences cheered the stars who raped their guitars.

Although Joplin claimed all the prerogatives of conspicuous self-indulgence that set rock stars apart, she gave them a distinct female form. Not content simply to command her woman's share of the proceeds, she carved out a competitive angle and reformulated the terms of seduction in the arena of rock music. The devil woman rose up to taunt and tempt men with her need for them and to dare women to be adventurous. As a commercial gimmick, it worked. There I'd been in Sam's, drawing my single-minded conclusions from her performance while the men drew theirs, neither they nor I minding that she might set us up with mutually exclusive fantasies. If Cavett suspected that she needed him only to enjoin the attack on his stuffed shirt, would he still squirm with the pleasure of her attention? Who cared? Uncertainty about the outcome heightened the fun—and enlarged the market.

Joplin's value and influence exceeded her modest musical talent because of her singular position among the loud and leading men of rock. From her commercial roost, she undermined any expectation that women would maintain themselves in a culture of silent anxiety and awe. She could tap the poorly disguised and explosive combination of propriety and sexuality in teenage girls. By letting her hair fly, her clothes pile up every which way, and her acne scars show, she defied the conventions of *Seventeen* magazine and its ilk. Fashion may be spinach, but someone had to *insist* that the world is bigger than a person's blackheads. Defiance of inexpressive neatness seemed plausible to her teenage following precisely because Joplin was a sex object, which demonstrated the appeal such flamboyance had for men. Within this nominally safe kind of rebellion, she opened up fanciful possibilities, not only of unconventional appearance but also of prominence, travel, controversy, money, achievement, and sexual freedom.

She associated success with sex, just as other rock stars did. In a sweepstakes whose grand prize, as *Rolling Stone* informed us, was to attract Plaster Caster groupies who made a mold from a star's dick and mass-produced replicas, what would Janis Joplin win? Obsessed with that question, she became the goddess of wanting "it," needing "it," and getting "it" when you can. She put the case for female dependence on men boldly and shrilly. But how she worked for "it"! From tapes of a concert in Calgary, in 1970, included in the record *In Concert*, Joplin can be heard pulling, pushing, and shoving her new and last band through "Try (Just a Little Bit Harder)," teaching them to follow her no matter where the music or thought took her. As Joplin emerged as the bandleader, the song's sexual metaphors became interchanged with the situation on stage where she told the men to "listen to the words, man." The leadership and ambiguity are both evident in such shouts as, "you're not going to get anywhere, if that's all you can do"; "put your heart into it, you ain't trying, man"; or "hey, there's a lot more talent around than that, man"; and so on, setting her rhythm and doubling the tempo in an exhausting finale. In moments like that, the line between dependence and command blurred.

Joplin found a tradition of assertive and outspoken women from which to take songs and styles of entertainment. She identified herself with the black women stars of blues and rhythm and blues. She dressed up like Ma Rainey and Bessie Smith and posed for photographs that imitated pictures of them. But there's no denying that Joplin's cover version of "Ball and Chain" is inferior to the rhythm and blues star "Big Mama" Thornton's original and that no just distribution of Joplin's money and fame helped Thornton. The history of rock and roll exploiting black music continued. By turning to this tradition, however, Joplin found a strong voice for women's angle on personal relations. No white source existed for stating women's case so bluntly. Her songs were peopled with women who lodged complaints, bemoaned male inadequacies, celebrated sex, sought out the male talent, picked up and left in disgust or anticipation, and so forth, through the somewhat narrow range of alternatives the topic offers for songs. At its commanding best, the tradition that Joplin revived gave us women who stood up, turned the tables, and told men, "put it right here."

Around Joplin's excesses—and despite them—women were turning a corner that had yet to be named during Joplin's rise and fall. Without offering or finding solutions, Joplin certainly sang out the news that it was a mess out there in the world of men and women. We played her songs in 1970–71 because we liked the music and because it gave us frantic encouragement to live with that mess. Sexual frustration and multiple orgasms were hot topics then, and we distinguished the artists who acknowledged them from those who didn't. Tina Turner's mind-expanding song "River Deep, Mountain High" replicated a male fantasy of female orgasm, which, yes indeed, seemed to go on and on in waves of feeling with intense peaks but ended in a finite chord, perfectly resolved. Joplin, in contrast, threw out that fantasy by never closing the chord of her great musical orgasms such as "Cry, Baby, Cry." (It is the same trick that the Pepsi song perpetrates on us to keep us singing the jingle for days, looking for an end to it.) Joplin, we thought, had made a political point – or so we called it in those days of feverish sisterhood.

Whether she announced doomsday or heralded change, Joplin mirrored that crazy struggle to define what was wrong and what good we were after. She was rowdy in a brief period when feminists gambled a lot on the consequences of speaking out about personal experience. If you make one woman happy one time, she charged men, that'll be the end of the world. Meanwhile, New York radical feminists saw fit to publish testimonials from women who announced that their sex lives were so unsatisfactory, they usually wished they were playing ping-pong. Joplin echoed elements of the B.I.T.C.H. Manifesto and acted upon Shulamith Firestone's "dialectical" contention that boys have more fun. And she was, after all, a working woman.

Faced with similar pressures from forces that are overtly hostile and from those that masquerade as friendly, I insist on resurrecting my old images of Joplin in defiance, as if to regain some images that will support my modest view of progress since those early days of resistance in 1970. After that commanding Calgary concert in 1970, Joplin and her Full Tilt Boogie Band headed back to California, cut the album *Pearl*, and the star died. Trouble about who she had been began immediately. There were two angles on her death: to associate it with the rash of rock music industry deaths, most of them drug-related and, if widely known, of men; or to associate it with the frailty of womankind. Neither version described the struggle for female satisfaction that made Joplin and her eccentric individualism attractive to me. I stuck with an image of Joplin shooting the works in a full tilt rush to prove that a woman could take charge in that most exclusive male domain she chose and to insist that women were a noisy lot. This was no Sylvia Plath, choosing death in the kitchen, but a woman on the scale of Catherine the Great, who died, it is said, trying to satisfy herself by having sexually aroused horses lowered on top of her. It wasn't a bad idea until the winch broke.

Crazy Music

R. Crumb

I collect old records, and so I have access to a lot of audial surrealism. Lots of it! Those old-time songsters were always doing nutty things with words and music. They made up nonsense lyrics and played weird homemade instruments like the "Gazoom" (Bob Miller's Hinky-Dinkers), the "goofus," the "kazoo," and the "slide-whistle" (Hoosier Hot-Shots, Ezra Buzzington's Rube Band, etc.).

"Mac" McClintock was himself a very interesting character – a Wobbly, a hobo, a cowboy balladeer who made some records in the late twenties for Victor and was on the radio from Oakland, California, I believe, in the thirties, when he was fairly old. He had a cowboy band called "The Haywire Orchestra." In the twenties, the hayseeds were nuts about hobo songs, and "Mac" wrote (or stole, I dunno which) some of the best. Such classics as "The Bum Song" (1928): "Come all you jolly jokers/and listen while I hum/A story I'll relate to you/of the great American bum."

He also did "The Big Rock Candy Mountain," a hobo's dream of heaven, where "the handouts grow on bushes" and there are "cigarette trees" and "little streams of whiskey" that "come trickling down the rocks."

"Ain't We Crazy" is another great song that's all nonsense: "It was midnight on the ocean/Not a streetcar was in sight/The sun was shining brightly/It rained all day that night"–and so on and so on. Actually it's kinda dumb, just a lot of puns and wordplay. But, see, I'm not even sure "Mac" actually wrote all this stuff. I'm sure he borrowed some of it ("little streams of whiskey" I know is from other, older sources). Probably most of it is stuff that was floating around in the great murky pool of "folk" songs. Nonsense songs were probably always popular. Take the song "Oh My Darling Clementine":

> *Light she was, and like a fairy*
> *and her shoes were number nine*
> *herring boxes, without topses*
> *sandals were for Clementine.*
> *Drove she ducklings to the water*
> *ev'ry morning just at nine*
> *hit her foot against a splinter*
> *fell into the foaming brine*
> *(etc. etc.)*

Anybody in the country over the age of 35 can dredge up all kinds of surrealist campfire ditties.

Another great cowboy wit and balladeer on old records is Goebel Reeves, "The Texas Drifter," who did such classics as "Station HOBO" (1930) and "The Cowboy's Dizzy Sweetheart" (1932). Then there's Bob Miller, who wrote a lot of nutty tunes around this time, his best being "Duck Foot Sue"; the lyrics are so weird I can't even remember them offhand, and besides, he and his partner sing them so fast you can hardly understand them.

Then there's the all-time weirdest, spookiest record, "The Fatal Flower Garden" by Nelstone's Hawaiians (actually a couple of hillbillies) recorded in about 1929. It's about a little boy, who is lured into a flower garden by a gypsy lady, who locks him in an attic to die: "Tether a Bible at my feet/a Testament in my head/if my dear mother calls for me/tell her that I am dead." But it has to be heard to be appreciated because much of the strangeness is in the mournful style of the singing and playing. The same is true of most of this old "folk" music.

The popular arts are a brimming treasure trove of strangeness, weird fantasy, and surrealism. It's endless, really . . . infinite. . . .

Great stuff! Great stuff! All suppressed by the goddamn bourgeois insufferable mass media of our time! Cuteness, in itself a monstrous "surrealism," imposed on us by corporate-cultural dispensers! A cultural curse instituted by the likes of Disney and his ilk.

I was just playing some more old records, looking for weird songs. A good one is "When the Moon Drips into the Blood" by the Taylor-Griggs Louisiana Melody Makers (1928), a string band. The words are from the Bible. Those old-time rural people loved the Book of Revelation and other parts of the Bible with fantastic or grotesque images and visions and used a lot of it in their religious music. Black country preachers and gospel and sanctified singing groups, as well as whites, used surrealistic religious imagery all the time. "Black Diamond Express to Hell" by Rev. A. W. Nix & Congregation or "A Coffin May Be Your Christmas Present" backed by "Death May Be Your Santa Claus" by the Rev. J. M. Gates (1927)– Christmas surrealism. Rev. F. W. McGee & Congregation did "Dog Shall Not Move His Tongue" and "Dead Cat On the Line," both around 1930. There are a couple of surrealistic blues songs that make about as much sense as a Hieronymus Bosch painting. One is "The Duck's Yas Yas Yas" by James (Stump) Johnson and his piano (1929): "Mama bought a rooster/thought it was a duck/brought him to the table/with his legs sticking up/in walks sister with a spoon and a glass/serves up the gravy from his yas yas yas."

"Rabbit Foot Blues," shown in the old Paramount ad for the Blind Lemon Jefferson record [in *Cultural Correspondence*, Nos. 10–11], is the other good surrealistic blues piece. But the thing about black music is that a lot of the "surrealistic" element is due to the heavily coded, "cabalistic" you might say, style of the old Southern blacks' way of communicating. All those weird references to animals ("Pick Poor Robin Clean") have specific meanings in the old down-home rural cosmology or whatever ya call it. "Black Snake

Moan" begins, "Black Snake crawlin' in my room." . . . Same thing with the "hillbilly" music. . . . "Hogeye" by Pope's Arkansas Mountaineers is really weird and senseless to the urban mind. . . . "Sally in the garden siftin' sand/Sally upstairs with a hog-eye man." What the hell does this mean? I *know* it means something, but I don't know what. . . . The song "My Name is John Johanna," or "Hard Times in Arkansas," is full of weird images, with that solemn, very dry rural humor that the "smart" city person always misses. "I wish I was a mole in the ground" (wish I was a lizard in the spring) . . . well, on and on . . . it's interesting, ain't it? What I like so much about all genuine rural and "folk" music is that it's not very conscious of what it's about and therefore it's infinitely deep. The singers and musicians are so much a part of their culture, their connection, and their ties are so strong, their identity so bound up with their culture, that they are more "carriers" of the culture than "artists" as defined by the class view of artists (basically the aristocratic-bourgeois view).

OK, Bob, get off it now . . . I'm clumsy and awkward when attempting to be analytic and academic . . . I should stick to the art stuff, eh?

Black Music:
Surrealism

James Spady

*Have you ever been in a Negro church? Not the whitewashed article
of respectable colored folks, but the shanty of the peasant Negro.
God, but they feel the thing. Sometimes too violently for sensitive
nerves; always sincerely, powerfully, deeply. Their theology is a
farce [in terms of western theology] (christ is so immediate); their
religious emotion, elemental, and for that reason, very near the
sublime.* (Jean Toomer, 1922)

You may note these words were uttered before the issuance
of Breton's Surrealist Manifesto. Toomer speaks to a third party.
Masking, somewhat muting the message. Shall we say translating,
translocating the immutable bonds of consanguinity tying him to
his primordial ancestral father? Blacks, among the most ancient of
people, have never tried to dichotomize the sacred and secular.

This is further illustrated in Charlie Parker's most legitimate
defense of black bards assembling in the cesspool of economic exploitation. New York's 52nd Street has both an alley meaning and
a street meaning. "Bird Lives" not because he didn't die but because
the orange flames never stopped licking out their tongue. Why

praise Billie Holiday as a precursor of surrealism? Does not her birth predate the charter? Is not the black belt of Baltimore a quarantined area? The issue of the black artist and his or her public/patron is one that bears examination. It may explain why both Cecil Taylor and Thelonius Monk so seldom work. The question is not *Kazi* but remuneration. Fair, equitable remuneration. Given the state of this human condition, it is not surprising that those who see and seek the ocean beneath reality most often are nonwhite.

Etienne Lero died at 30. Charlie Parker at 34.

And yet another witness just south of us in Haiti. Another witness to the antiquity of surrealism.

La grande cite, l'enorme cite mangeuse de reve, la devoreuse de songe, la croquese d'illusions, la grande metropole materialiste est audesous de nous. . . . Les fourmis humaines s'agitent. La grande cite ressemble a une enorme fleur de reve, mais plus elle s'avance, plus elle perd peu a peu caractere erd pour devenir, l'absurde, l'inhumaine, la terrible ennemie et l'Imaginaire.

Such is the vision of one of the great surrealist artists of all times, Jacques Stephen Alexis, recorded in his tale "Le Roi des Songes." The big city that devours fantasy and crushes illusions is preeminently the terrible enemy of the Imagination. But even within this materialistic metropolis *he*, voice of the group, called for the intervention of the marvelous in a powerful social and dynamic realism. This realism exists beneath the surface. It is truly subterranean, analogous to the Funkadelics doing it under water. That is the lush terrain of those who practice the marvelous. Unencumbered by the stench of the metropolis. They go underwater, underground. Their spirits lift the tides. Their humming frightens the beachcombers. They are mask-wearers. Claude McKay understood and carved a mask.

Dr. Willis James, an Afro-American musicologist, folklorist, and musician used the drum as a metaphor in much the same way

James Spady

Stevie Wonder uses the synthesizer today. In the hand of a blood, it is a machete and a flute.

The African believes in rhythm as a musical entity, whereas in the Western culture, musicians use rhythm as an adjunct of melody, as an organizational force. But the African not only does this, but he uses rhythm as a complete aesthetic expression. For instance, in Africa we have several different types of drums which are comparable in some cases of speech, and in some cases which bear peculiar hypnotic influences, and in some cases which we could say are particularly stimulating for dance, and in some cases where the drum is used almost with occult impact and high medicinal qualifications. The African is perhaps the world's greatest drummer. He has within him a kind of rhythmical feeling, which some say is innate and some say is acquired. This we will not argue. It is sufficient for our purpose to note that he has it, and that he uses it in a very singular way. The African drum is a very highly appreciated and in some cases almost worshipped musical instrument.

It is because Alex Haley's ancestor Kunta Kinte did not listen to his father's drum that he became enslaved. Could this be the same reason King Lear has beckoned Haley to the forbidden ground where the orange flames encircle the very tentacles, slice the marrow of tradition? Shall the circle remain unbroken? How many? Many thousand Gone!

Did you say a precursor of surrealism?

There is another voice. I heard it first as a whisper. Later a drum began moving slightly above the voice. When did the voice and drum become one? An ex-slave narrative from a 77-year-old woman reads:

I know there was one song, and the voice sounded like a woman's, and it was raised up from the graveyard. At first they just thought it was somebody coming through the graveyard for a short cut home and they didn't pay no 'tention to it; but in a little while it come up over the house and then went back to the graveyard. I've heard white people tell it as well as colored, and it caused quite a stir around there, 'cause the white folks said they couldn't understand it. Yes,

*it went like this: "I come to pray, I come to sing/I come to do my
master's will/By waiting on the Lord."* (Indigene, 27)

Was it the voice or Guede? Dark glasses. Moving rapidly. Sun
moves across the planet. Crystalline effects. Rapidly the moaning
turns into midday. And then: "At the end of the dawn; this town,
flat, displayed, brought down by its commonsense, inert, breathless
under its geometric burden of crosses." These are the words of
Aimé Césaire in his prophetically moving *Cahier d'un retour au
pays natal.* It is no wonder that this poem caused quite a stir
around there. Breton says: "Movement was a little slower than
necessary, the noise too clear, as though coming through the
stranded wrecks. In the pure air the continuous ringing of a distant
alarm bell."

It was a bell like a distant voice. The voice sounded like a
woman. They knocked on the windows. Daring to frighten paled
faces. Daring to enter their world, a world enclosed by brick walls.
A world of books. It was in the library. Buses continued to pass
along Walnut Street. The Outsiders remained on the other side of
the window. The storm clouds rose atop the city.

Césaire watches the sunshine. The dawn has ended. "Blood!
Blood all our blood roused by/the male heart of the sun/those who
know the femininity of the moon/with her body of oil."

John Ciardi, possessed by the orange flames encircling his
sky, raged madly, walking off the stage in the midst of that great
tornado. For instance,

*James Baldwin in back-Switzerland where no black man had
    even been, and they thought he was the devil,
saw a mountain, trapped in a Harvard accent, and listened for
    months to Billie Holiday records.*

Ciardi failed to recognize that despite a Harvard accent Baldwin had been baptized. In Florida they had called his name. "Nig-
gah, we know who you are. You's James Baldwin." Named in the
streets. He had led the camera crew (West German, Voice of
America, Newark) into the merciless bottom of the pit, a housing

project in a city manned by a black mayor whom Baraka had called "A Messenger for Prudential Life Insurance Company."

He had ended his message of moral redemption by saying Repent or Perish! That teenage preacher had returned to the stage for the last time. Jimmy Baldwin, named in the street, had come before Ciardi. He had heard the voice of Billie. Ciardi had never heard or understood the voices of his darker brothers in Sicily. Never never alone. He promised never to leave his children alone. What plunderers they were! So insecure. Hallucinatory? No. We witnessed Ciardi's walk from the stage as Ntozake Shange was sharing a common history. Wilfred Cartey not yet risen from the Amen Corner. How Long? Not Long.

Comics

Reprinted by permission of Johnny Hart
and News America Syndicate

Surrealism in the Comics I: Krazy Kat (George Herriman)

Franklin Rosemont

Next to "What is Truth?" the question "Who is Krazy Kat?" is the most perplexing in the annals of philosophy.

Rather than to even attempt a definition, let us begin on more modest terrain with a simple *description* of George Herriman's magnificent creature and the drama that unfolds around it.

Nominally a cat (or at least a kat)—albeit with few typically feline characteristics—and of indeterminate gender, Krazy is a gentle, wistful, poetic, eccentric, innocent, impractical, exuberant, inspired, idealistic, and amorously passionate dreamer wildly in love with a mouse named Ignatz. If Krazy is not like other cats, Ignatz is not at all like other mice. Inordinately strong, Ignatz is not easily frightened. He regards himself as coldly logical, realistic, rational, materialistic, practical, and unsentimental; he is also hot-tempered, shortsighted, and malicious. He is by no means scrupulously honest; he is sometimes hypocritical and is always thoroughly cynical and pugnacious. In contrast to Krazy's unabashedly lowbrow tastes, Ignatz prefers Mozart, Beethoven, the classics. Perhaps the mouse's most endearing quality is his wholehearted disrespect for the law; indeed, we can forgive him much (and even grow fond of the little demon) because he is such an incorrigible sinner.

Far from returning the kat's affection, the mouse insists that he despises his krazy admirer and, to demonstrate his scorn, hits the kat again and again—many thousands of times over the years—with a brick. Krazy, however, does not interpret Ignatz's overt aggression as hostile. For the kat, the brick is the proof, a veritable symbol, of the mouse's deep devotion. Time and again, Krazy is anxiety-stricken that no brick has hit his head that day; time and again, following such moments of despair, the kat is duly clobbered in the end and sings, "Now I'm a heppy, heppy ket."

At this stage in the drama, we meet the third and last of its central figures: a sort of bulldog, Coconino County's official representative of "law 'n' order," who happens to be in love with Krazy, and who is ever vigilant in protecting his love from the violence of the mouse. As often as Ignatz tosses a brick, Officer Pupp tosses Ignatz into jail.

Officer Pupp, also known as Kop, may be more or less doglike, but he is hardly coplike. Aside from his touching fondness for the kat, his incessant philosophical soliloquies—delivered with old-time oratorical grandiloquence and accompanied by exaggerated theatrical mannerisms—make him, as a law enforcer, odd indeed. And if he does, several times a week as a rule, apprehend Ignatz and lock him in a cell, nonetheless, the mouse—repeated offender though he is—is always back on the street the next day: rather a poor showing, by police standards.

It is necessary to emphasize the peculiar *symbiosis* of these three characters. They are engaged in a complex contest in which there is no question of our "taking sides." They are all in it together. In one strip, Officer Pupp has lost his memory ("lost about a quart of memory where but a pint existed before"). Leaving the doctor's, he runs into Ignatz but fails to recognize him. Upon questioning, he admits that he does not know the name Krazy Kat. Gleeful at this turn of events, Ignatz rushes off, brick in hand: "At last I'm free to toss this 'brick' at that 'kat' without the kop's interference." But by the time he finds the kat he has forgotten what he intended to do; indeed, he has forgotten who he is and, face to face with Krazy, does not recognize him. Whereupon an alarmed kat runs off shouting "Oh-h doctor!" But when Krazy finds the doctor, he too has a memory failure – can't remember what he wished to say. The final panel shows all three – mouse, kat, dog – together in the amnesia ward of Dr. Ambrose Phleeze's sanitarium, each ignorant of the identity of the others.

Through it all, year in and year out, we are treated to a laugh a minute – or oftener. Fortunately for us, we know now that laughter – like everything truly desirable – must lead *somewhere.*

Herriman's magisterial strip has elicited numerous paeans, a few detailed commentaries, several widely conflicting interpretations and, most plentifully, polite confessions of despair to the effect that, tantalizing as the strip is, it doesn't have a bit of meaning. Although it is "universally acclaimed as the greatest comic strip of all time," as Bill Blackbeard says in *The World Encyclopedia of Comics*, surprisingly little light has been shed on Herriman's motives, methods, or achievements.

Traditional critical approaches will always shrivel to nothing before this unpretentious yet sublime work. The arduous search for "sources," with which philologists like to commence their exegeses, has turned up little more than the faintest clues. It is unquestionable, for example, that Herriman was influenced by Cervantes. This is plain from any number of internal details (there is even a character in *Krazy Kat* named Don Kiyote), as well as from abundant affinities of atmosphere and theme. Krazy is very much like Don Quixote: a romantic, errant knight who faces impossible odds in a madcap effort to revive the Golden Age. And the perils that Krazy confronts, like those of Don Quixote, are all the greater, all the more hilarious, because the kat does not see them the way we do. All that Krazy Kat does, moreover, surely qualifies as *quixotic*. Society, for Herriman as for Cervantes, is a welter of meretricious schemes and devious designs, all working at cross-purposes – over which a solitary dreamer may somehow, almost "accidentally," triumph, doubtless thanks to his perseverance in his solitude and to the integrity of his dreams.

Franklin Rosemont

If Krazy Kat is a passable Don Quixote, Ignatz is rather a poor Sancho Panza. And Officer Pupp is wholly unsatisfactory as Rocinante. Some critics have attempted to compensate for these shortcomings by compounding the confusion. It has been suggested, for example, that Krazy is not only Don Quixote but also Parsifal; and Gilbert Seldes proposed, no doubt jocularly, that Ignatz is not only Sancho Panza but also Lucifer. We could add that Krazy is both Romeo and Juliet, and probably also Hamlet and Ariel; the kat has much in common with Immalee in Maturin's *Melmoth the Wanderer*, and embodies the principal qualities of Queequeg, Tashtego, and Daggoo in *Moby Dick*. This sort of thing, of course, can go on forever – but does it help us understand anything?

If the Don Quixote analogy collapses in a heap after a few faltering steps, e. e. cummings's effort[1] to see in the strip an allegory about democracy versus all extremism – in which Krazy represents democracy struggling against the individual (Ignatz) and society (Officer Pupp) – never even gets to its feet: Herriman's mighty epic just does not conform to such shallow and lukewarm prejudices. A more recent attempt to read the strip through the double lens of Kierkegaard and Sartre is no more helpful.[2] As hard as it may be for the partisans of easy solutions to accept, *Krazy Kat* clearly is not reducible to any simple formula: literary, philosophical, political, psychological, aesthetic, or otherwise.

There are indeed very real difficulties posed by Herriman's many-sided message. The strip developed, day in and day out, for more than 30 years; and if its thousands of incidents retain an unmistakable coherence – and form what can be regarded as a "unified whole" – still there were countless digressions, sidelong glances, and a multiplicity of subtle ramifications. The very magnitude of the work and its incontestable complexity – together with the mediocre attempts made thus far at critical interpretation – have led some critics to conclude that it is not in fact interpretable at all; that it is "meaningless." The most assertive proponent of this view, Robert Warshow, bluntly stated: "We do best, I think, to leave Krazy Kat alone."[3] For Warshow, and for others who have followed his lead, Herriman's strip is without significance except perhaps as a symptom of the "extremity of . . . alienation" in *"Lumpen* culture." Behind this abstentionism we cannot miss the ill-concealed sneer of the snob. He perceived that once it was admitted that the "mass image" deserved the same consideration as any other "work of art," traditional aesthetic values (and beyond those, traditional *social* values) would stand exposed as laurel wreaths whose leaves have long since withered to dust.

As if to illustrate the extreme backwardness of American critics as far as the "popular arts" are concerned, Warshow's bitter polemic has sometimes been mistaken for an "appreciation" of Herriman. It is further indicated that there is more than a little hypocrisy in the voluble acclaim of *Krazy Kat* by the fact that 70 years after the kat's initial appearance and 35 years after Herriman's death only a minute portion of his complete works has ever been printed in book form. Surely the prerequisite for serious evaluation of any artist's or writer's contributions is that the work under consideration be accessible. To read Herriman, however, one must pour over musty and crumbling newspapers or scan mile after mile of microfilm.

The many and disparate attempts at analysis to which *Krazy Kat* has been subjected have at least the virtue of demonstrating the extraordinary and lasting power of fascination that this comic strip has exerted on minds very different from each other. If one recalls, first, that it was a highly *popular* strip, perhaps less widely read than *Blondie* or the later *Peanuts* but nonetheless appearing daily for decades in dozens of papers, and, second, that although its publisher was William Randolph Hearst (the most demagogic and reactionary figure in the U.S. news media of his day), it aroused the sympathetic interest and even devotion of many who were generally antipathetic to everything Hearst stood for, it becomes clear that with *Krazy Kat* we are in the presence of an extraordinary phenomenon. Such coincidence of taste between "advanced intellectuals" and "the masses" testifies to Herriman's rare prescience, which reveals in turn a deeper truth: that *Krazy Kat* expressed, in a uniquely captivating way, the latent content of the historical drama that convulsed the first half of the American twentieth century.

Franklin Rosemont

The following notes are offered as jottings from a "log," so to speak, of repeated journeys through the kat's enchanted domain. I have never been able to view Herriman's work as primarily a "problem" to be "solved." It is rather a gift to be enjoyed. To avoid misunderstandings, it is necessary to begin with some introductory principles – a trayful of kategorical aperitifs:

1. *Krazy Kat* is not only a work of "fantasy" – it is, much more importantly, a work of *nonsense*: indeed, one of the masterpieces of nonsense. This does not mean, of course, that it therefore lacks "significance"; on the contrary, there is more significance and worth in the best nonsense than there is in the great bulk of what passes for "sense." It so happens that the significance of nonsense lies outside of formal logic, but this in no way diminishes its interest, for logic itself is almost negligible as a factor in human affairs.

The strip's dialogues often have the flavor of Zen koans or of the surrealist "one-in-the-other" game or – at times – of the excruciating ambiguity of certain mystical paradoxes, such as St. Teresa's "I die because I cannot die." A riot of rhyme and "reasons beyond Reason" and therefore situated outside any traditional discipline, *Krazy Kat* drinks from sources deeper and more far-ranging than philosophy or religion. "The world as it is, my dear K," Ignatz explains, "is not like it was, when it used to be." To which Krazy responds: "An' wen it gets to be wot it is, will it?"

2. *Krazy Kat* is, above all else, a *poetic* work, and George Herriman is one of the greatest American poets. It is astonishing that no one has yet taken the trouble to approach Herriman's work from the linguistic angle. Such an exploration could not help but yield important discoveries. Herriman's language was drawn more or less equally from lush Victorian prose and the Yiddishized street lingo of New York's Lower East Side; something like a synthesis of Emily Brontë and Groucho Marx. This gives his dialogues a very special rhythm, a *baroque pulsation*, found nowhere else.

Herriman's wordplay is invariably loose and lively. The kat would never say, "Of course I wouldn't," but, rather, "If coarse I wooden"; Richard Wagner becomes "Rigid Vogna"; "solar eclipse" is "solo eeklip." In strip after strip we find enticing queries ("Do the moom always come ova the mountin? Dunt the mountin evva come ova the moom?") and grand assertions ("You turn off the light and turn on the dark. You turn off the dark and turn on the light. Positivilly marvillis!" and "I like my kit fits in riddim—I do").

3. *Krazy Kat* was not "conceived," not "born"—it "jes grew."[4] Herriman was as surprised as his readers were by the doings of his kat, whose "marvelous secrets," moreover, were as elusive to him as they were to us.

Consider these words by Herriman himself, which I think may be taken as a kind of testament: "You have written truth, you friends of the 'shadows,' yet be not harsh with 'Krazy'—he is but a shadow himself, caught in the web of this mortal skein. We call him 'cat'; we call him 'crazy': Yet he is neither. At some time he will ride away to you, People of the Twilight. His password will be the echoes of a vesper bell; his coach, a zephyr from the west. Forgive him, for you will understand him no better than we who linger on this side of the pale."[5]

It is evident in all his work that Herriman had more than a vague "sympathy for the underdog"—that he shared an active spirit of solidarity and revolt and was very much on the side of the outcasts. In addition to *Krazy Kat* and his other strips, see his review of Charlie Chaplin's film *The Gold Rush* and his illustrations in the volumes of satirical verse by Don Marquis, featuring Archy the anarchist cockroach.

A particularly subversive aspect of his work is also discernible. Krazy is not only a cat but a *black* cat. Long a fixture of folklore, the black cat as a symbol of *bad luck* is second to none. At the time Krazy began to appear, however, the black cat was enjoying an unprecedented notoriety as an even more specific symbol: the symbol of workers' *sabotage*, or "striking on the job," bringing bad luck to the bourgeoisie.

Throughout the American labor movement in that era—most especially in the IWW and the Socialist party—sabotage was a major topic of discussion and debate. Numerous pamphlets and articles hailed it as an important form of class struggle. Its praises were put in rhyme by leading Wobbly songwriters such as Joe Hill and Ralph Chaplin. Black cats abounded in IWW cartoons. It is noteworthy that this literature and art favoring workers' sabotage was characterized – like *Krazy Kat* – by a genuine lyricism and an all-pervasive humor.

Herriman himself, in the finest IWW spirit, is known to have practiced sabotage. As a teenager he was unhappy with his parents and hated his job in the family bakery. Once, to get even, he poured salt on several hundred doughnuts. Another time, when he buried a dead mouse in a loaf of bread, he was kicked out of the house, never to return.

It was under the sign of sabotage, therefore, that the man who would create *Krazy Kat* gained his freedom. From then on, George Herriman was on his own.

Herriman's deep affection for "the wretched of the earth" also underscores the overriding *utopian* quality of his work: utopian in the best sense, signifying the imaginative critique of existing values and institutions and the presentation of imaginary alternative societies organized on lines completely different from our own. It is not often remarked that the early comics appeared in the heyday of American utopian fiction. But to a greater extent than has been acknowledged, comics (the best of them, in any case, such as Herriman's and Winsor McKay's) are an extension – we could even say the *flower* – of this important critical/utopian current.

Ethereal and earthy at the same time, incorruptible in his infinite tenderness, Krazy confidently reaches out for values that do not yet exist. Here we have a "kounter-kulture" resonant with everything the heart desires. Against odds that seem impossible to everyone else, the Kat holds out for nothing less than dancing in the streets, poetry created by all, total love, permanent festivals of what Edward Young, in his *Night-Thoughts*, called "unprecarious bliss."

The world of a comic strip might seem small, but Krazy Kat's world looms larger than "life as we know it." Emphatically inconclusive, neither Herriman nor his kat pretended to have "the" answers. Rather, they proceeded – and we proceed with them – by means of a continual *questioning*. "Nobodda but me," the kat once said, "would care to got where I'm going, an' ivvin i dunt know where I'm goin' until I get there." And so it is that we as readers must make our own way, by our own means, over this magical terrain: there are no shortcuts.

But one thing is certain: the specter of Krazy Kat will long continue to haunt the world.

Notes

1. e.e. cummings, "Introduction" to *Krazy Kat* (New York, 1969).
2. Arthur Asa Berger, *The Comic-Stripped American* (Baltimore, 1973).
3. Robert Warshow, *The Immediate Experience* (New York, 1962).
4. On the notion of "Jes Grew," see Ishmael Reed, *Mumbo Jumbo* (New York, 1972), which is, by the way, dedicated to George Herriman.
5. Quoted in *Krazy Kat*, 168.

Surrealism in the Comics II: Dick Tracy (Chester Gould)

Franklin Rosemont

In the comics, as everywhere else, the struggle between the marvelous and the miserable is waged unrelentingly. We want comics that dream and inspire dreams; comics that challenge musty traditions and overturn mental habits; comics that give the "impossible" a chance (the mask behind which the "desirable" is so frequently forced to hide). Is it necessary to add that virtually nothing that matters to us—nothing inspiring, subversive, emancipatory, poetic—will be found in the plethora of comics devoted to family life, soap operas, spies, military exploits, sports, pets, or the shenanigans of "bobby-soxers"? There are, here and there, a few rare exceptions, but they serve only, as usual, to prove the rule.

Still less should we expect to find subversive/poetic qualities in those comics that consciously aim at the glorification of detectives and cops. And yet, though the great majority of these comics are irredeemably dreary, the exceptions are both sufficiently numerous and of such indisputably high quality that we are confronted with what might seem to be an anomalous circumstance. The problem, however, is easily solved: the extreme intensity of conflict in these comics, their fevered acceptance of the omnipresence of crime and malevolence, their dark obsessiveness and constantly recurring violence are such that the artists often are carried away by their creations. On such emotionally charged terrain, conscious intentions count for little: it is the *latent* content that commands our notice. What do these comics show us? A mercilessly steady stream of snapshots: brutally altered primal scenes, traumatic memories, oedipal rages, savage impulses, fits of ferocity, lust, and vengeance. The seven deadly sins multiplied a thousand-fold cavort and grovel in these stark panoramas of unconscious mental processes. In Will Eisner's compelling *Spirit*, in *The Shadow* (drawn by several hands), and in Jack Cole's admirable *Plastic Man*, we are presented with shattering, nightmarish dramas—as gory and disfigured, perhaps, as Grunewald's *Crucifixion* or Goya's *Disasters of War* but also just as authentic in their passionate portrayal of the return of the repressed.

Pride of place among the comics' detectives belongs to Chester Gould's pioneering Dick Tracy. Starting on October 4, 1931, this laconic, angular, trench-coated knight ventured boldly through the streets of Chicago to do battle with an astonishing cast of villains. In the very nerve center of America's criminal underworld, Depression/Prohibition Chicago—the Chicago of Al Capone and Bugs Moran, whose rival gangs of bootleggers were machine-gunning each other all over town—Tracy was the first to begin, in Chester Gould's words, "fighting it out face to face with crooks via the hot lead route" in comics.

Gould has expressly denied being influenced by Dashiell Hammett or other "hard-boiled" mystery writers. But there is no doubt that the work of such writers, which enjoyed widespread popularity from the mid-1920s through the 1940s, helped prepare an audience for Tracy. And Tracy, in turn, has influenced the crime/mystery genre, not only in comics but in literature, radio, movies. Ellery Queen has credited him with being "the world's finest first procedural detective of fiction."

However, Tracy himself is of decidedly minor interest, always peripheral to the strip that bears his name. The central figures of the strip, its prime attractions, and the reasons for its success, invariably have been the "bad guys." The real theme of *Dick Tracy* is: the fascination of evil.

Look at its unparalleled roster of grotesque rogues: Little-face, B-B Eyes, Mole, Flattop, Pruneface, Mrs. Pruneface, Mumbles, the Brow, the Blank, Shaky, and a host of others. It is these incarnations of Satan—these insatiably cruel, deformed, horrible abominations—who hold the spotlight as they move from outrage to outrage, gun or dagger in hand, through an immemorial darkness splattered with moonlight and blood. We are in the old Gothic wilderness; it has been industrialized and urbanized, of course, and the moldering castles have been replaced by skyscrapers, but the atmosphere remains essentially the same. A cold metallic solitude rings through the Tracy epic in its early years. The streets glisten with greed and fear as we follow crazed killers in their gloomy sedans, roaring through the shadows to an inexorable doom.

It is beyond question that Gould consciously—with all his heart—is on the side of the cops. He is an inveterate champion of law and order, a hater of crooks who likes to spend his free time visiting police stations to see how the boys are doing in their war on crime. But at night, when he shuts his eyes, he can't help dreaming; and sometimes dreams enjoy the sweetest revenge. "I don't outline the whole story when I start," Gould has admitted. "I feel if I don't know how it is going to come out, then the reader can't, and if you keep enough punch and enough interest, the intervening ground seems to be covered automatically."

Even such a casual concession to automatism has serious consequences. In spite of Gould's precautions, poetry wreaks its own havoc and achieves its own infallible justice. To cite an example: when one of the *Dick Tracy* villains, the psychopathic killer Flattop, died

Gould received half a dozen telegrams from people who offered to claim the body. . . . The day of the funeral, several floral offerings and a stack of sympathy cards arrived at the office of the syndicate which distributes the strip. That night a crowd of bereaved citizens gathered . . . and held a wake, complete with a coffin and candles, for Flattop. Many people have since written Gould touching letters, expressing their deep sense of personal loss. . . . A woman living on the West Coast asked the ageless question, "Why did he have to die?" and added sadly, "All America loved Flattop."

We read *Dick Tracy* the way we read Cotton Mather's *Wonders of the Invisible World*. Both are works of apoplectic puritanism, bursting at the seams with an uncontrollable and "righteous" fury. But we are as little interested in Gould's respect for the law as we are in the fine points of the old witchhunter's theology. What interests us is the insuperable violence of the dramatic collisions and the dazzling profusion of obsessive detail.

Let us conclude by paraphrasing Blake: the reason Chester Gould writes in fetters when he portrays Law-Abiding Citizens and Cops, and at liberty when he portrays Evildoers and Criminals, is that he is—unconsciously at least, and in spite of himself—"a true Poet and of the Devil's party without knowing it."

As the Artist Sees It: Interviews with Comic Artists

R. Crumb and Bill Griffith

R. Crumb: Do I feel like I'm still trying to attain the kind of cohesive intensity achieved by the early Kurtzman *Mad* comics? Is it still an unrealized dream of mine? The answer is . . . naturally . . . I think that's the way "culture" works . . . artists are always trying to equal the work that impressed them in their childhood and youth . . . I still feel extremely inadequate when I look at the old Mad comics, or early Walt Kelly, or Carl Barks, or Frank King (Gasoline Alley), or Segar (Popeye), or Thomas Nast, or James Gillray Posad . . . going back to the granddaddy of them all, Peter Bruegel . . . but this is a different time, and of course, I know I'm saying different things in different ways from these past cartoonists . . . I know I'll never be the craftsman that some of them were . . . I'm too lazy . . . but that too is a sign of the times . . . our generation lacks the drive it takes to be really advanced craftspeople . . . but it's alright . . . it can still be good . . . there's a charm in the "looseness" of the culture of our generation, in its lackadaisical approach . . . besides, our parents threw all the old traditions in the garbage can without a second

throught and left us to root around for the remnants in the back alleys of the culture, so, hell, it's not our fault if we're crude at our
crafts . . . actually I'm amazed to see so many people my age and
younger who can do good work with their hands . . . and it's part
of our struggle to maintain what's left of the old crafts in the face
of the "exploding plastic inevitable" . . . you take a simple thing
like pen and ink drawing . . . it gets more difficult as each day
passes to find stores that sell good drawing paper, ink that's fit for
use in a crow quill pen . . . pen points have declined drastically of
late . . . the price of drawing paper has skyrocketed, et cetera, et
cetera . . . but you can get all the 47-cent felt-tip pens you want
in any short-stop or Seven-Eleven open all night . . . it's like
that . . . and anybody involved in any handicraft activity has a
similar tale of woe. . . .

And another thing . . . the comic-book medium has gotten
so stiff and restrictive on the big-time mainstream level that the individualistic cartoonist can't make it even if he or she *wants*
to . . . underground comics being the only alternative and they
are so low-budget that there's almost no economic incentive for the
majority of the artists. Everyone has to do their own color separations using shitty Zipatone screens . . . Kurtzman tells me that in
the fifties, you just did a color indication on a photo-stat made for
you by the company you worked for, and then the final color work
was done by old German immigrant printer-craftsmen . . . the
point is that everything was much more together on the material
plane in those days . . . but, of course, the main point of the underground comics is absolute freedom, which they never had back
then, and have even *less* today, in the big-time.

Since the beginning of modern mass culture, artistic accomplishment has become less the work of isolated individuals and
more the result of time and place . . . the artists, musicians, et
cetera involved being more anonymous in relation to the phenomenon as a whole, such as, say, comic books, 1935 to 1955, or pulp
magazines, or, say, jazz music, or the golden age of country music,
1925 to 1935 . . . of course, there are artists who stand out, but
they don't stand out as much, especially to someone who really
studies any one of these fields and knows the hundreds of various

and different works produced. . . . I guess this was always true of culture, but more so now I think, in the age of mass media . . . it's sort of a modern version of the old anonymous tribal and folk art . . . it involves looking at cultural phenomenon not as outstanding individuals so much as various movements, eras, and like that . . . the artist is the product of a time and place, no matter how "great" his or her "genius" . . . art is de-mystified: "creative genius" is seen as mostly bool-sheet . . . good, even great, art is achieved as much by a whole cultural group and a period of time as it is by an individual. . . . The artist deserves merit only for "integrity," not for "genius" . . . man, do I hate that genius shit when it's heaped on me . . . it can only serve to fuck up an artist's head. (How I do prattle on, eh?)

Imagine being Bob Dylan . . . ten years ago he was worshipped as if he was a god by millions of "leftist" college kids . . . it's a wonder he's still alive to tell about it . . . but what does this do to an artist's ability to spontaneously create anything? Well, you can bet it makes the guy very, um, self-conscious . . . fortunately for me I never got as famous as that poor devil Bobby Zimmerman. . . . I can still hope to work in some kind of unfettered atmosphere, but believe me, media notoriety is not an easy thing to deal with . . . my silent period of the early seventies was a time when fame and money had fucked up my life and complicated it to the point where I could no longer work . . . my work ground to a painful halt, and I was forced to deal with the world around me . . . to get it off my back, essentially, so that I could get back to work. . . . I have yet to finish this task, but my life is a bit simpler now and I am able to work some. . . . Of course, I too was affected by the disintegration of the optimistic sixties' youth movement, but the early seventies for me was mostly a period of figuring out how to deal with fame and money, neither of which I had the faintest notion of how to handle when it was dumped on me in the late sixties. . . . At first I ate it up, naturally . . . oboy, lots of attention, glory, love . . . they love me. . . .

I'm slow to realize things, so it took several years and a long, long succession of fast-talking con-men, rip-off lawyers, publishers, movie producers, painted women, mooches, bums, desperadoes, fan boys, and other pests stomping all over me before I started squirming my way out from under. . . . I'd probably still be there except that for a couple of years I was just never able to get any work done.

Bill Griffith: I don't consider myself to be under the influence of either dadaism or surrealism (although I make nods in both directions)—I'm too interested in telling stories. The discipline of cartooning pretty much excludes the self-indulgence which is associated with dada. Dadaists relate to the world from an outsiders point of view. I'm more of a burrower from the inside—with a case of terminal ambiguity. That quality (ambiguity) of my work may explain the apparently irrational (dada, surreal) strain. Using Alfred Jarry (daddy of 'em all) as a character enables me to deal with the subject of irrationality without becomeing completely enmeshed in it.

I have no illusions about America or capitalism (down with 'em both!), but I take *people* as my subject matter—and so I feel affection for them. I'm also afraid of them, which is simply the other side of the same coin. Comics are a tremendously flexible medium—virtually nothing is excluded—from escapist fantasy to psychological probing to your basic slapstick. But they have this tradition, through the newspaper strips and "aboveground" comic books, of being primarily a kid's entertainment medium—and thus a stigma is attached to them. "We don't get no respect," as Rodney Dangerfield so aptly put it. That's okay, though; it's better that we're left alone to do our work. . . . The same thing that's happening to comics now (through ARCADE, etc.)—a bending, stretching of the medium process—happened to film long ago—and to painting, literature, et cetera.

I tried being a painter for a number of years—but the joker in me was always poking through. I was starving a major tendency—it was a startling revelation for me to see the early Crumb stuff in the *East Village Other* and *Zap*. Within six months, my oils were drying up on the palette, and I began to struggle with the discipline of cartooning. I found out that you really have nothing to say until you know *how* to say it.

Perhaps I could end with a line Bukowski wrote in a letter to the Print Mint when we were trying to decide on what story of his to use in ARCADE: "Underground cartoonists are all a bunch of Baptist ministers in Popeye suits!"

Radio and
Television

Bruce Kaiper *Aerial Attack* (montage, 1974)

Radio Voices:
A Child's
Bed of Sirens

Philip Lamantia

Activity is the faculty of receiving.
Novalis

Whatever its limitations, it was generally acknowledged that American radio between 1920 and 1950 had the virtue of providing a stimulating vehicle, albeit a technical one, for exercising the listener's imagination. Determined by radio's intrinsic structure, the listener was "forced" to "see" by responsive imaginative activity the invisible content of what is, by contrast, given and visualized in movies and television. For adults such imaginary collaboration may have been, more often than not, confined to what was directly suggested by the broadcasters, but for children up to the age of puberty certain radio dramas sparked realms of terror, desire, and reverie which infinitely improved and heightened the content far beyond the limits set rationally and consciously by the original producers. In some adventure and mystery programs of radio's "golden age" (as a child, between 1934 and 1942, I was listening intensively), radioland was peopled with figures, images, and mythic concepts that served as formidable initiators of poetry and enchantment. I can trace a profound awakening of the poetic sense of life and language directly to the exemplary magical myth of "The Shadow" and to those disquieting transgressions–veritable sagas of symbolic patricide and matricide–revealed by "The Whistler."

Among the programs aimed primarily at children, along with the science fiction genre represented by "Buck Rogers" and "Superman," were the realistic adventure serials: "Jack Armstrong the All-American Boy," "Dick Tracy," "Jungle Jim" and "Terry and the Pirates." Though not devoid of some spirit of risk, adventure, and exoticism, the whole group was a varied expression of diurnal mentality, characteristically broadcast in the afternoon hours that followed school. Most of these daylight dramas more or less reinforced old-fashioned ideas and morals of capitalist culture and the clichés of "law and order." But beginning in the early evening, the purer mystery fantasies were featured: "Fu Manchu," "Chandu the Magician," "Mandrake the Magician," and "The Shadow." Deeper into the night, fantasy fiction came on: "Lights Out" and "The Witch's Tale," aimed presumably at adults and adolescents but certainly heard by the more precocious or less disciplined children, by those of us who possessed secret handmade crystal sets or managed to acquire personal bedside radios, dropping off to sleep at least once or twice a week by means of a kind of audial *Weird Tales*, the Lovecraftian pulp magazine many of us would not discover until the brink of adolescence but for which we were being adequately prepared by radio late at night. For those who lived in the Western and Mountain areas, around nine or ten in the evening, radio on Sundays transmitted the long-running series of individual dramas linked by a basic structure fictionalizing "heinous crimes" of capitalist greed: "The Whistler." "The Whistler" and "The Shadow" were conceived no doubt under the rubric of escapist adult fare, along with the detective adventure group, which was also aired usually at prime time, such as the very sympathetic "Alias Jimmy Valentine" (based on O. Henry's genial safecracker) and "Boston Blackie," both prototypes of the "good-bad guys," as well as "Bulldog Drummond," an exotic lone wolf from England. But what was intended by the radio producers and what occurred in a child's imaginary reception and associational development of the thematic materials from these au-

dial sources was often contradictory—and humorously so considering the rigorously adhered-to serious intentions of the producers
and writers behind the formulas.

For children the excitement and crystallizing imagery gener-
ated through audial reception of violence, mayhem, murder, and
terror far outdistanced and superseded in imaginary grandeur any
possible parallels of thought and feeling an adult might have experienced. For sophisticated adults most of the radio dramas were
received as variants, often banal, of the formula-fictions of the
pulps; the great mass of listeners, often too tired after a hard and
anxious day of work or the fatiguing anxiety of looking for work in
the Depression, may not have been hearing too distinctly at all. Gilbert Seldes insisted in "The Great Audience" (1950) that radio was
not, in the strict sense, a mass-media cultural form; hence, the
dramas were mostly the creation of connoisseurs of certain genre-
literatures who, representing a minority of the reading public,
projected their special interests onto everybody, at least onto who-
ever was listening throughout the evening hours. Seldes also noted
that the broadcasters were well aware of the positive effect on and
high responsiveness of children to the more violent programming,
so that "fifteen hundred murders take place each week on the air.
This does not include murders meditated or suspected in daytime
serials, but it does take in manslaughter specially arranged for children's programs."

Such shows of violence were generally salutary for children
and carried for them necessary degrees of representational non-
repressive sublimation, as parallel expressions in comic books and
movie serials (and, long ago, fairy tales) had adequately conveyed.
All the more the interventions of marvelous figures, or even merely
fantastic ones, such as the Shadow, Fu Manchu, Chandu, or Mandrake the Magician, some attaining mythic dimensions, themselves
transforming-agents of violence and terror, transmitted audially to
children, continued in new forms the unbroken line of fabulous oral
literature, legend, and myth of earlier times, when the magician
such as Merlin, that counselor of vengeful battles, and the mul-
titudinous transformations of the Shadow served as permanent cultural motifs. If for adults the Shadow or Mandrake may be said to

connote signs of regression and narcissism, for children these beings can represent truly effective symbols of triumph, power, and necessary ego-building–interacting with the child's psychical needs during the successive stages of the latency period. On the poetic plane, the Shadow and Mandrake are paragons of hermetic knowledge: modern forms, respectively, of the fairy tale wonderworker and sorcerer. The opening theme of "The Shadow" is among the most memorable for those whose childhood games were often sparked and charged with imaginary adaptations of this potent figure. His literal visual image was known to us from two sources: graphic conceptions from the covers of the widely circulated pulp magazine devoted to him and the Saturday matinee movie serial in which he was adequately portrayed by Victor Jory, who resembled some of the magazine portraits.

Psychoanalysis long ago located correspondence between practical magic and ritual in primitive societies and certain phases of our childhood psychical development. The child's psychical reality is structured in early infancy by a high sense of omnipotence continuing dynamically and transformationally through the "magical" power of words and gestures, "calling," in Geza Roheim's theory, "on all the child's sources of pleasure within its own body." Roheim wrote:

Magic in general is the counterphobic attitude, the transition from passivity to activity. . . . It is probably the basic element in thought and the initial phase of activity. . . . We grow up through magic and in magic, and we can never outgrow the illusion of magic. Our first response to the frustrations of reality is magic; and without this belief in ourselves, in our own specific ability or magic, we cannot hold our own against the environment and against the super-ego. The infant does not know the limits of its power. It learns in time to recognize the parents as those who determine its fate, but in magic it denies this dependency. In magic, mankind is fighting for freedom.

Simultaneously with the daytime heroines and heroes of the earliest mythology came the beings of the Night. For example, to Spaniards, *la Sombra* (the Shadow) is to this day a familiar figure, often the name of a restaurant, café, or other popular haunt; and charmingly depicted graphically with cape and sombrero, silhouetted in black on the label of a popular wine. In folkloric investigations, Alexander Krappe found superstitious variants of the identification of "the double" or "soul" with the Shadow. By 1925 Otto Rank completed his milestone psychoanalytical study, *The Double*, in which he interprets innumerable appearances and transformations of this subject from anthropological and literary sources. Maxwell Grant's pulp magazine version of 1931 – perhaps inspired by Dickens and Poe – united the sense of the Shadow's earlier superstitious traditions to those of a nearly omnipotent and mysterious personage with an Avenger motif; adapted for radio, the Shadow was altered to possess, as well, perhaps the most appealing of magical powers. The opening theme of the program clearly delineated both "the double" and the extraordinary power: "The Shadow is in reality Lamont Cranston. . . . Several years ago in the Orient, Cranston learned a strange and mysterious secret . . . the hypnotic power to cloud men's minds so they cannot see him."

During radio's golden age, children were generally trained rigorously to respect institutional authorities; thus, any representation of the police as weak and ineffective, which is how they were portrayed in "The Shadow," may be interpreted as an effective communication of a subversive sign, all the more enhanced by its weekly repetition. Since the depiction of police impotence was conducted within the context of comparison to an "improbable" power, the broadcasters probably rationalized the subversive quality as having been rendered diluted in a manifestly irreal form. But for children who would grow up to question or reject institutions that uphold the generalized criminality at the base of capitalist society, the subversive dimension of "The Shadow" may have been more germinal than any rationalist adult could suspect.

The Shadow and the radio magicians possessed magical power. It is the imaginary intervention of this power, in the urban landscapes of daily life, which suggested the precariousness of normal social relations and hence the possibility of extraordinary transformations (here suggestions of the marvelous, but always generally intuited by humanity as rationally possible). For children who were defending themselves against the repressive demands of their parents and were capable later of questioning societal norms, great magical beings furnished the sign of a "conscience" deeper and nobler than that enforced by capitalist morality. Just as another mythic figure of the night, the Vampire, can be seen as a symbol of the latent power of the proletariat rising "from the dead" of social existence, so can the Shadow be viewed as the Avenger of the victims of the "hidden" criminality of capitalism which has been internalized in psychical reality: "Who knows what evil lurks in the hearts of men? The Shadow knows." Although the radio producers counterbalanced the exceptional qualities of "The Shadow" by the use of a conventional device, that is, by enlisting him as an "aid" to "the forms of law and order," this manifest sign of accommodation was itself rendered "improbable" by the logic of the magical context in which it operated and the magical response of children nullified the device entirely. A hypothetical rationalist or positivist "sociological" argument that the Shadow and other fantastic and mythical night-beings are reducible to mere "defenders" of capitalist law and order by adult rationalizations via mass-media ideological reinforcement misses the point; it errs by not taking into account *the determining significance of psychical life materially interacting with socioeconomic structures.* The rich layers of latent meaning or the uncovering of inferences that signify the specific *logic of the poetic marvelous* could never emerge with such rationalist reductionism, which is totally inept at understanding cultural exchanges. Any effective interventions of the marvelous impose their own logic on events, including even those fictionalized moments in crime stories that otherwise progress "realistically" but are capable of transmutation by the determinations of a magico-marvelous symbol such as the Shadow, the Vampire, Mandrake, or even Chandu. Although it has been understood in the historiography of Hollywood movies that certain filmic representations of "private-eyes" – foremost, the prototype of the "bad good-guy" or "good bad-guy" in Sam Spade of *The Maltese Falcon* – are "ambiguous" vis-à-vis established law and order, all the more the magico-mythic hero intervening in ordinary human affairs is able to turn the conventional context of cops and robbers inside out and by his superimposition of improbable means and ends implies a profound subversion of societal norms.

For a highly anticipatory imagination, such as a child's, not yet corrupted and overwhelmed by associations of routine reality, the narrations of many of radio's "opening themes," repeated ritually week after week for years, formed some of the most lasting germinal impressions emanating from popular culture. It was these thematic crystallizations that resonated with a poetic insistence and inspired all-consuming moments of fervent exaltation throughout my childhood. Spells they were, auditory enchantment; talismanic voices cabalistically conveying us in vehicles structured by breathtaking excitement, irresistible affective surges of our eyes on fire beating on winged corridors of sound; waves and rivers of pulsating phonemes that swept us immediately from the first phrases into deliriums of anticipation. . . . And as we continued to "grow up" in the remaining few years, with the underlying sense of having conquered lost ground in the passionate embrace of newly arriving landscapes emerging ever more clearly from the steamy vermillion mists, we continued almost semiconsciously to hear the radio voices of anticipation and insatiable desires for the unknown—in a great headlong rush into whatever was to be: "invitation to the voyage," "on the road to Xanadu," "coming on like gangbusters."

The following few examples, dense as I have become, still flicker from having once been bathed *in the first lights of glowing words*: The quoted narrations and sound effects directions are from the opening themes of, respectively, "Lights Out," "Fu Manchu," "Bulldog Drummond," "The Witch's Tale," and "Boston Blackie":

(Announcer's voice:)
It . . . is . . . later . . . than . . . you . . . think!
Lights out . . . e-v-e-r-y-b-o-d-y!
London at midnight
a great city wrapped in a heavy shroud
of dense yellow fog
. . . street lights weird as elfin lamps
grow mistily as something fashioned
in a dream. . . .

Philip Lamantia

*The murmur of creeping traffic. Behind an ancient wall, a vast
gloomy mansion crouches like an evil beast of prey. . . . The
prince of evil . . . a superman of incredible genius possessing a
brain like Shakespeare and a face like Satan . . .
the shadow of
Fu Manchu.*

(Sound effects:
Foghorn blasts, slow footsteps, gunshot, police whistle.)
*Out of the fog
out of the night
and into his American adventures
comes . . .
BULLDOG DRUMMOND.*

(Sound effects:
Tower clock tolling, eerie music, howling wind.)
*The fascination for the eerie . . . weird, blood-chilling tales told
by Old Nancy, the Witch of Salem, and Satan, the wise black cat.*

*Boston Blackie
Enemy to those who make him an enemy
Friend to those who have no friends!*

If in realms of a child's wish fulfillment the Shadow represented the sign-symbol of an ultimate defense mechanism, that is,
the power to appear invisible to others ("the cloak of invisibility" is
a concomitant of legendary shamans, magicians, and yogis), Mandrake, who stepped into radioland from the pages of a nationally
syndicated daily comic strip, was a twentieth-century interpretation of the traditional Magus displaying "all the powers" that have
been universally ascribed to this archetype immemorially in history
and myth. He was also characteristically "American." Although I
imagine one could by exhaustive research find any number of "reasons why," the fact remains that the United States has *not* had in
its history a mythic figure corresponding to Merlin in Britain, Faust
in Germany, the historically authentic Cagliostro in eighteenth-
century Revolutionary France. Cagliostro—who fascinated half of
Europe, from kings and courtiers avid for his "secrets" to great

masses of people who eagerly sought him out for thaumaturgic cures – was perhaps the last truly popular of the modern great magicians; he is doubly interesting for his antimonarchical and subversive influence in the Free-masonic secret societies of his time, "the friend of liberty" who died in a dungeon in Italy as a victim of the Papal Inquisition.

Many of the fictional accounts of the modern magus, from Bulwer-Lytton's *Zanoni*, a seminal popular novel of the Victorian age, to *Doctor Strange* in the recent comic book extravaganza, have their sources directly and indirectly in Cagliostro and his more esoteric, royalist counterpart, the Count of Saint-Germain, who also distinguished himself in the resurgence of magical belief, which curiously paralleled the rationalist enlightenment and the birth of capitalism. In this latter connection, the sociologist Marcel Mauss, writing in France at the turn of the century, stated in his *Theory of Magic*, "Magical beliefs which are active in certain corners of our society and which were quite general a century ago, are the most alive, the most real indications of a state of social unrest and social consciousness."

Although by powers and accomplishments Mandrake was easily the equal of his European counterparts, his comic strip inventors during the Depression years chose to depict him, interestingly enough, in the guise and attire of what from the standpoint of "high magic" signifies a mere caricature of the Mage. Mandrake was drawn to look exactly like a conventional stage magician, hypnotist, or mentalist. Could it be we were confronted with another appearance of "the double" or (also implied ironically) that hard times in Depression America had forced the truly great magician Mandrake into "selling himself" in the more credible and lucrative disguise of a theatrical performer of legerdemain? But as they say here, "it worked, man," and presto – behold! – the heir of Merlin, Faust, Cagliostro, and "the great unknown magus" arrived in full morning or afternoon daylight replete with evening clothes, black tie, tails, short cape, tophat, and pencil-thin mustache, as if he had just finished his act on a vaudeville stage of 1920s' America. Among his superior attributes were the ability to go through solid steel walls, levitate himself and others, paralyze enemies and oversee events at a distance, divert lethal objects from attaining their mark, and cloud men's minds to the pitch of producing prodigious hallucinations to their disadvantage, et cetera. He even sent his seductively beautiful companion and accomplice, Princess Narda, unscathed, through a full-length mirror.

This combinational adaptation by his inventors turned Mandrake the Magician into a veritable theatrical dandy of the occult whose stage of operations was basically the whole world *of certain interiors* of an urban landscape. He was commonly depicted inside luxurious Manhattanlike apartments, fashionable restaurants, and cocktail lounges of the 1930s. And he was invariably drawn into *interiors* of all kinds, as if fulfilling the old hermetic-magical invitation "into the insides of the earth," to acquire knowledge and power. So, to the extreme delight and wonder of children, Mandrake took off one day for what was to be perhaps his longest adventure; he descended into another universe, into another inhabited planet, which existed in the subatomic spaces within the interior of an ordinary American coin! Among childhood friends and acquaintances, this series of comic strip adventures "inside the coin" was the source of endless reveries at every turn in the long chain of phantasmagoric events.

Although we had ample visual prefiguration of Mandrake from the comic strip, the opening theme of the radio series in 1940 had the surprising quality of an extraordinary, anticipatory annunciation. We listened to a truly oracular summons, the Latin words intoned slowly, as if coming from a deep cave and swept by a whirling wind to float over the world: *"Invoco Legem Magicorum!"* Whether or not we understood literally the English equivalent, "I Invoke the Law of Magic!," these Latin sounds communicated perfectly the "cabalistic" meaning of the emblematic motto which, joined to the provocative words, "Mandrake the Magician," was instantly received as a doubly crystallized sign, an efficacious *password* into the deepest realms of the marvelous, perfectly serving our real needs as children for the pleasures and excitement of an authentic magico-poetic experience: poetry invoked and provoked.

Because language is basically an audial system, for those in the process of extending their recently acquired capacities for language-acquisition, poetic crystallizations of verbal signs received directly by the ear were complementary to the poetic and mythical expressions on the visual plane offered in some comic books and films, for example, the Saturday matinee serials: "Fu Manchu," "The Shadow," "Black Dragons," and "Dr. Satan," the latter a primitive masterpiece of the marvelous featuring one of the great Hollywood actors, Eduardo Ciannelli. For me, three fertilizing rivers of popular culture—certain radio dramas, comic books, and movies—often interchanging subjects or content, were the authentic sources of poetic and life-transforming expression a child of the Depression and war years was offered, in contrast to the poverty of institutional culture, in the schools and elsewhere, whose results we would confront soon enough in the general miserablism mercilessly enforced in adolescence and young adulthood. As in other fields, the high quantitative content of dross was immediately dissolved by certain exalting words, purified images and sounds, all the more so with radio materials, which the producers deliberately structured, they believed, to last but a day and be forgotten. But as I have tried to indicate, rich thematic matter was ritually repeated and latent messages were received and often recreations of exceedingly subversive and mytho-poetic information was heard *as if for the first time.*

Backyard Bombs: Horror Movies on TV

Nancy Joyce Peters

Late at night and in the dark, after the legitimation comedies and the frauds passed off as "news" have left the air, we are likely to find roving our television screens ubiquitous and disquieting figures—vampires, werewolves, mummies, zombies, abortive creations of diabolical doctors, and other masked and mutant beings. Monsters and magical practitioners have always been inseparable from the human imagination, a fact confirmed in ancient civilizations, rites and myths of tribal peoples, folktales of peasant societies, the fantasies of childhood, and the dreams of "civilized" adults. Only the means of expression changes.

At the end of the ancien régime, on the eve of explosive industrialization, when D. A. F. de Sade was working out his brilliant theories in prison isolation, the modern horror tale grew in European literature and blossomed in the dark gardens of gothic romance. Matthew Lewis's *The Monk* and Anne Radcliffe's *The Mysteries of Udolpho* (1795) coincided with others of the type that set the scene with images of the castle, the night, the dungeon, the storm, the mysterious ruins haunted by specters. In the early nineteenth century, four poet friends wrote stories that were to give form to characters still seen on the late show: Percy Shelley's *St. Irvyne*, Lord Byron's *The Giaour*, John Polidori's *The Vampyre*, and Mary Shelley's *Frankenstein: Or, the Modern Prometheus* (1813). Through them and their heirs, the gothic tradition, with its marvels and terrors, its amalgam of cruelty and love, its quest for supernormal power, and its acts of violent transformation, carries into the late twentieth century in essentially the same outlines.

Tales of terror and the supernatural were among the first to be translated into film. Melies made *Le Manoir du Diable* (vampire) in 1896, and *Cleopatre* (mummy) in 1899; Edison's *Frankenstein* was filmed in 1910. Many others were to be made before the 1920s when the first surrealists in Paris recognized in *Nosferatu, eine Symphonie des Grauens* the revelation of the *poetic marvelous*, heralded by the words, "on the other side of the bridge, the phantoms came to meet him." Mass audiences in the 1930s and 1940s, sitting in rococo movie palaces, thrilled to the oneiric delights of scores of films: *Dracula* (Bela Lugosi), vampire par excellence, evoking another, more seductive world for his "children of the night"; *Dracula's Daughter* (Gloria Holden), unable to awaken from her nightmare of perverse sexuality; or *Night of the Zombies*, two women in their nightdresses almost sleepwalking through the shadowy cane fields suddenly encountering the spectral Carre Four on their way to voodoo rites.

Generally, it is possible to follow in these pictures a fusion of themes and imagery with historic moments, in the present era with the cataclysms of capitalism. Certainly the direction of horror films after Auschwitz, Hiroshima, and Vietnam was more overtly violent and sadistic – from the bloody Hammer productions to Franju's elegant and hallucinatory *The Eyes without a Face*; and it tended toward mutants – from the Japanese *Godzilla* saga, in which Tokyo is compulsively and repeatedly destroyed, to films like *The Split*, in which a horrific double emerges little by little from the suffering hero's shoulder. Recent audiences have responded strongly to *Night of the Living Dead*, in which all the dead of the world rise to avenge themselves in an orgy of cannibalism, leading to an ironic climax where imbecile politicians and murdering cops reveal their own zombie nature.

The second film in George Romero's zombie trilogy, *Dawn of the Dead*, extends a view of the eclipse of human values in a mechano-SWAT-bureaucracy out of control. The 1970s – decade of mass carnage, cult suicides, nuclear menace, urban disintegration, monetary terrorism, technological catastrophe – has been *the* decade of the horror genre, with a new focus on impotence, anger, and revolt: science fiction apocalypses *(Star Wars, Close Encounters, The Alien)*, cannibals *(The Hills Have Eyes)*, demonic possession *(The Omen, The Exorcist)*, and telekinetic adolescents *(Carrie, The Fury)*.

Television has altered the social context of the ritual aspects of horror films; it moved the landscape of the transfigured collective dream from the communal warmth of Depression movie houses into the isolated living room. Yet the sheer frequency with which these films are available for viewing on television gives them a peculiarly *obsessive* quality. *King Kong's* immense head and eye at the window of Faye Wray's hotel window – yet another metropolis devastated by a gigantic insect; Dr. Pretorius displaying his enchanting homunculi dancing in their little jars; or Henry Hull *(The Werewolf of London)* in the mists of a Tibetan plateau, bitten by a mysterious animal, searching for the *marifasa lupina lumina*, which blooms only in moonlight: one sees these images over and over again until they are granted a kind of mythic privilege.

As for plodding realists and cynical purveyors of "camp," they can have their impoverished and reactionary horrors: the "horror" of Watergate, the specter of so-called terrorism, airline disasters and condominium fires. Beware the enemies of poetry who try to foist on the public the idea that the horror film is beneath contempt, fare fit only for children – revealing an awesome denigration of childhood, that stage of life in which imagination has not yet been wholly exterminated by this society. In spite of constant subjection to ridicule and scorn, more horror films are being made now than ever before, and they seem destined to remain an immensely popular cultural form. Undaunted, filmmakers proceed with rock-bottom budgets, so it is no surprise that "masterpieces" are rare.

Backyard Bombs: Horror Movies on TV

Technical achievements are often crude, scripts sometimes banal, actors inept. Yet, even when great strains are placed on the "willing suspension of disbelief," the poetic marvelous may emerge astonishingly even in those films termed "bombs," those apparently made in an ordinary backyard with homemade materials. Potentially explosive, any object can be an object for transformation. A flying saucer fashioned from an automobile hubcap, a monster composed of three people inside gunnysacks stitched together, a rubber and seaweed humanoid lurking in an ocean cave: these images, which I have recently seen on late night television, summon a sweeping nostalgia for childhood, the delirious transports at the Saturday matinee where the incomparable Eduardo Ciannelli as *Dr. Satan* ruled the world from a control panel made from a cardboard box and his adversary The Mysterious Copperhead could become unrecognizable to his own family and friends simply by donning a stocking mask. This was an inspired game anyone could play.

The horror genre can be considered today to be in an embryonic stage; it had an auspicious beginning in the magical images of Melies; it has far to go, and there is an infinite road ahead. Because it forces the imagination to operate in a surrealist manner, this kind of tale issues a profound challenge to the filmmaker (and the viewer), an invitation to transform reality, a prospect with dizzying potential. Realistic conventions can be dispensed with: the logic of time and space and proportion does not apply here. Barriers between external and internal, dream and waking, the monstrous and the beautiful, desire and fulfillment, the categories of mineral, vegetable, animal, human can dissolve in a second through the magic eye of the camera. The intrusion of the poetic image might occur at any moment in the most unusual places: I think of *The Night of the Lepus*, a pedestrian effort with a farfetched theme if there ever was one, featuring mutated hares. Yet what a delicious and strange charm was exerted by the moonlit apparitions, giant rabbits floating over an ordinary American farmyard with an air of totally unexpected menace.

In poetry, content, especially latent content, is always sovereign over form. Sometimes the maker of a film is quite unaware of the resonances of the marvelous it emanates. Dream figures of animals appear as regularly as they once did in legends told around fires on starry nights in the past, and their sense of enchantment is not limited to the dialogues concerning radioactive mutation. Transformation into cat, wolf, ape, spider, cobra, alligator, plant, owl, bat, vulture, wasp: an uncannily familiar scenario expressing universal impulses to live outside social regulations prescribed by human law and to recognize deeply felt bonds with earth's other creatures. Here is a potential meeting ground, in film, with the wisdom of non-Western cultures, a hint of a future myth for all humanity which might break the chains of habitual conventions.

"So on his nightmare, through the evening fog, flits the squat fiend o'er fen and bog, seeks some love-wilder'd maid with sleep oppressed" begins botanist Erasmus Darwin's poem on the incubus vampire. The capacity for transformation, particularly of humans into animal forms, has an erotic basis. Psychoanalyst Ernest Jones in his classic *On the Nightmare* traces how the masochistic and sadistic components of the sexual instinct come to expression in the figures of the vampire, werewolf, witch, and demon; how these creatures of popular belief and folklore derive from nightmares and anxiety dreams; and how these dreams, in turn, arise out of tabooed sexual impulses. Unconscious desires and repressed sexuality become visible on the screen in fangs, fur, teeth, and claws, materializing before our eyes in the forms of beasts. The modern viewer, no longer believing in the old superstitions, nevertheless is not immune from dreaming or from the fascination of encounters with transformational symbols in movies or on television.

The horror film is the terrain where heroes and heroines dream their sexuality, *where the repressed image is allowed.*

It is not difficult to discern parallels with primitive ceremonies that mediate untempered infantile wishes, the Oedipal passage, motifs of cruelty, guilt, revenge, perversions. The power of eros appears with the force of inevitability: "Even a man who is pure at heart and says his prayers by night may become a wolf when the wolfbane blooms and the moon is full and bright," says the old gypsy to poor Larry Talbot (Lon Chaney, Jr.) who succumbs to his sadistic wishes in the excesses of lycanthropy. What heroine in her passive, virginal beauty could resist the spell of Dracula with his promise of the eternal ecstasies of the night? Recent Draculas' victims, I note, experience even less reluctance. And who can forget the haunting image of triumphant desire as Imhotep (Boris Karloff), despite 4000 years of death in mummy wraps, hypnotically draws his lover, the reincarnated Princess Anck-es-en-amon, to him across the deserted streets of London?

Under the surface, horror films deal with *essentials*: the exaltation of desire, wishes for the excessive possibility, the truth inhering in the nonrational, and the absolute necessity for transmuting and surpassing present reality. The protagonists are on a quest as authentic as that of a medieval knight or a historic revolutionary. The dreamers are not satisfied. And although the passages of transformation are dangerous, dreamers will change the world. Some have seen in zombies and monsters the sleeping people, the workers of the world, awakening and rising to seize power from their exploiters. Deprived of love, experiencing a living death, disoriented among the electric rays of the nineteenth-century's magneto apparatus and twentieth-century weaponry, the monster destroys an alienating world. By portraying in fantasy the images of defiance, negation, and revolt, the horror film grants a powerful assent to freedom.

Bilko:
A Sitcom for
All Seasons

Daniel Czitrom

You don't know this, but you're a poet. Your comedy is not just a comedy, its the masses crying for recognition.
Charlie Chaplin complimenting Phil Silvers

All I'm trying to do is be funny. It has no underlying social significance.
Phil Silvers

Sure, I think I'm the best, and every other professional comedy writer who's any good thinks he's the best . . . But don't let them kid you. I'm really the best.
Nat Hiken

Nearly a quarter century after their original broadcasts, the miracle of syndication keeps alive some of the best work in early television. It offers a unique chance to watch, in a sense, the historical evolution of the medium. For comic relief, when one tires of the shrill, "relevant" products of the Lear assembly line or the "swinging" single professionals that populate the MTM empire, there is still Lucy and Ricky, George and Gracie, Ralph and Ed. And, if you live in the right area, "The Phil Silvers Show," a.k.a "Sgt. Bilko."

In so many ways, the "Bilko" show remains the best of the classic television situation comedies, holding up very well indeed over the years. The series ran four seasons over CBS (1955–59), winning high ratings and a bushel of Emmies. It was the first show ever to knock Milton Berle out of the top spot. It had everything: the tremendous comic talent of Phil Silvers, the writing and staging genius of Nat Hiken, and a superb supporting cast. All these principals brought decades of experience in older forms of popular entertainment to the new medium.

Beyond this, the "Bilko" show offered comedy built on situation, and a nondomestic situation at that, an exception to the traditional family setting, which has dominated television comedy from the start. The appeal of this situation made the show more than the sum of its parts and a true work of television art. Analyzing what makes comedy funny is a notoriously risky business but, in the case of the "Bilko" show, perhaps not a wholly fruitless one. Chaplin's remark at the beginning of this chapter has a ring of truth; what follows is some speculation on why such an unorthodox show became so popular.

By the time he came to television, Phil Silvers was a seasoned 35-year veteran of show business. Growing up in the Brownsville ghetto of Brooklyn, the son of Russian immigrants, Silvers typified a whole generation of Jewish-American entertainers. He started singing in the streets, local movie houses, and talent shows for nickels and dimes. In 1923, at the age of 12, he was found by vaudeville impresario Gus Edwards, discoverer of Eddie Cantor and George Jessel. After a boyhood career in vaudeville, Silvers spent years as a burlesque comic, learning his craft on the old Minsky circuit. In the 1940s, Silvers made a string of B movies playing the "Blinky" role, the friend who always told Rita Hayworth or Betty Grable in the last reel that the guy really loved her. Over the years he starred in several Broadway musical comedies and played the nightclub and hotel circuits as well.

Silvers managed to incorporate all sides of the Jewish-American comic tradition in his humor. He could fast-talk and insult with the flair of a Groucho Marx, but he also had a sweet, ingratiating, almost effeminate side, recalling Cantor or Al Jolson. "I'm kind of a louse," he once said, "but I'm a lovable louse." The story goes that Silvers at first shied away from several television offers in the early 1950s, on the advice of Jack Benny and others. He feared overexposure and maintained a stage person's distrust of the new medium. After all, in a Broadway show an actor knew that people paid money to see him perform. But the "Bilko" series soon made him an international celebrity, and it was as if the 35 years leading up to it had never happened. Interestingly enough, the show was filmed live before an audience; it was like doing a Broadway play each week. Silvers would warm up the crowd before shooting began, introduce the cast, and perform for about 15 minutes. Thus, early television performers stubbornly kept one foot in the older show-business traditions.

CBS hooked Silvers by the lure of working with Nat Hiken, whom Silvers described as "the most fertile TV comedy mind of the 1950's." Silvers knew what he needed to make it on television: "I'm a plot comedian and don't like standing up and telling jokes." Hiken began writing radio and nightclub sketches in the 1930s. He eventually wrote for the highly regarded "Fred Allen Show" for seven years, and later wrote and directed for two early television stars, Martha Raye and Jack Carson. In 1954 CBS tapped Hiken to create a television comedy vehicle starring Silvers. Together, the two worked five months dreaming up several dozen potential plots for the new series. Both Hiken and Silvers were aware of the crucial quality needed for a successful sitcom: durability. "Comedy on television," Silvers once observed, "is a lot like comedy in burlesque. It's not how funny you are; it's how many weeks can you be funny."

Hiken's idea of a con man/sergeant in business for himself did not appeal to Silvers at first; but he soon came around, convinced it could work and last. In fact, the Ernie Bilko persona represented the kind of character Silvers had almost always played in musical comedies and burlesque. The similarities to the real life Phil Silvers could not have been lost on him either. Silvers enjoyed the night life, was an avid sports fan, and gambled compulsively on horses, cards, dice, or whatever game was in town. He counted well-known underworld figures such as Bugsy Siegel, the founder of Las Vegas, among his friends. Perhaps this fusion of fiction and real life accounts for Lee Strasberg's reputed description of Silvers as one of the great "method" actors of all time.

Once they had decided on the plot, Hiken and Silvers wrote a pilot script and cast the show. They paid close attention to finding suitable faces to inhabit Fort Baxter and also paid off some old cronies. They came up with several former boxers and fight managers (Walter Cartier, Lou Nova, Maxie Shapiro, Mike O'Dowd, and Jack Healy); Rocky Graziano, a friend of Silvers, brought in the majority of these men. Herbie Faye (Cpl. Fender) had been Silvers's old vaudeville mentor. Hiken found both Maurice Gosfield (Pvt. Doberman) and Paul Ford (Col. Hall) and created characters to match their looks. Often, Gosfield would do no more than stare into the camera, and the rubbery-faced Ford would provide a perfect foil for Silvers's fast-talk. CBS began filming episodes even before it had a sponsor, reportedly spending a huge sum before even placing the show up for sale. Then, confident it had a winner, CBS placed the new series opposite NBC's top comedy hour, which alternated Milton Berle, Bob Hope, and Martha Raye. Soon, the Bilko show reached a regular weekly audience of 23 million viewers.

This success, I think, reflects the touching of a universal *gestalt* in the popular consciousness. Originally, Silvers believed the show would have a made-to-order audience of men in the army, enlisted men as well as veterans. But "Bilko" soon surprised everyone by reaching far beyond this core group and attracting legions of fans from every demographic group including women and children. The show's success was even more astonishing because it did not use the traditional sitcom setting: the family at home.

"Bilko's" comedy situation had universal appeal because everyone could identify with the burlesque of authority, particularly in that most disciplined of institutions, the army. Bilko constantly presents outrageous scams aimed at beating authority in all its guises, turning it on its head to line his pockets and the platoon's. At the top of the pyramid, Col. Hall proves to be the one character most vulnerable to Bilko's conning, either face-to-face or indirectly through Bilko's blandishments toward his wife. The assorted captains and lieutenants who periodically try to clean up the motor pool are simply no match for Bilko's ingenuity or high-powered enthusiasm. More often than not, it is Bilko's reputation alone that frightens his superiors. With his key position at the center of Fort Baxter's transportation (the motor pool) and communication (girlfriend Joanie), Bilko subordinates the entire army structure to his insatiable passion: gambling.

Gambling of all kinds becomes the dominant activity at this Middle American (Roseville, Kansas) army base; it is the hook that begins many of the episodes. By risking all, the men manage to subvert the military chain of command; this affirmation of the need to gamble no doubt won many fans from the millions of Americans who gamble regularly. Along with his henchmen Barbella (Harvey Lembeck) and Henshaw (Allen Melvin), Bilko creates a private empire within the army. To keep the men in line, he must rely on his wits to supply a neverending string of bread and circuses. Bilko supplies an oasis in the desert of army routine, a haven for an endless succession of raffles, lotteries, all-night poker games, and Las Vegas Nights. Most of the everyday action takes place off-camera. The weekly plots usually center on truly grandiose gambles: either platoon versus platoon bets (eating contests, sports events) or get-rich-quick schemes (getting into movies, convincing the Yankees to sign a new recruit phenom, etc.).

The challenge to authority is almost always linked to the gambling fetish. For example, when the colonel decides the men should acquire some culture, he brings in a nervous WAC officer to lecture on classical music. Bilko, depressed over cancellation of one of his beloved dances, manages to turn the talk on Beethoven into a hilarious pool, as the entire base bets on how many times the notorious "Twitcher" will twitch while speaking.

The motor pool platoon itself is a combination of the Dead End Kids and the ethnically balanced units featured in World War II movies. A truly proletarian army, these Italians, Jews, blacks, Poles, et cetera, are united by their distaste for work and their fear of being taken by Bilko. The platoon serves as the "family" for the series, with Bilko as the only shyster-patriarch in television comedy history. Hiken's beautiful ensemble staging visually enhances the theme of the platoon as a tight-knit family. We frequently see a dozen or more actors at once, each in just the right place and with the perfect facial expression.

The platoon represents an even more complete rejection of order, often rebelling at the work place (where much of the action takes place) and forcing their sergeant to shed all the inhibitions implied by his three stripes. When the Hungarian Pvt. Nagy goes AWOL and returns to his home in Chicago to get married, Bilko is deputized as an MP to retrieve him. At the Nagy house, Bilko innocently learns a new Hungarian card game, promptly takes the entire family, and causes a fight between the parents of the bride and groom. Later, he patches things up and convinces the soldier to rejoin his platoon before marrying. Of course, "our friend Beelko" is guest of honor at the ceremony; he dances up such a storm in the raucous wedding finale that Col. Hall has to send a real MP to drag him back to the base.

Bilko himself looms as an authority figure in his own right, torn between protecting and ripping off his men. The platoon frequently rebels against his greediness, playing upon Bilko's very deep guilt feelings. This is his tragic flaw, as reflected in the show's original title: "You'll Never Get Rich." His streak of sentimentality makes him the con man who can't con when the chips are down. This contradiction is revealed most clearly in one of the more famous episodes, "Bilko Goes to Monte Carlo," which begins with Bilko working five days and nights, alone, perfecting a system for roulette. Everyone watches warily, then scrambles to scrape up cash when word comes out that the sarge has found a system. Bilko's request for a weekend pass to visit his sick aunt in Las Vegas is naturally refused by the colonel. Doberman, ever alert, suggests Monte Carlo. Using his base contacts and the bait of making a killing, Bilko disguises himself successively as a jet mechanic, military courier, and MP. He reaches Monte Carlo with a $10,000 stake, ready to test out the "can't miss" system. But once inside the casino, Bilko sees apparitions of his men and their money, and he gets cold feet. Lost in thought, he wanders onto a ledge where the pit boss, fearing a messy suicide attempt, brings him to the manager, who gives Bilko $10,000 to play with. Naturally he loses it at the wheel; he then fakes a suicide leap, gets another ten grand, and loses that too. Finally, the pit boss, wise to him, offers a pistol, "compliments of the manager." As Bilko leaves, with the original money intact, he throws down the gun crying, "Put this on the red."

The tension between Bilko's conning and confessing, the alternation of scheming and "schmaltz," afford the best comic moments in the show. Silvers, flattering, insulting, mugging, and cloying supplies the perfect performances in fleshing out Hiken's situations. The comic portrayals of the various officers, elaborate slapsticks of the work routine, and the tension built into Bilko's dual role of huckster and honcho made identification with the show easy for millions.

Like other popular arts, the art of the situation comedy is based on testing the limits of a carefully conceived formula. But unlike the vast majority of television sitcoms, the "Bilko" show did not base its humor on the standard formula. Rather, it gave its audience endless variations on the theme of challenging authority and the opportunity to gamble without the risk of losing. Here was a chance to watch the Dobermans of the world demand and get recognition or at least achieve the center of attention. Bilko did not provide a neat Robert Young-ish affirmation of the American way; he offered a subversive assault on propriety and the work ethic. As we watch Bilko go for broke, the outrageous reversals of the larger social order still hold today as a vital brand of comedy and comic truth.

Prime Time
Jesus

Michael E. Starr

Church and state are separate in America, religion and culture are not. In its prime, in the late nineteenth and early twentieth centuries, before Madison Avenue and television domesticated it, revivalism represented threats or promises to community comparable to those effected in a later day by Black Power, or the New Left, or the forces of urban backlash. The destiny of local and national communities seemed to be involved in the fateful decisions made by people confronted by evangelists. Revivals, camp meetings, fiery preaching, and personal conversion set the tone of the evangelical sects. By renewing the spirit, they struggled to free persons of the sins of the flesh, convinced that good public policies and practices could be achieved only by a cleansed people. In many parts of rural America until at least the 1950s the touring tent revival and camp meeting provided a form of people's theater. Now the tents have almost vanished. Churches still mount crusades for Christ, but much of the drama of salvation is played out on television.

From its inception, the modern revival has made abundant

use of the electronic media. In the early postwar years, it was a healing revival led first by the redoubtable A. A. Allen. Allen was a colorful mixture of style-setting evangelical innovation and Elmer Gantry flimflam. He preached to racially mixed Southern audiences in the 1950s, and testified to have gotten out of financial difficulty on one occasion by praying that the one-dollar bills in his pocket would turn into 20s. Through "The Allen Revival Hour" on radio and later on television, Allen pointed out the direction revivalism would take in the 1960s and 1970s, without fully making the transfer himself. Allen's impact was dramatic. After he reported in his *Miracle Magazine* in March of 1966 that two children had been raised from the dead at his headquarters in Miracle Valley, Arizona, followers began shipping him the bodies of loved ones for resurrection. Allen had quickly to explain that God did not choose to raise everyone before Jesus' return and that disciples should bury their loved ones within "a reasonable period of time." With Allen's success, others came forward to broaden the healing revival. Oral Roberts, Kathryn Kuhlmann, and C. W. Burpo, founder of the Bible Institute of the Air, Incorporated, all enjoyed great success with healing services in tent revivals, on radio, and later on television.

The healing revival that had flourished in the postwar years mainly among lower-class people began to die out about 1958. Several unseemly scandals cast a blight on the movement. In a campaign in Miami, Florida, in 1956, the Reverend Jack Coe of Dallas annointed the head of a three-year-old polio victim, who had been carried through the healing line by his mother, and shouted, "Jesus, heal this boy!" He then instructed the mother to remove the boy's braces. For three days the child stumbled and fell, but his mother refrained from putting the braces back on lest her lack of faith rob the boy of a miraculous healing. Finally she took the boy to the doctor who found irreparable bone damage. Brother Coe was arrested for practicing medicine without a license, and the nation was treated to newspaper accounts featuring a picture of Coe behind bars and a sensational account of how he had amassed a fortune of more than $500,000 in just five years of faith healing. Oral Roberts also came under attack following an incident in a 1959 Detroit campaign. A diabetic woman believed Roberts had healed her with his touch. Even though she had required daily shots to keep her condition under control, after Roberts laid hands on her, she threw her insulin away. The next day she was admitted to the hospital in a diabetic coma and died. Roberts was concerned but could not recall praying for the woman specifically. "I had no particular feeling that this woman had or had not experienced a significant improvement," Brother Roberts explained, "yet it was not for me to determine. That was a physician's responsibility." Before long, critics and industry executives were seriously considering limiting the access of faith healers to the air waves.

With the move to television, modern revivalism underwent a transformation and at the same time came into its own. Clerics of all stripes were quick to perceive the potential of the new medium. Bishop Fulton J. Sheen saw television as a positive blessing. "Radio is like the Old Testament, hearing wisdom, without seeing; television is like the New Testament because in it the wisdom becomes flesh and dwells among us." When the healing revival waned, a movement better suited to the special gifts of television took its place—the more respectable, subdued "charismatic" revival. In the charismatic revival, the healing ministry takes a back seat to other "charisms"—gifts of the spirit such as speaking in tongues, prophecy, and the baptism in the Holy Spirit. The message of the movement is finding salvation from sin and peace of mind and self-renewal in a ravishing experience with God. The charismatic revival began to spread among the middle classes and within the more orthodox denominations including the Roman Catholic. This presented the evangelists with a vexing dilemma. The class base of their ministry was changing. The tents were giving way to hotel lobbies and stadiums. Television required massive budgets. The revivalists could either stick with the poor and disenfranchised from whom they had sprung or they could ascend to the middle class. A. A. Allen chose the former route and, as a result, few outside of his own circles ever heard of him. Oral Roberts, on the other hand, joined the Methodist church, founded a university in Tulsa, and dropped the healing ministry in favor of soft-spoken prime-time religious variety shows. He is now introduced on his weekly program, "Oral Roberts and You," as an author, educator, and last as an evangelist. In many ways, television was the key to Roberts's, and others', upward mobility.

When the revival shifted to television, its message changed in subtle ways as well. The new revivalism moves, in a qualitative way, beyond the methods of Dwight Moody or Billy Sunday, partly as a result of its employment of all the technical contrivances of modern popular culture. Nowhere is this more clear than in the curious celebrity status of Billy Graham. Not since the prime of Billy Sunday had Americans come to know and recognize one outstanding mass evangelist. Not since Dwight L. Moody had they turned to a premillennialist for an interpretation of history. But they turned to Billy Graham. Moody had expressed the dark vision of the premillennialist well. "I look upon this world as a wrecked vessel. God has given me a lifeboat and said to me, 'Moody, save all you can.'" Graham spoke in similar terms. The only substantial change in history, Graham argued, will occur with the apocalyptic Second Coming of Christ, followed by a millennium or thousand-year reign of peace and justice. Graham predicts the imminence of the millennium on the basis of his interpretation of the signs of our time — communism abroad and immorality at home set in the framework of a literal reading of the scriptures. What is remarkable about all this is not that Graham should hold such views but that his extremely particular and specifically Protestant point of view does not seem to have offended anyone except Reinhold Niebuhr. By the mid-1950s, mass evangelism had become domesticated and its only well known advocate of the time regularly appeared among the ten most admired men in the country. Both Catholic bishops and pious Jews soon found him acceptable. Secular people on television, editors of popular magazines, and presidents of both national parties considered him to be a comfortable and congenial symbol of the American way of life.

Much of Graham's acceptability and nearly all of his celebrity status came from his televised crusades. The moral atmosphere surrounding television is congenial to pictures and sounds but not always to language and meaning. Most successful television shows do not depend on the meanings of words or the logical patterns they create. What is important to producers and consumers of television are the impressions and identifications created by the high-speed chase and the shoot-out, or the gestures, facial expressions, and habitual phrases of characters; consider, for example, Archie Bunker and Mary Hartman. Evangelists like Billy Graham create similar images with masses of people streaming toward a lighted stage while a choir croons, "Just as I Am," and the voice of the evangelist soars heavenward appealing to "all you who are weak and heavy-laden, come unto me." The traditional meanings of historical Christianity, particularly of Graham's premillennialist variety, were lost in the warm images of masses of people finding succor at the evangelist's feet. The televised setting of the revival lent to it an air of mass fantasy closely akin to advertising on television.

Graham himself further contributed to the haphazard linking of contradictory images by adopting the tack that "everything at any moment can become almost everything else." Even as he spoke of a "world aflame" rushing headlong toward Armaggedon, Graham could also speak in optimistic terms about America as "the last bulwark of Christian civilization." In spite of the "corruption, crime, and moral decay" he chronicled in horrific detail, he still maintained that "we [in America] were created for a spiritual mission among the nations." So, as Graham said in *World Aflame*, Christians should wait for the Second Coming to bring peace and racial justice, but, at the same time, they should "maintain strong military power for defense at any cost."

The acceptance of Billy Graham demonstrated how theologically inclusive and ethnically diluted the televised revival had become. The churches of the 1950s were not notable for their devotion to the cause of racial justice. The issues of world population, hunger, poverty, and disease were minor emphases in Billy Graham's *Peace with God*, Fulton J. Sheen's *Peace of Soul*, and Norman Vincent Peale's *The Power of Positive Thinking* Sermons. Each of these men, in their writings as well as in their successful television programs, advocated a kind of escape from the world, even though they implied that serene souls would help to transform it. The essential pessimism of Graham's message was overlooked in his association with these optimists. Television's subtle subversion allowed the culture that made him a celebrity to ignore his expressed meaning.

Oral Roberts carried this transformation of the revival one step further when he returned to television and combined the techniques of Lawrence Welk and Monty Hall for the greater glory of God. Roberts began television broadcasts in 1954 with a program of healing. As early as 1955, the response to these programs was overwhelming. Roberts's mail tripled and he became so famous that he wrote, "I was recognized by children, taxicab drivers, business people, and almost everybody," But this was too good to last. The healing scandals of the fifties, Roberts's own flamboyant platform style, and the complex intricacies of his huge financial resources became sources of severe criticism. By the 1960s, Roberts began to initiate changes in his ministry. He started phasing out his televised faith healing programs. He dropped half the stations in 1966 and went off the air entirely in May 1967. He became an educator with the founding of Oral Roberts University, which made him president in 1967. In April of 1968, Roberts shocked his followers by leaving the Pentacostal Holiness Church to join the Boston Avenue Methodist Church in Tulsa. Many of his old supporters never forgave this last drastic act. Across town Billy James Hargis, leader of the Christian Anti-Communist Crusade, thought these changes indicted Roberts as a closet intellectual. Hargis accused him of having read 50 books on existentialism – a charge Roberts significantly did not deny. Although this transformation certainly caused Roberts to lose support in some precincts, it opened up a whole new mission field for him as he headed back to television. He debuted again on television in March 1969, no longer the faith healer who had signed off two years before. The preacher who had declared in 1956 that he "consider[ed] Hollywood and all its works unclean," now returned as the star of his own Sunday television series and the superstar of quarterly prime-time specials offering a veneer of piety and featuring some of Hollywood's biggest names.

Roberts's weekly programs, and particularly his televised specials, treat the viewer to a slick professional production of song and dance performed by nubile young women and bronzed young men (all students at Oral Roberts University) garbed in denim jackets and bell-bottom Levis. The performances stop considerably short of the overt sexual suggestiveness or the artistic anarchy of rock and roll, but, they are, nonetheless, contemporary—"in the now," as Roberts is fond of phrasing it. Like Tony Orlando, Sonny and Cher, or the hosts of any other variety show, Oral Roberts features "guest stars" from the world of entertainment, sports, or politics—Johnny Cash, Dallas Cowboys' quarterback Roger Staubach, or Senator Mark Hatfield. Roberts does not preach or even really sermonize on these programs. Rather, in a subdued, conversational style, Roberts relates the stories of believers who have been cured of illness, restored to solvency, or found peace of mind and self-renewal, all beneficiaries of the Lord's goodness and power. Nothing is ever said about the principles of Christian belief or of the obligations of Christians to love and actively seek the good of all humankind. Billy Graham still mentions these, but for him, as for Roberts, personal needs and hopes are the center of concern. The message of these programs is that a viewer who wants them badly enough can enjoy happiness and prosperity "in the now." As Roberts's slogan promises, "Something *good* is going to happen to you!"

Other evangelists were quick to adopt Roberts's techniques. Television ministries now are often skillful amalgamations of evangelical religion and the modes and rhythms of mass entertainment; a fusing of revivalism and popular culture so tight that the former has, in fact, become the latter. The programs from Rex Humbard's Cathedral of Tomorrow in Akron, Ohio, although still within the mold of traditional church services complete with altar call, also manage to include guest stars and a full orchestra to accompany his choir of several hundred. Half of Jimmy Swaggart's program each week is devoted to singing up-tempo country gospel songs in the style of Swaggart's cousins, singers Mickey Gilley and Jerry Lee Lewis. Swaggart regularly offers to viewers records, cassettes, or eight-track tapes of these songs. The televised services from Robert Schuller's drive-in church in Garden Grove, California, called "The Hour of Power," are very much in the variety-show genre too. A recent show, for example, featured, in addition to the latest installment of Schuller's "possibility thinking," a guest appearance by Earl Ravenscroft – the voice of Tony the Tiger – who appeared to testify that Jesus is GRRREAT! On that same program, in the slot Ed Sullivan once reserved for animal acts or acrobats, Schuller presented a quadraplegic who draws pictures by holding a pencil between her teeth. As she drew, the young woman told of all the blessings God had brought into her life since he had seen fit to test her faith by paralyzing her from the waist down. The late Kathryn Kuhlman remained a part of the healing revival throughout her career, yet she was also an accomplished performer with a following of millions and a television personality every bit as dynamic as Dinah Shore's and Barbara Walters's. Reverend Ike, the apostle of the "good life" here on earth, has all the effusiveness of a game-show host. The revival even has its own talk shows in the widely syndicated "700 Club" and in Morris Cerullo's "Helpline." Cerullo runs "Helpline" like a telethon; there are rows of telephones in the background of the set, and people answer calls from viewers desiring prayer. While this is going on, Cerullo interviews converts who have been touched by the healing power. Occasionally Cerullo telephones notables such as George Wallace on the air and solicits testimony and encouragement. Entertainers such as Pat Boone and Skeeter Davis drop by to witness God's work in their lives and to perform a number. Clearly, Jesus has made it to prime time and He is a hit in a continuing series.

In addition to the variety and talk-show formats mentioned above, the evangelists' television ministries also have an affinity for country and western music and sports, especially football. These are, of course, very popular expressions of our national culture. Country music has had a strong religious bent since its inception. Furthermore, it speaks to a kind of moral nostalgia for a mythological frontier past that was cleaner and more virtuous than the present. In some ways sports makes a similar claim to our patriotism and religious feeling. There is a kinship between Americanness, godliness, and the manly graces of sports. The National Finals Rodeo begins with a prayer thanking God for his greatest handiwork – America. During this prayer even the horses bow their heads. At every football game the flag is raised and the national anthem is played. Nothing is so touching to the spectators as a linebacker transformed by an encounter with Jesus or a team huddling in prayer before rushing out to "hit 'em hard for Jesus." These affinities further testify to the disappearance of sectarianism from the revival. It has become part of a homogenized civil religion promoting a kind of social order based on an acceptance of the commonplace as the way things are and must be.

Like everything that is successful in America, the modern revival grows out of popular demand. After the American religious depression of the 1930s and the preoccupations of World War II, it became clear that by the 1950s many Americans were in a mood to settle down. They needed a means of justifying their complacencies, soothing their anxieties, and producing benedictions on their way of life. Millions turned to religion. The television evangelists are symptomatic expressions of this widespread yearning to be relieved of the anxieties and despair of our time. They offer shelter in simple beliefs and strong convictions. America's crisis of meaning and self-confidence has brought large numbers into the fold of pietistic and evangelical religion. Robert Schuller's "possibility thinking" is but another episode in the American success myth. Schuller's tips for self-improvement are designed to solve the immediate personal problems of his white middle-class parishioners and, at the same time, to reassure them that they are on the right path. Schuller, Roberts, and others, as well as the recent "I found it" campaign of the Inter-Varsity Christian Fellowship, give voice to a central idea of the charismatic revival: that if I put *myself* in a state of proper reliance on God, I will be granted *my* miracle. In a cruder fashion, Reverend Ike performs the same service for the black middle class. In the "Science of Living," Rev. Ike's success plan, God is not:

Someone else, somewhere else, sometime else; but God is the Presence of Infinite Good within you HERE and NOW . . . and this Presence is within everyone. . . . The Science of Living teaches you how to become a dynamic person. You UNLEARN sickness and know health. You UNLEARN poverty and know prosperity. You learn how to break every limitation and solve every problem YOURSELF. Sickness, age, fear, worry, tension, every human tor-

ment drops away, and a NEW YOU begins to live more abundantly.

This "science of living" that Rev. Ike preaches amounts to success hints like Schuller's or Norman Vincent Peale's with the added assistance of devices like prayer cloths the faithful lay on their driveways to encourage the divine provision of a much-needed new car. "You can't lose with the stuff I use," Rev. Ike declares, "and the stuff I use is mind power." These evangelists pronounce a benediction on the hard-working, saving, unspectacular lives of the middle class. There is no need for guilt, they say; you are living according to God's plan. As Rev. Ike points out, Jesus never said, "Don't drive a Cadillac." Thus the religion provided by the television revival is a religion of immediacy and feeling, not of philosophical reflection. The television evangelists offer religion as a prepackaged, homogenized lifestyle shorn of the sectarian individualism of past revivals. There is no trace of the world negation, or the living toward death that is at the heart of historical Christianity. Jesus has become simply a helping friend with magical powers, no longer the judge and renouncer of the world who charged rich and poor alike to take up the burdens of the cross and to never look back. All you need to do is smile, be happy, and praise the Lord, and you will be sure of your place at the Rapture with Pat Boone, Johnny Cash, and the World Action Singers.

The Christ to whom all evangelists appeal is virtuous because He loves God with all His heart and soul and His neighbor as Himself. Many fundamentalists and evangelicals see themselves as virtuous because they do not drink, smoke, or dance or tolerate those who do. The television format of the revival in some way mitigates this censoriousness and harshness of spirit. But even as the television evangelists offer a personal miracle to all who would participate, a certain coldness and hardness of heart remains to indict the moral bankruptcy of this Christian revolution. In the end what is important are the modes of presentation. And these are the styles, techniques, and sentiments of popular culture that express the true character of the moral space we now occupy. The television evangelists represent the desperate hopes and cries of millions of people who feel lost, sick, and hopeless but who have not given up. What the revival has to offer them is expressed in the hymn they often sing as they surge down the aisles toward health, salvation and dignity: "Only believe, only believe. All things are possible. Only believe."

Spelling's Salvation Armies

Bob Schneider

From Nat Hiken, Desilu, and Lekordova to the contemporary laugh factories run by MTM Enterprises and Norman Lear, the sitcom has always had its auteurs. In the action-adventure genre up until now, the only really prominent producer with an identifiable signature has been Jack Webb. His austere and ascetic heroes, generally coupled, generally male, have ridden the freeways of Los Angeles in car ADAM-12 wearing Badge 714. Their short, staccato speech patterns were derived from Hammett out of Hemingway and reflected Goldwater, Murphy, and Reagan. The trademark of these shows was their claim to documented veracity. "The names have been changed to protect the innocent" entered into the language as a fixed syntagm signifying absolute credibility and affirmed moral integrity. The zombies of Webb-world walked and talked as androids from Disneyland do and functioned with a preprogrammed ethical code formulated in the never-never land of the nationalist noumena. Fundamentalist flatfeet in Webb-world believed in the sanctity of the law and renounced as sacrilege any defense derived from psycho- or socio-logical realms. These perfect footsoldiers of the 1950s waged their modern Manichean war against the forces of evil armed only with a righteousness capable of embarrassing a card-carrying Old Testament prophet out of his beard and sandals; and, when self-righteousness wasn't enough, police specials were always available.

By 1968 the Vietnam War, and its media-induced spinoff, the generation gap, had sorely divided the nation. It was in fact so divided that it was in the process of electing Nixon, the Gollum in a Brooks Brothers suit, who had in a moment of zen inspiration co-opted the militants' peace-sign and subtitled it with the phrase "bring us together."

It was the seven o'clock news that had made a hit of the war and of the protests – the war's domestic concomitant. It also fell to television to "bring us together," to minimize the murderous potentials of the ideologically induced yet psychically sanctioned split in the generations. Within this context the mondo-jingo world of Webb was no longer tenable. These shows in fact became another in the series of constantly escalating provocations that were pushing both sides of the generation gap ever more deeply into the trenches of their media-manipulated Maginot line. What became necessary were mediative shows. In the area of action-adventure, this call for a mediative series was answered by Aaron Spelling. His "Mod Squad" featured the best of both worlds in a visionary compromise. Youthful exuberance modified by adult (parental) pragmatism presented a paradigm of intergenerational co-operation in the post-1960s' world. At the same time it presented visions of the family affirmed. The "Mod Squad's" racially mixed, extended family concept was an attempt at floating an alternative to the nuclear one, under attack as it had been for two decades, clearly eroding, and, as a result of the everbroadening polarization of parents and progeny, seemingly on the verge of annihilation.

"Mod Squad's" three central characters were all former hippies who had decided to apply their searing social consciences to the saving of like-minded souls of a more muddled meddle by joining the LAPD as undercover cops. They worked under Captain Greer, a strong father figure, who always made the right decision and always scolded them at the psychologically proper moment. The squad members were Pete, a rich kid and frat member who had fallen into drugs, Linc, an appropriately named, former black militant, and Julie, the show's sexual fulcrum, a dreamy-eyed blonde with a big heart, who had gone through unspecified young adult trauma.

The "Mod Squad" was a bizarre version of the commune, an extended family of enormous scope. It was racially integrated, nonsexist, socially conscious, and its Tim Leary was a captain in the police force. That is the brilliance of the formula. Spelling combined only the positive elements from each of the polarized factions and activated them for the purpose of helping people out and protecting the "community," a word with as much power in Great Neck as it has in Bed-Stuy. Spelling provided a strong father figure who could give orders that would be obeyed and three dedicated children desirous of seeing their peers protected from each other and from the corruption of those older souls who had not grown as straight and true as Captain Greer, their guru.

In "Mod Squad," Spelling had detected the growing conservatism of the people, young and old. In 1969 he produced a new show for ABC called "The New People." It was a mistake. "The New People" was about forty college-age kids who were on their way to Southeast Asia (a.k.a. Vietnam) on a goodwill tour in a chartered plane. A forced landing on an isolated atoll in the South leaves them to create a better world than the establishment one they had left behind. Utopia didn't last through the second season. America was changing. "Easy Rider" (Dennis Hopper, 1969) and his Sancho Panza had died for the hippies' sins. Before dying they even acknowledged what a mistake it had all been. Middle-class genes reasserted themselves when economic and psychic depression pushed the young back onto the societal conveyor belt. It was time to work for change from within. Whereas "The New People" fled the real world, the "Mod Squad" stayed behind and reaped the reward of a healthy Nielsen rating.

In 1972 Spelling released a new series, "The Rookies," in which the "Mod Squad" formula was embellished and perfected. In a year when, except for Massachusetts, Manhattan, and D.C., every place went for the Nixon/Agnew team in a big way, it was all right to have the "Mod Squad" turn in their bell-bottoms and tie-dyeds for uniforms and a "black and white." The basic family unit was extended to include one more child. Another Spelling step toward the relegitimization of the family unit was accomplished by having the lone female costar married to a rookie. (Defusing the possibilities presented by unattached and sexually attractive female characters.) Mrs. Danko was a nurse, which, outside of making her a nun, is the quickest way of establishing compassion in a character.

"The Rookies" takes place in a small, unnamed town in southern California. As a result, the alienating effect of the big city is undercut. All roads lead to the same hospital floor, with the same nurse/wife on duty. The precinct is a comfortable nineteenth-century brick building that could easily pass for a school. It is not the computerized glass skyscraper of "Police Story," in which everyone walks around not only with their badge of office but with their badge of identity as well, a concession to the paranoically inspired inner security force. In "The Rookies" clubhouse, the files have pictures and data written in English to be looked for and at manually – not programmed, punched file cards to be fed into the big machine that services *Metropolis* (Fritz Lang, 1926). In "The Rookies" you get the personal touch.

"Tell the boys and girls of the United States this world is theirs. If they have hearts of gold, a glorious new age awaits us. If they are honest, riches shall be theirs. If they are kind, they save the whole world from malice and meanness. Will you take that message to the boys and girls of the United States, Jack Armstrong?" So spoke a (Calvinist) Tibetan monk over the radio to Jack Armstrong in 1939. He could have been saying it to the rookies. They were so terminally sincere that they made the Mod Squad look like followers of Bakunin.

Lieutenant Ryker provided the rookies with a powerful father figure. The fact that he held a lower rank than his predecessor Captain Greer produced a partial moderation of his blustery and Jehovan personality. He was not the final source of authority, the end of the chain of command. He was a worthy and worthwhile teacher, and in his military-mystical way, he actually seemed to care. He was above all a strict disciplinarian. He had an incredible temper. During one outburst he defined the ongoing ethic of the Spelling universe of mod rookies. While dressing down Danko and Terry for a breach of discipline borne of idealism—an idealism very often negatively reflected as antisocial when it manifested itself as the behavior of the angered, hirsute, ideologically inspired perpetrators of crime that haunted these shows like the ghosts of decades past—Ryker claimed in his close-mouthed, staccato style (trademarks of his orthodox adherence to the religion of corporate- and self-discipline): "When you're on your own time you can be hip, and groovy, and right on, but when you're here, you're an aware bunch of squares and don't you forget it!"

The formula of "Mod Squad" had a built-in defect—they were undercover, ergo, they had to remain incognito. The world they traveled in had by necessity to remain an alien one. "The Rookies," who did not have to worry about covering up their identity, could fall back into the comfortable pot-boiler soap formula of the small world where everybody knows everybody else. There was a built-in mechanism of audience reassurance in the intimate relations of the characters including the transient ones—the victims. The only strangers in town were the perpetrators, the furthest distillation of the 1950s' hysteria over invaders that had led to the production of nuclear amnesia movies like *The Thing from Another World* (Christian Nyby, 1951) and *Invasion of the Body Snatchers* (Don Siegel, 1956), as well as television shows like "Andy Griffith" and "The Real McCoys." In the 1970s the body snatchers had been transformed into junkies, pimps, and corrupt city officials. "The Rookies," like their even more paramilitary brethren "S.W.A.T.," provided a kind of psychic mosquito netting that kept out repellent thoughts and creatures and maintained the sanctity and purity of the neighborhood. The McLuhan global network formula was transformed by ABC via Spelling into a universal police blotter.

Rhoda moved east and started life anew from Mary and the gang. The Jeffersons moved to the city and the Bunkers attended their housewarming. Bionic Jamie got her own show and a visit from Steve every so often, while Oscar pulled double duty as nursemaid to his matched pair of übermenschen. When Spelling wanted to introduce his new "S.W.A.T." show, he made a two-hour television movie that had the rookies assigned to S.W.A.T. on temporary duty. "S.W.A.T.," which moved into the time-slot originally occupied by "Monday Night Football," had to counteract the resistance it could meet as a result of the urban napalming of the SLA. that had first propelled it into prominence. By assigning the rookies to S.W.A.T. and having them accept S.W.A.T.'s actions as being in the public's best interest, the problem was defused. At first Terry resisted the S.W.A.T. team, thinking them rash and brutal. But after S.W.A.T.'s rescue of an entire building held captive by a gang of supercriminals, a rescue in which Hondo, the team leader, stopped a bullet, Terry and the rest of the rookies–and the audience as well–were won over. The gap that the end of the football season had left in the schedule was filled with a worthy replacement–a paramilitary precision outfit that could red-dog the PLO. ABC had it, and, for a while, it was the most popular show in the South Bronx, a neighborhood referred to by the local gendarmes as Fort Apache.

"S.W.A.T." was an ethnically mixed show reinforcing the American melting pot myth. The four principals on the S.W.A.T. team were two all-business WASPs, one very together black man, who was Hondo's Mr. Spock, and an eternally lovelorn Italian man. Two of "S.W.A.T.'s" most memorable episodes from its first season illustrate its broad appeal. In one episode, the S.W.A.T. team is given the heinous task of defending a mafia chieftain who has turned state's evidence. Having already been blasted within an inch of his life, the don is in need of protection. S.W.A.T. must seal off the entire floor of the hospital wing where he is being nursed back to health. Luca meets the daughter of the don and promptly falls in love with her. He keeps saying how happy his mother will be now that he has found a nice Italian girl to bring home. As it turns out, the daughter is an inside plant, ordered by the syndicate to snuff out her father in case their frontal assault fails. In the nick of time, Hondo and Luca dash into the godfather's room and stop the patricide. The unremorseful young woman explains, "The family is my only family." The contrast between Luca, with his innocent incomprehension of the young woman, compounded by his zeal at pleasing his mother with an ethnically sanctioned mate, and the mafia-mad young woman bent on patricide, throws into sharp relief the good and bad ways to deal with the concept of family.

In another episode, the best guard in pro-basketball is an old college chum of Street's, the noncom S.W.A.T. WASP. He visits him on the afternoon of the championship game. The plot thickens when a band of ruthless criminals hijack the entire squad at half-time claiming that they are representatives of the PLO. If their demands for a cool million and a fueled truck aren't met, "There'll be a lot of dead basketball players around here!" S.W.A.T. is called in. They eventually rescue the jocks, including Street's friend the superstar. In the Spelling universe, law enforcement was a personal thing, not a 9-to-5 job but a passionate dedication to the protection of their fellow men who were so often also their friends.

The "Mod Squad's" bell-bottoms, beads, and body shirts were part of the bring-us-together strategy that in the end produced "The Watergate Hearings" on daytime television and spawned Spelling's prime-time menagerie of activist assimilationists. Like Audie Murphy, a country ancestor from that precious paradigm of a world war, Spelling's characters had been *To Hell and Back* (Jesse Hibbs, 1955). By virtue of that fiery cleansing, they were now ready to cure the ailing collective superego through weekly doses of soporific sincerity. Spelling's reworking of the ontological argument went like this: the status quo is saved by a holy trinity of mod squadders and (tautologically) its mere ability to think up the mod squadders proves the viability of the society. The soundtrack was modernized also, with polyphonic chants by Perotin replaced with psychedelic hymns by The Beach Boys. The strategy required that this psychedelic salvation army be outfitted in the uniform of the day, thereby gaining the immediate trust of the young adult contingent (to whom the Romilar commercials meant something quite special). It gave hope to the woe-filled wombs and freaked-out papas in the audience that their own brood of rebels, experimenting with god-knows-what lifestyle in some college dorm or inner-city ghetto, might someday drag their hirsute and haltered bodies onto the front lines of the war against evil.

When "Starsky and Hutch" were cloned, these tendencies had

reversed. Undercover assimilation had transformed itself into paramilitary reverence. Starsky and Hutch swung the pendulum another full semi-circle; they bought their clothes at the Gap. What was once the verbal symbol of ideo- and psycho-logical fury is now the source of baroque denims and chambray shirts. These plain-clothes parallels to ADAM-12 out of Mettachine via Barracuda, dress not out of Darwinian necessity (the mod squad would not have lasted two weeks had they dressed like the rookies) but out of an evocation of the ethic of the 1970s reflected best in Burger King's admonition to "have it your way." Going underground is no longer indicative of a point of view, as it was in the 1960s; it is now a state of mind, it is all-pervasive.

Starsky and Hutch are the ultimate orphans of the Aaron Spelling/ABC stormy universe. They are street kids, smart and tough, yet proscriptively humanized, armed not only with police specials but with terminal sincerity, which is their genetic link to Linc, Terry, Julie, Hondo, and the rest of their ancestral line of idealistic public defenders. With the absence of a viable father figure, the evolution of the young adult as savior is brought to the end of the line. Instead of direction being supplied by a stern yet caring papa in the Greer/Ryker mold, it is the katzenjammer kids themselves who represent father-figuredom to punk, lovable Chicano street urchins and concupiscently cute, toothsome teenage girls, long on adolescent lust but short on street smarts.

Spelling has achieved on television what Sam Goldwyn, David O. Selznick, Samuel Z. Arkoff, and Albert Zugsmith had achieved in the movies: that rare recognition of producer as auteur. Spelling's vision came in response to the psychedelic, sexy 1960s. LSD and the pill had exploded on the cultural horizon with all the impact of a matched pair of 50-megaton bombs, threatening to send marriage, the family unit, and the rest of the ball of wax into an oblivion already shared by the hula hoop and the deposit bottle. His vision united the best of all possible worlds. His was an integrated nirvana inhabited by sanely hip, hard-core young people, directed in their zeal by stern yet caring father figures. In Spelling-heaven, parents and children fight side-by-side to protect, defend, and expand the notions of loyalty, law and order, and the boundaries of the family.

Bob Schneider

Unlike his eclectic rival in the cops-and-robbers field, Quinn Martin, who produces one kind of show for CBS ("Barnaby Jones" and "Cannon") and another for ABC ("Streets of San Francisco") and, as a result, is a packager and not an auteur, Spelling has stuck by ABC and together they have managed to legitimize "The Young and the Restless" without forsaking "The Guiding Light" of "Father Knows Best."

Hegemony and Me

Jim Murray

A child is born into a world of phenomena all equal in their power to enslave. It sniffs—it sucks—it strokes its eyes over the whole uncountable range. Suddenly one strikes. Why? Moments snap together like magnets, forging a chain of shackles. Why? I can trace them, I can even, with time, pull time apart again. But why at the start they were ever magnetized at all—just those particular moments of experience and no others—I don't know. And nor does anyone else." (The shrink in *Equus* by Peter Shaffer)

Number seven is Mickey Mantle. The hegemonic ("hedge-a MON-ik") figure of my media youth. If you don't think in terms of hegemony ("ha-GEM-a-knee"), that's okay. It's a helluva powerful word ("it's a hell of a powerful world").

Hegemony is the power that you cannot see. But it explains why I *can* see Mickey Mantle's lefty crouch, his running, backhand, over-the-shoulder reach to catch a bases-loaded, inning-ending liner deep in left center.

Mantle could hit it out or lay it down and beat it out, from both sides of the plate. When he popped it up, the out took longer. The opponent's only hope was to strike him out. Mick often went down swinging, sometimes looking. But he always came back up.

Mickey Mantle played only in black and white. (In those days you had to go to the game to see what the players looked like. Now you *have* to watch it in color.) When he batted fourth in a home night game, my domestic politics hit home. I had a bedtime. As early as 8:30, as late as ninth grade.

That's okay. I thought every kid had the same bedtime.

If Richardson, Kubek, or Maris didn't get on, Mantle's first-at-bat would get into bed with me. "AW-ka-mon, Mom. *Whitey's* pitching. Three outs in three minutes. Lemme watch Mickey come up."

Hey ump! Time out! Notice the social forces in that quote. Mickey Mantle provided me with a reason to function, a mediated object, a useful, necessary disguise. I am *not* saying, "Mom, come on, be with me." It was Mickey who was coming up. Mom had already hegemonically ("hedge-a-MON-ik-lee") changed the channel. My mind was on the next morning's box score.

When Mantle retired, he addressed 70,000 emotional fans at Yankee Stadium: "I never understood, until today, how a man who knew he was going to die, could stand here and say, 'I am the luckiest guy in the world." (He was referring to Gary Cooper's Lou Gehrig.)

A few years ago Mickey was asked, "Are players better today?" Number seven gave a brilliant history lesson. "Yes, I think so. I've never subscribed to that Old Timer myth that the old guys are always better."

In other words, "There is no sense comparing me to Reggie Jackson. What *matters* is that I was better than DiMaggio." The next question, in the era of Reggie Jackson, was, "What about the money they're making today?" Mickey choked up, "The players or the owners?"

The hegemonic figure of my sister's media youth was Superman, the man of steel sent here to humiliate petty criminals. Now she lives a very good life in a community of women. All of them are married, engaged, or otherwise pursuing a relationship to God. Four times a day they kneel to pray and stand to sing their living praise of men they do not see. "Hegemony, hegemony, I'd give my life for thee!"

As for me, I am a journalist sitting desk. When I was eighteen, I went up to the Resistance table and said, "I want to change my life." A week later I was sitting desk.

If you pass by, with your "Hey, what's new?" or your "Gotta rush," I'll give you the long rap (coming right up!) or the short rap with (if I can) a little extra.

"Ya know what, Mick? I hate competition more than anyone."

The Sitcom Decade: The 1970s

David Marc

Like sands through the hourglass, so are the days of our lives.

The starchy Victoro-suburban realism that had Iked even the J. F. K. years on television gradually conceded primetime (along with the news) to Levittown surrealism as the 1960s flowered. Eddie Haskell, Lucy, and Edward R. Murrow had yielded the homescreen to Jethro Bodine, Samantha the witch, and Les Crane. Through it all, however, the sitcom remained king. Although a whole lot of shaking had gone on, nothing had happened to America so drastic as to eclipse the narrative breadth of the classic twenty-four minute commercially segmented comic serial. The problem facing television, just as the television babies were starting to shell out for their own color sets and living rooms, was not formulaic revision (as had been advocated by NBC's Big Event nut Paul Klein) but rather a return to realism—a restylized realism that would reflect the growing interest of Cutback Era consumers in living the good life to the left of Hubert Humphrey. Dr. Bombay, Jeannie and the astronaut, Herman Munster, and Arnold the pig shared the cultural limelight with Timothy Leary, LSD, and the paperback reissue of

On the Road. When CBS dropped its "rurally oriented" programming in the early 1970s, however, the Age of Straights and Freaks ended. Clearly it had been necessary to be one or the other to watch "Nanny and the Professor," "Gilligan's Island," and "Green Acres." The new CBS popular front dropped both ends and reestablished the middle. Norman Lear fixed the ideology. MTM Productions defined policy. Jed Clampett and Eva Gabor passed the torch to Archie Bunker and Mary Tyler Moore, and so the 1970s began.

The early days of Lear were in some ways remarkable. The producer emerged as the tube's first publicly recognizable *auteur* (despite the fact that Paul Henning had dominated the 1960s incognito with "Beverly Hillbillies," "Petticoat Junction," and "Green Acres"). He was hoisted upon the shoulders of the earth-toned bourgeoisie and celebrated as its socioartistic champion. This new Émile Zola of the airwaves had given guilty, self-improvement oriented television watchers a rationalization that extended beyond the fringes of "Masterpiece Theatre" and the news, right into the heart of prime time. Problems of racism, poverty, transportation, communications, women's liberation, and so on, were given the same half-hour resolution as were Beaver's lying to Miss Landers and Ricky's forgetting Lucy's birthday, and it was all kept in the family to boot.

If the old-fashioned Bunker living room was the heated political battleground of the generations, sexes, and tribes, Mary's one-room studio (with breakfast nook) was behind the lines of television's liberated zone, and here, in the brave new world of swinging Minneapolis singles, the fine points of post-revolutionary habitation of space could be honed by the well-paid media workers. Lear's obsession with the politics of politics in, for example, "All in the Family," "The Jeffersons," and "Maude" shared the CBS transmitters with "MTM's" obsession with the politics of embarrassment. MTM, Phyllis, and Rhoda defined the manners of post-Vietnam television living in episode after episode. Gross and mellow had replaced wrong and right as the moral praxis.

Although CBS had almost single-handedly coordinated the logistics of this return from "Gilligans Island" to the mainland, it was ABC, under the programming and promotional aegis of der Silvermensch (recently arrived from CBS), who navigated this return to normalcy. It is Garry Marshall's "Happy Days" and "Laverne and Shirley" that will be remembered along with the end of cheap Molotov cocktails and Ricardo Montalban and Tatoo as emblems of the 1970s. Owing to their relentless social consciousnesses, the Lear and MTM shows are more likely to be recalled by "love generation" geriatrics as being shows from the 1960s, even though they did not air during that decade. Marshall, in a stroke of Madison Avenue/Hollywood genius, frankly flashed his cosmos back past the 1960s, inventing the instant cliché that history was an entropic bell curve and the 1970s were really like the 1950s. By incorporating the sexual "freedoms" won by Lear and MTM into the old "Father Knows Best" setting, Marshall performed the cosmological bypass operation that created the sitcom of the 1970s. The Marshall shows, along with the giggling, jiggling "Three's Company," lead the pack as the decade fizzles.

The first hint that the 1960s might be in for a little recuperation and resurrection occurred with the sudden hit "Mork and Mindy" in the final two years of the "me decade." An old idea, "My Favorite Martian" (CBS, 1961-65) is salvaged from the pre-Beatles ancient world and an extraterrestrial visitor moves in with an American single person. Instead of Tim and his "Uncle Martin," we have in this post- "Three's Company" science-fiction sitcom the male alien Mork living with earth woman Mindy in no less a mecca of jogging boutiquedom than Boulder, Colorado. The action takes place in equal parts in Mindy's Marylike apartment and in her father's record store. Ostensibly from Ork, Mork, with his striped shirts and suspenders, druggy nonsequiturs, and innocent love for all that treads upon this earth, seems more like a time traveler from the "summer of love" than a star warrior or extragalactic anthropologist.

Whereas many generic mainstays faded from the home screen (westerns, weekly variety shows, and half-hour anthology dramas among them), the sitcom, although not totally aloof to the crowds in the street, sat squarely on its throne in the never-threatened palace.

Making a Production of It

Sam Hunting

I don't have a television and maybe for that reason I more carefully watch people react to it (in places where there happens to be one). The story I have in mind is a short one. It's about a Teamster, six months out of work because of an arterial bypass operation. He was a short, wiry man who had earlier that day carried a cedar chest into the house on his shoulder and needed no one to open the door for him to do it, sick as he was. The television was a huge, ghosting, off-color oblong in a paid-for-on-time "Mediterranean"-style cabinet. We sat in the living room, and there was a certain constraint between us. I was, to tell the truth, waiting to take his daughter out. We both stared deeply into the screen.

The movie was a thing called *The Beast with a Million Eyes*, but I didn't get a chance to watch it all the way through. It certainly rated a D-minus. Camp, some might have said. But after ten minutes of tight-lipped study, "this is stupid!" came from my opposite number. He was a French Indian, and hot-tempered; there was a real depth of bitterness and disgust in his tone. I had been engrossed. I wanted to say: No, look at it! Why are the doors made out of plywood? Why are there only five characters? Why is that supersonic whistle that says the aliens are around and about so hackneyed? Why is the acting so bad and the script so predictable? Because they're trying to compete with the Japanese wage scale of the late 1940s, and they can't do it! El cheapo sets, five actors and a dog to get ripped up mysteriously, that's in the budget; they can't afford an alien of their own, so they got a secondhand one from some other movie, and they're afraid we'll catch them at it, so they give us that whistle till the last ten minutes; they hired the best actors and scriptwriters they could. What do you want? In short—making my theoretical intervention—if you look at the movie as it was *produced*, you can take into account the conditions under which it was produced and learn to love it in spite of its flaws—*because* of its flaws. People like you and me made it, right? (To Marie's brother, I would have quoted Frank Zappa: "I love monster movies. And the cheaper they are, the better they are.")

Had I not held my tongue, Mr. DuBay would have come back with something like: "Why tell me?" Six months is time for a lot of television; he has probably seen *The Beast* at least twice. "Why tell me?" indeed. On the Left, we hear a lot about what television is supposed to do, how exactly what goes on the screen organizes consent to the rule of our permanent government, but we rarely hear about how this hegemony is worked out in real life. We rarely see what people *make* of television. People say, "this is stupid," when Buck Rogers heaves boulders "as if" they were made out of cork. People scoff when an obligatory chase scene screeches to a halt—on gravel. Naturally so. But why exactly?

Somewhere Marx argues that as the division of labor increases, the individuality of the worker shows up, not in the useful finished product but in the imperfect product. In the first case, cooperation has succeeded; in the second, the production process has broken down. When International Publishers ships 10,000 cases of *Capital*, the cooperation of many workers has attained its end; when one of those cases is off, number 19 will get the finger. In other words, detecting bad work and fixing blame are essential parts of the production process. That is what International's little slip of paper, "this case inspected by number 19," is for.

It's commonplace that people take their work habits home with them and that home is where the television is. What was it that set our friend off? It was, in fact, a car "screeching" on gravel – a case where what was on the soundtrack manifestly did not match up with what was on the screen. More than scoffing, it seems, is involved here. Hank Malone's useful notion of "scoffability" implies that directors deliberately show ridiculous happenings so that audiences, by scoffing, may feel they are themselves superior to the work and, hence, enlarged in their sense of themselves as persons. But the touch of the unreal our friend detected was not deliberate. He noticed bad work – in the same way that he would have noticed it at work. He did not simply *feel* superior, he *was* superior. Check out the television "Bloopers" column in any issue of the *National Enquirer* and you'll see that this happens on a collective scale. For instance, one reads in part:

Jaclyn Smith – who plays the sexy Kelly on television's "Charlie's Angels" – may be a good detective, but she has proved to be an even better quick-change artist. At least that's what viewers thought during a recent episode of the show when Jaclyn hopped into her car wearing one outfit and hopped out a few seconds later wearing an entirely different outfit. Blooper snooper Tammy Huber of West-vale, Ind., was the first to tell the Enquirer *about the TV boo-boo she had quickly spotted.*

"On the September 13th episode of 'Charlie's Angels,' Kelly was wearing a shirt, white vest and white pants when she walked to her car and drove off," Tammy said. "But when she got out of her car at a racetrack she was wearing bibbed overalls. She couldn't have changed while she was driving the car and she didn't stop anywhere. So it had to be a blooper."

Jeff Kibbee, production assistant for the show, admitted the goof and explained how it happened. "We shot one scene in Las Vegas and one in Los Angeles about three weeks later," he said. "In the second scene we had Kelly in the wrong outfit. It was a mistake – as simple as that," explained Kibbee. (Enquirer, 7 November 1978)

Mrs. Huber has completely bypassed any hegemonic, ideological, what-have-you sort of message. Her eye is focused elsewhere. She has learned to read the screen through a practice that academe (and, to its shame, the Left) has yet to pick up on. She has detected bad work. Perhaps, in her mind, Jeff Kibbee is her boss, and she fixes blame as well. We do know that thousands take this form of "popular revenge": the *Enquirer* gives T-shirts to blooper-spotters. Here mass culture happens, a process that takes my "intervention"–the notion of the artist as producer–for granted.

I'm not sure what the political implications of this achievement might be. One way to approach them might be through the notion of "continuity." Most movies are made with a continuity person, whose duty it is to make sure that the star's hair is styled the same way in successive scenes, that furniture, rings on whatever finger, vests, overalls, all objects carried from scene to scene remain constant. A lapse in continuity means, to the sharp eye of Tammy Huber or my Teamster friend, a blooper. (The cheaper the movie, the more likely these lapses are.) Does official reality, the way it is currently manufactured in the United States, achieve continuity? Is Nixon's 18-minute gap an alien manifestation, or are there little gaps, lapses, visible splices, discontinuities, bloopers, all around us?

The cheaper our politicians are, the more likely this would seem to be. As I mentioned, I have no television, so a "yes" or "no" answer from me would be pure speculation. I read the news that's printed to fit the columns of the *Times*, and who knows what the sharp eye of Mrs. Huber would read between those lines? To me, our official reality reads very much like a science-fiction story called the *Penultimate Truth*. World War III is still going on, and the U.S. is fighting the USSR. Ninety-nine percent of the U.S. lives and works underground in gigantic fallout shelters called tanks. The tankers make robots by the hundred thousand, for the surface is so radioactive and germ-warfare ridden that only "leadies" can fight on it–commanded by the remaining 1%. Periodically, a missile breaks through one of the force bubbles that shield the cities; the destruction glows from the tankers' television screens, and the face of the "protector," Tablot Yancy, appears to console them, inspire them, to up their production quotas. Above: a lead suit or "the stink of shrink"; below, quarters so cramped that the furniture must be folded into the walls. Ninety-nine percent of the USSR lives and works in the same official reality. What none of the tankers know is this: there is no war at all, and the surface is perfectly safe. The war was settled decades back by the Supreme Council of War game computers in Mexico City. The 1% use the "leadies" the tankers make to hunt down any tankers who tunnel their way to the surface and to function as retainers in their "desmesnes." The 1% – called "Yancemen" – serve the Supreme Council by constructing an official reality. They produce miniature holocausts in their studios and program speeches into the robot simulacra, Talbot Yancy, all for the consumption of the captive tankers. At the beginning of the story, Carol Fugate, who has been taping Yancy's speeches, notices a queer thing: Yancy, in that day's speech, pronounced "coup de grâce" without an "s," whereas one week ago he had pronounced it correctly. A blooper! The reader knows that the Yancement let Yancy slip a cog. Will Carol lose her faith in reality? Will she work it out that if a camera were to get at the back of Yancy's talking head, it would show only a mass of circuitry? Will the tankers, having detected bad work, fix blame? Will Yancy's blooper initiate a tanker drive upsurface?

Why *does* CBS show Walter only from the waist up? Speculation cannot detain me; but certainly "our" official reality – styled by Yanceman Ragshoon though it may be – increasingly lacks continuity. Will the habits and practices of mass culture lead Mrs. Huber and Mr. DuBay to say – provoked by one blooper after another by our permanent government – "this is stupid"? For my part, when I think of the collective Mrs. Huber seeing through the finished product to the process that made it and asserting her mastery over that process, I recall some hundred-year-old words: "Let us now picture to ourselves, by way of a change, a community of free individuals, carrying on their work with the means of production in common."

The Niagara that visitors to Manchester in the 1840s heard, when the whole city's machinery roared into life at dawn, finds its echo today in the upward flick of the sanitation engineer's flowmeter at commercial time, when millions of people take their "breaks" at once. One day the working class will awake and demand a cup full of joy.

Recent
Literature

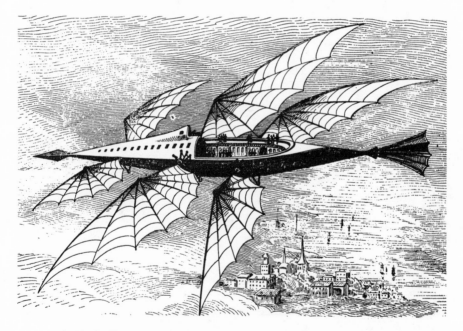

Artist's Conception of Future Aircraft, as Suggested by
Thomas A. Edison (1880)

Science Fiction: Philip K. Dick

Sam Hunting

Death is Dick's friend. It supplies him with his germs of inspiration.

The basic thing that motivates me is that I have met people in my life who I knew deserved to be immortalized, and the best I could do — couldn't guarantee them immortality, but I could guarantee them an audience of maybe 100,000. Especially I like to write about people who have died, whose actual lifetimes are over with, and who linger on, say, only in my mind and the minds of a few other people. I happen to be the only one who can write them down, and get their speech patterns down, and record incidents of great nobility and heroism which they have shown under very arduous conditions . . . and leave that as a permanent or semipermanent trace in the stratum of society in which we live. (A Skanner Darkly)

This elegiac thrust is the basis of Dick's art. His characters live in our collective memory. They speak to us. We feel as if we have met them.

In what stratum of society does he seek to leave his traces? At first sight, this stratum is the science-fiction community, and indeed he takes his place as a master there. Dick started as a letter hack and was given his first break by Horace Gold's *Galaxy*. Science fiction, at the time when Dick turned pro, was incorporating both concerns and personnel (Fred Pohl, for example) from Madison Avenue, and the hidden persuaders theme runs through the work of that period and through Dick's science fiction from that day to the present. His first novel, *Solar Lottery*, pictures a world of conspicuous consumption where the state is run like a game-show. *The Man Who Japed* concerns a piece of "japery" perpetrated by the head of Moral Reclamation, the glorified ad agency that runs the world. Dick is a master of social-science fiction.

At the level of production, Dick is a master speedwriter. He typically sets up an interlocking set of premises early in the story, then gives his germinative characters the ball and lets them run with it. The results of Dick's mad rushes to make a week's worth of pennies-per-word pay off are good. Damon Knight gave *Solar Lottery* unqualified praise: "Dick states his premises and then puts away his maps and charts for good. . . . [He catches] the bare nerves and tautness of our own society at its worst and puts it on paper so you can hear, feel and smell it."

Dick's Hugo winner, *Man in the High Castle* (1962), kicks speedwriting to a whole new plane. *Man in the High Castle* was composed by letting the I Ching decide the plot in places where Dick couldn't. The character Breton advises, "put your trust in the inexhaustible nature of the murmur." In *Man in the High Castle*, the murmur of the speedwriter's unconscious association is objectified in the spontaneity of the 87 yarrow stalks. And Dick was right to trust the oracle as orator. This novel is the best treatment of a theme that Dick returns to again and again: the fascist state.

Maybe that's it [Juliana] thought as she put the magazine back on the rack. The Nazis have no sense of humor, so why should they want TV? Anyhow, they killed off most of the great comedians. Because most of them were Jewish. In fact, she realized they killed off most of the entertainment field. I wonder how Hope gets away with what he says. . . . Like the joke about Göring. The one where Göring buys Rome and has it shipped up to his mountain retreat and

---

then set up again. And revives Christianity so his lions will have something to . . .

(Göring, by the way, is not a misprint. It is one of the little details which indicate that *Man in the High Castle* is an alternate world story – one in which the Nazis won World War II.)

The theme of the fascist state derives from authentic conviction on Dick's part. Dick's treatment of the fascist state raises the hidden persuaders theme to a higher power. But this theme is also very useful to Dick as a speedwriter. An all-powerful, arbitrary evil state comes in handy again and again at crucial plot junctures – its very arbitrariness being, for the temporarily blocked writer, a measure of its usefulness. For Dick, the fascist state functions in the capacity of what Henry James calls a *ficelle* – one of those interesting characters whose role is to forward the plot and let the characters unfold themselves.

Dick thus makes his early mark as a social-science-fiction writer via the typicality of his characters, his plottiness, and the warp and weft of his multicolored fascist background. He achieves his status with a superb command of science fiction's technical resources. But Dick means to leave his traces in a second stratum of society. He means to be judged within the milieu that gives him his germs, as well as in that milieu which is his market. He remarks that he wishes these people would judge him, even though they probably don't pick up books at all. Around 1964, this "noble," "heroic" community changed both the character of his inspiration and the nature of his plots. In 1977, the need to speak to this community led Dick, in *A Scanner Darkly*, to abandon science fiction altogether.

What happened to Dick, as a Marin county resident in 1964, was LSD. 1964 was his miracle year. It saw *Martian Time Slip, The Three Stigmata of Palmer Eldritch, Penultimate Truth*, and *Clans of the Alphane's Moon*. Each of these works is marked by a strong family resemblance to the others. Their germinative material clearly derives from the "transpersonal experiences" so characteristic of Grov's "psycholytic therapy": a therapy whereby the key of LSD opened many minds.

Enter death. *The Three Stigmata of Palmer Eldritch* shows

the effects of the acid test most clearly. It is an ad-agency novel with an added ingredient. The sun is heating up. Earth is becoming un-livable. The U.N. is forcing emigration to Mars. Force is needed be-cause Mars is unlivable, too. In their "hovels," the colonists spend their time building "layouts," doll-sized replicas of earth. Via the "transsubstantion" drug, Can-D [read (LS)D], they leave their bod-ies and reincarnate themselves in "Perky Pat" and "Dick," the two dolls who live in the perpetual, earthly weekend of the layouts. (Mattel's Barbie and Ken dolls must have been Dick's inspiration here.) For a few minutes, the colonists can gaze on Terra again. The hero, Barney Mayerson, works for the ad agency that markets the dolls, the layout components, and – illegally – Can-D. Into this cozy arrangement enters Palmer Eldritch, interplanetary industrialist, marketing his own out-of-body drug, Chew-Z. Can-D wears off; Chew-Z does not. Eldritch's slogan: "God promises eternal life; we can deliver it." Mayerson is inveigeled by his agency into taking Chew-Z as a test subject. Gradually, it dawns on Mayerson that the Chew-Z user can never find his way back into his own body and "real" time again. In fact, all Chew-Z users begin to turn into El-dritch himself. (This is a typical reaction of the naive user of LSD: "they're *all* on it." So is the ego death that lies at the heart of the novel's experience. At one point, Mayerson becomes Mars – Grov's "planetary consciousness.") The world becomes a bundle of sensa-tions tied together in one mind: Palmer Eldritch's. They chew; he chooses. *The Three Stigmata of Palmer Eldritch* has the sweaty palms and "acid" stomach of a using world. Grey flannel werewolf, meet Tiny Doctor Tim.

It's a long way from 1964. LSD, like the coinage, can be dated by its purity. From Sandoz to those formaldehyde-filled little yel-low barrels: what a falling off there was for the experienced taster! From Neal Cassady juggling his steel mallet to the coarse gibes and stark gibberish of the decade's finest political journalist, Dr. Hunter Thompson, the adulteration of LSD ran parallel to the sophistica-tion and decay of the counterculture. Yet surely the acid test, as a sacrament and conversion experience, was at the heart of that di-verse grouping of nuclei and trends. Even the Weathermen tried to use it to dope out the latter-day *Pinkertons* among them. But as the troubadours of the "me decade" sang: "All those dayglo freaks/who used to paint their face/they've joined the human race/ some things will never change." Thus sings Steely Dan on the demise of Owsley and the Merry Pranksters. Only nuclei of an exceptional toughness – the Grateful Dead, the Hell's Angels, the Whole Earthers – survived this trend. The light had failed. For many, the locked briefcase and bloody stumps of the Haight's last days were all the "further" there ever was. This, then, is our second death. *A Scanner Darkly* partakes of the disillusionment that followed in the counterculture's wake.

A Scanner Darkly is cast in the form of a detective novel. The hero, a narc, is posing as an ordinary salesman in a Blue Chip stamp redemption center in L.A. "Fred" is assigned to record his own movements (as well as those of his circle of friends) with a "scanner," a holographic bugging device. One of the attractions of the book is the authenticity of Fred's circle. The problem Fred has is that he must edit these conversations to present his film to his superiors. When he does this, he must edit himself out (but creatively, selectively, so as not to give the editor away). He must do this because the agency avoids penetration by keeping its operatives' identities secret – even from one another. Under the intolerable strain of editing himself out of his own life-movie, he begins to take the most popular drug of the period, Substance D, which, although it gives relief, has the side effect of eroding the corpus callosum; thus his right brain is separated from his left. While his personality is being split, it is also being pulled back and forth between the two lobes, owing to the mental contortions he must undergo in the editing process. His mental censor helpfully conceals all traces of these changes from his consciousness, even rendering his hallucinations faithfully in the holos while he watches them, thus putting him beyond all help. After his personality destructs, it is brought back to the vegetable level at a fascistic Synanon-type therapy clinic. "Bruce," as he is renamed, doing fieldwork as therapy, conceals a little blue flower in his shoe.

Bruce saw only the flat of Donald's hand bring the light, and he stared at it a thousand years. It locked, it had locked; it will lock for him, forever for dead eyes outside time; eyes that could not look away and a hand that could not move away. Time ceased as the eyes glazed and the universe jelled along with him, at least for him, froze over for him and his understanding, as its inertness became complete. There was nothing left to happen.

"Back to work, Bruce," Donald, the executive director, said.

"I saw," Bruce said. He thought, I knew. That was it.

The "it" Bruce saw—the little blue flower he concealed in his shoe—is the raw material for Substance D. It turns out that the clinic uses its patients to grow the drug which addicted them.

The most striking thing about *A Scanner Darkly* is the thoroughgoing way it adopts the conventions of the detective story. Fred sinks from being an agent (a conscious representative of the state) to being a medium. These are the two poles of the detective as hero. The one pole is represented by Holmes, the rationalist whose case always depends upon money. Sax Rohmer's Morris Klaw is at the other pole. His slogan and theory, "thoughts are things," lets him pluck the identity of his antagonist, the least likely suspect, out of the ether every time. By the end of *A Scanner Darkly*, Fred becomes a medium for Substance D. Fred is a mouthpiece through which Substance D says, "I am here," to his agency. The little blue flower—concealed by a person whose brain readout is so automatic that, for example, he cannot look away from a hand covering his eyes—resolves the case.

In detective fiction, the case to be solved remains at the compositional center of the work. Fred slips from *having* a case to *being* a case. He has also been someone else's case all along. The stimulus-response loop—"if you love her, bring her flowers"—which causes him to pluck the blue flower was implanted by his girlfriend, Donna, who is (unbeknownst to him) also the federal agent who set him up by dealing him his first dose.

In *A Scanner Darkly*, death retains its germinating force. Its theme is the ego death of Substance D. Its characters and incidents are drawn from the dying counterculture. Superficially, this novel is Dick's best science-fiction work. The characters are drawn from life, and it has a powerful description of a fascist state. But the complex web of premises we have come to expect from Dick does not exist. Furthermore, the book is not speedwritten. That is why Dick had to adopt the conventions of detective fiction to move the story forward. In *A Scanner Darkly*, one's own personality is split by watching oneself. In a science-fiction story, it would be by *meeting* oneself – via a time-travel paradox, cloning, a matter-transmission screw-up. When Dick abandons the premise and speedwriting as techniques of production, he abandons science fiction. He himself admits that it is not science fiction. It is a deviant work. Why?

In *A Scanner Darkly*, Dick is speaking to the community that gave him his germs. The fruit, which seemed so sweet in 1964, turned sour by 1977. At the end of the novel there is a list:

To Gaylene	*deceased*
To Ray	*deceased*
To Francy	*permanent psychosis*
To Kathy	*permanent brain damage*
To Phil	*permanent pancreatic damage*

The cause of these deaths and maladies? "The greatest single contribution of the counterculture to the American way of life: unbridled use of drugs." *A Scanner Darkly*, then, is a memorial dedicated to a collective memory. This rules out the use of the premise as a technique. No disbelief need be suspended in science fiction's core readership because the book is explicitly about events and real people in the past. Belief is demanded, for joined to the memorial nature of the book is an equally explicit didactic purpose. The message engraved on the marble of it is: "don't use." That is Dick's message for the stratum of society on which he hopes to leave his traces.

I think we can see how important it was for Dick to get the message of *A Scanner Darkly* across if we remember that to achieve it, he throws away the techniques that make him a great science-fiction writer. This decision is symptomatic of larger problems that science fiction is just beginning to face. LSD – for which we can read (Substance) D, if we recall the ego death at the heart of the LSD experience – is a science-fiction premise come true.

It is a brain-frying experience which seems to drop from nowhere. Like the lethal JJ 180 in Dick's *Now Wait for Last Year*, it

Sam Hunting

is a weapon of war loosed upon a civilian population. Dick is forced to abandon science fiction to make his didactic point precisely because a moral judgment and a warning cannot be conveyed by making this danger an imaginary one. I think he succeeds in his object; but, in terms of fiction, I prefer a work in which he is in his element.

Science Fiction: Ursula K. Le Guin

Paul Buhle

Ursula Le Guin is the bearer of a promise long hidden in American literature. She is the greatest utopian writer in the English language since William Morris. She has also done more than any writer in a given generation to bring science fiction from the level of a "space western" toward a mature and meaningful form. She has introduced a feminist-ecological critique of Western civilization so well constructed and deft that few will charge her with propaganda and many will find insights they had shunned in radical polemics.

The critical literature on her work has grown by leaps and bounds and by no means is all of it the usual effort to stuff creative insights into academic pigeonholes. A special issue of *Science Fiction Review* (November 1975) and *Ursula K. Le Guin, Voyager to Inner Lands and to Outer Space*, edited by Joe De Bolt (Kennikat Press, 1979), along with her own collection of essays, *The Language of the Night: Essays on Fantasy and Science Fiction*, edited by Susan Wood (Putnam, 1979), carry the discussion on narrative description and technical grounds as far forward as the average reader will want to go. With this material as a given, there is more to say about

Paul Buhle

Le Guin as a quasi-political writer, as a feminist revolutionary, and as an anthropological-literary emancipator – that is, as a little-used resource of democracy's future potential.

In content, she has drawn a sad picture of revolutionary failure in the nineteenth and twentieth centuries, illustrating the strength of our conditioning over our best interests and even our fervent desires. Le Guin's characters are, by and large, culturally determined, whether they be earthling primitives or technologically advanced aliens, oppressor or oppressed. And like the protagonists of *The Word for World Is Forest*, creatures with a lustrous dream-life who can smash their invaders only in self-defense – a clear analogy to Vietnamese culture – the circumstances of their entry into history is tragic. Once drawn together for violence, no matter how valid, they have lost a primeval innocence (of neolithic matriarchal culture?), which cannot be regained. The universe is a perilous place, most of all because we can do so little to alter ourselves.

Not suprisingly, her main protagonists are marginal and alienated. Like our twentieth-century cultural heroes – especially in the U.S. – they are outsiders in one way or another, and, for that reason, they are able to see what the insiders cannot perceive or understand. Often they are no better off for the knowledge they gain; certainly they are no happier. But they are an avant-garde, as surely as Kerouac's mad hipsters are. They speak to us, especially because they represent a fragment of ourselves and of Le Guin's self in a steadily declining society.

If a source of hope exists, it is in the familiar resource of that avant-garde to make the most of its outsideness, to reach beyond the everyday in all directions. Sometimes as an individual, like the doctor in *The Word for World Is Forest* who suddenly realizes his fellow soldiers are torturing and enslaving beings more worthy than themselves; sometimes as a collective, like the Odonian anarchists in *The Dispossessed*, who live on a planet apart determined to show humankind a better way. The cost is heavy. But the alternative price for subservience is more degrading and self-demolishing. And there are possible compensations of an inwardness, a hidden knowledge gained or merely glimpsed, which makes existence more whole and meaningful. As Larry Tifft and Dennis Sulivan say quite eloquently for Le Guin and her characters: "The hope for survival is the ever continuous breaking down of barriers, never pausing, but never pressing revolution. It entails continuous change, a never-wavering commitment to risk, to the negation of certainty."

In form, Le Guin seeks to return to the basis of a richer and more universal literature than we now possess, the oral cultures which were almost eradicated by mass society. In her essays, she has illuminated the fairy tale at the root of fantasy literature, the journey into the darkness of subconscious thought. Here right and wrong no longer apply in the ordinary sense; and the only rule is that by instinct, the animal – the animal within us – "knows the way home," out of the madness we call civilization. The dark brother, the shadow soul, has not gone away, however much Christianity might seek to tame him (or her) and however hard industrial society of every ideological variety tries to attach certain standards of "progress" on each action. By reaching back toward pre-Christian and premodern fantasy, which she does most clearly in her *Earthsea Trilogy*, Le Guin strives toward the poetics of oral culture: *Beowulf*, the Finnish *Kalevala*, or the many lesser known epics. In so doing, she dissolves that arch-pretentious literary form, the novel, much as Novalis, Breton, and Ishmael Reed have proposed its dissolution in the last two centuries: back to storytelling, with language serving as a shamanistic resource, back to the magical power of words to live and love rather than merely describe.

In the name of emancipation, two kinds of criticisms can be made. Le Guin has been hard put to find the latent potentialities in daily life and most especially in the laboring classes, which have been the basis of most revolutionary movements. Perhaps she is too pessimistic about the fate of the West. Perhaps she does not feel rooted in her own experience when dealing with an earthly, lower-class subject. No one can, or should at any rate, ask the fantasy-weaver to be responsible for the realistic perception of circumstances and prospects: she writes in another world.

More serious is the very control that has made her so readable but at the same time, "literary," in a sense that many pulp science-fiction readers find high-toned and aesthetic. She made some offhand criticisms of H. P. Lovecraft and his work ("an exceptionally, almost impeccably, bad writer. . . . Derivative, inept, and callow . . . extreme psychological oddity" [*Times Literary Supplement*, Mar. 26, 1976]), which suggest an uncomfortableness with the volcanic, obsessive urges that bring many a pulp fantasy writer to write for days on end before falling into a stupor. H. P. Lovecraft, Clark Ashton Smith, and the early Ray Bradbury of *October Country* are powerful, not because they are frightening but because a kind of automatic writing *pushes them over the edge* where the litterateur loses control and the hysterical "visionary" takes over. One wishes a thousand times that the instrument panel would go blank in Le Guin's writing and that the nightmares we all possess would speak as if unaided.

In her most recent work, Le Guin has acted on one if not the other of these limitations, and has walked on new ground. *Malefrena*, like *Orsinian Tales*, is an antiauthoritarian political gesture with echoes of the French Revolution not evident before in Le Guin's writing. She is moving closer, one believes, to the hard political questions that the most incendiary of anarchists must wrestle with in practice and which the litterateur avoids by references to the high purpose of art. Le Guin means to say things and to be heard. *The Beginning Place*, a strangely allegorical work, reminds us of the classic pulp, *Wandering Jew*, by Eugene Sue, in which the traveler can find the end of his road only by meeting the woman whom he has imagined. There is eros, more direct and forceful than the Le Guin reader expects, and she takes a stab—not a very successful one but honestly undertaken—at treating the lives and dreams of workaday people of the present. Still, they seem brutalized and diminished, narrow rather than complex. But they *can* make the leap toward freedom of sorts, at least toward the freedom of genuine love.

Whatever is problematic in her work, Le Guin is a revelation to our times. The keen analyst Lawrence Krader, describing the accomplishments of Le Guin's father, A. L. Kroeber, remarked that his quest encompassed an organicism beyond the oversimplifications of Lewis Henry Morgan, Engels, and the other nineteenth-century anthropological writers, beyond the bland pluralism of twentieth-century academic anthropology – toward a statement of the whole universal human. Ursula Le Guin has carried on the search for that human, and we are all richer for it.

Getting a Handle on the Cranks

Dave Wagner

"Strange armies, transparent cohorts and phantom hordes, heralded by ultra-sonic trumpets, are beginning to descend upon our civilization," wrote Louis Pauwels in 1960. He was right, and his own book, *Morning of the Magicians* (Avon, 1963), was among the first of the merely sonic trumpets to announce the arrival on the market of those bizarre gentlemen who claim to have proven that the human species was conceived in a relatively quick one-aeon stand between our ancestral ape mothers and a band of wandering spacemen.

That's the claim. Somewhere back in the vague dawn of the Neolithic, or even earlier, a crew of exogenous astronauts surveyed the planet and found it fair, or at least found its primate females attractive enough to make a direct sexual intervention into the history of the species. Eventually the astronauts left, abandoning our hybrid new race to its destiny with nothing more than a few hints on how to go about building civilizations of our own.

No doubt about it: the cranks and dreamers, the fantasists, the eccentric theorists and weird speculators whom Pauwels predicted are no longer "descending," they have fully arrived. They have burst out of the quietly aging science fiction and UFO traditions to declare themselves the prophets of the new age, the thinkers who have synthesized anthropology, theology, and literary criticism into a force that will drag a fussing and bitching humanity into the Third Millennium to meet its makers. Now if Erich von Däniken were the only (or even the most interesting) writer to argue that humankind has extraterrestrial origins, there would be little point in studying this set of claims, despite his reported 14 million readers and the publicity he has gathered from all corners of the media. But among devotees, von Däniken is considered a theoretical lightweight. There is more to this movement than its most famous popularizer.

There is, for example, the brilliant and Byzantine mind of Jean Sendy, a Frenchman, who in *The Coming of the Gods* (Berkeley Medallion, 1973) begins soberly enough with a reference to obscure works on astrophysics by Russian and American scientists and then erupts with metaphorical brimstone into a denunciation of all science since the Renaissance and a militant defense of "medievalism" and cabala. The man is a walking avatar of the fifteenth-century intellectual.

A host of other Frenchmen are also working on the cosmic sperm theory (no one has yet suggested that the originators were spacewomen). Robert Charroux (*Masters of the World* [Berkeley Medallion, 1974]), whose approach is very close to von Däniken's, was working on it back in the early sixties; Andrew Thomas (*The Home of the Gods* [Berkeley Medallion, 1974]) at heart a nostalgic Atlantist, has developed the theory out of that branch of mystical literature; Jaques Bergier (*Extraterrestrial Visitations from Prehistoric Times to the Present* [Signet, 1974]), Pauwel's collaborator in the earlier book (which did not accept the theory), has contributed the corollary that we are all laboratory specimens under the scrutiny of *someone*, apparently a group of interstellar behavioral psychologists.

And there are also Italians, Germans, and Americans hot on the trail of the thesis, among them the U.S. team of Max H. Flindt and Otto Binder (*Mankind—Child of the Stars* [Fawcett, 1974]),

211

who maintain the high empirical standards of American crankdom by disdaining the romantic archaeology of von Däniken and the others to concentrate on the data of respectable anthropology.

All of them agree, naturally enough, that the theory is not simply a fad, and the steady sales of new entries in the field indicate that it is not. If that is the case, then crankdom will have graduated from its obscure beginnings in mass culture to the status of an international movement. Which raises the interesting question: how and why did this particular set of ideas become a springboard for the crank to leap into prominence as a force, however marginal, in contemporary popular culture?

For the answers we have to consider briefly the history of crank literature, a term (it should be explained right off) that is not used here in the usual pejorative sense. There is simply no other word in the language (Raymond Williams in *Culture and Society* notes that the word "crank" first entered the language early in the English industrial revolution. The German expression for the same phenomenon is the word *Kauz*, literally a kind of bug-eyed owl), which covers the full range of those highly unorthodox but systematic ideas that claim to have rational underpinnings. They have a tradition and a continuity of their own, and, if pressed to describe it, one could say it's the tradition that combines the range and sweep of Hegel with the anarchic spirit of Daffy Duck.

It is nearly as old as respectable science itself, of course, but with the earliest appearance of mass communications, the cranks were able for the first time to find each other, organize their strange committees, and lay the foundations for the modern wave of the baroque imagination we are dealing with here.

Ignatius Donnelly, H. P. Lovecraft, and Charles Fort are the chief American architects of the tradition, at least in their collective influence, and the period they span–from the Civil War to World War II–might be called the heroic age of crankdom. Each of these men was a literary original, the prototype of the failed genius. Or perhaps they were only premature. In any case, their work did not reach into the popular imagination in any big way until the flourishing of the paperback market in our own time.

At that point, after the mushroom clouds had barely cleared

from the skies of Japan, the primordial Lovecraftian horrors began to slither through the comic books and Fort's speculative extraplanetary beings started to appear in a chronic rash of UFOs. Most significantly for our purposes, though, was the resurfacing of Donnelley's catastrophic theories of history in a burst of public enthusiasm that sent academic scientists into a rage. The book that fired the scientific ire was Immanuel Velikovsky's *Worlds in Collision,* a gentle and even detached work that argued against the gradualist evolutionary theories of history in favor of "catastrophic mutations."

Today it's hard to imagine why the university scientists went to such lengths to suppress the book (among other things they banded together with threats of official boycotts against Velikovsky's publisher), or why only one of the literate American magazines found the pluck to point out that, after all, the man should not simply be denied a hearing by overly exercised scientists. But that was also the period that saw the hysterical suppression of horror comics and official signs of anxiety about UFO sightings among the military. The spirit of dread was loose upon the land, a kind of cultural McCarthyism that tried to root out the last traces of the marvelous and the fantastic from popular culture, the very themes it had always taken as its strong points. (If there is any way to relate the crank tradition to the larger history of popular culture, it is as a part of that genre known as Gothic literature, which embraces mystery, horror, and science fiction. The principal difference is that the cranks, except for Lovecraft, have written under the aegis of nonfiction and therefore may be said to have invented the form of Gothic speculation.

In retrospect it is clear that when Velikovsky updated Donnelly's theory of history, he provided the starting point for von Däniken and the other members of what we may call the school of popular Euhemerism, most of whom accept the idea that natural disasters and not evolution have shaped human history. But that idea is less important than Velikovsky's method. He had spent years comparing the myths and legends of early Western, Asian, and archaic cultures and believed he had found in them the remnants of real (though symbolically interpreted) convulsions of nature. "The answer to the problem of the similarity of the motifs in the folklore of various people," he wrote, "is as follows: A great many ideas reflect real historical content." And with that, the method was launched in its modern form.

Euhemeros was a Greek philosopher of the third century B.C. whom we can call, if we stretch a point, the Erich von Däniken of classical thought. According to tradition he (like his modern counterpart) spent a lot of time traveling around the known world, digging up material for his best-known work, the *Sacred History*, which was far more historical than sacred. He drew plenty of critical fire from the devout by asserting that the myths and legends of the gods then current in the pagan world were actually nothing more than idealized versions of real people who'd once trod the common earth. As he saw it, the original "gods" were ancestral heroes and conquerors whose exploits were preserved by succeeding generations with the only historical art they knew—the oral tradition. The tales of Homer and Hesiod were in this sense completely historical: the throne of mighty Zeus was revealed as a rude bench in some Bronze Age warrior's shack.

Euhemeros was not hasty enough to claim that the ancient heroes and conquerors were planning to come back someday (that part of the saga is unique to the modern school), but he did manage to make himself unwelcome among those who remained faithful to—in Lovecraft's phrase—the "elder gods." His only support came a few centuries later from among the Christians, who were understandably anxious to prove the historical and therefore superstitious character of the pagan pantheon.

Now the wheel has turned again. Today's Euhemerists are ransacking the Bible, particularly the Old Testament, for evidence to support the ancient astronaut theory. There is enough hairsplitting over certain passages of Genesis to appall the scholars of Byzantium, and it hardly helps that so many of the cranks like to split their hairs with an ax. Sendy, for instance, interprets the story of the Lord's displeasure with Adam for biting into the apple as a note that the cosmic immigrants were upset when they "learned that a native gardener had disobeyed orders." By the same token, the account of a rib extraction from the side of the native gardener was actually a fuzzy version of a cloning experiment. And so forth.

It's easy to resist these arguments even when they do not come down to particulars because they are finally no different from any other interpretation that goes busily about supporting a belief. For all their protestations of being strict rationalists, another side of their efforts sometimes sneaks through, such as when Sendy makes the curious admission that "one must believe in something, and I believe in rationalism." (We can only ask, in that case, whether there isn't something decadent in the state of rationalism that it should become a matter of *belief*?!)

Yet it's too easy to jump on the cranks for the detailed excesses of their books. After all, in their own way they reflect the tendencies of dominant ideas in the larger culture and even give us valuable glimpses into intellectual movements from "below." When Andrew Tomas writes, "It is easy to call legends mere fantasy and laugh at the traditions of many peoples [but] it is much more difficult to appraise history in its entirety," he is appealing to the discipline of universal history, whose practitioners include not only Hegel, Spengler, and Toynbee but Lewis Mumford in our own time. Whole intellectual movements of the twentieth century, for that matter, are preoccupied with prehistory, mythology, and oral traditions. Archaic art and music have been academically habilitated, linguistics has freed itself from written texts and turned to the spoken word, ethnology has been accepted as a legitimate science; and not least of all, the reconstruction of rational systems of thought from the myths of archaic cultures has been taken on as a special task by Lévi-Strauss and the French structuralists. Under the circumstances, who will deny the cranks their method?

It may even be true that the instincts of the cranks are as finely tuned as those of their more established colleagues. In the social sciences today there is an enthusiastic convergence on anthropology, a race to prehistory to discover the "lost" elements of human culture that were abandoned by a civilization which now finds that it can't do without them. Energetic debates about the political significance of the Neolithic for the present are commonplace, to take one example. The cranks are participating in all of this in their own way, at their best taking a position solidly in favor of the imagination being a necessary ingredient for a "restored" science. Meanwhile, widely respected thinkers in the natural sciences (like astrophysicist Carl Sagan and biologist Lewis Thomas) are writing playful and imaginative books, including in them speculations about extraterrestrial life. Who knows? The vigor of the cranks in any culture may be directly related to the imaginative strength of its scientists, and to a certain extent, the reverse may be true as well. At least popular interest in von Däniken's books has finally spurred the archaeologists to thoroughly investigate the pre-Incan civilization of Chan Chan.

The unanswered question is why so many of the current Euhemerists are French? Perhaps it's because French science has remained more unabashedly romantic than that of other Western countries, and their cranks simply follow the larger impulses of the culture. It's interesting, at any rate, to find that the only movement of self-declared Euhemerists to appear within the last few centuries was in France, just before the Revolution of 1789. Its members were men like Mirabeau and Claviere, well-bred revolutionaries whose deism (like that of Washington and Jefferson in America) shared the underlying pathos of our modern cranks in their belief that an unknown "Intelligence" created our species and then, soon after the act of creation, abandoned it to an uncertain destiny.

Immanuel Velikovsky's theory that catastrophic events and not evolution propel humans through history takes on additional meaning when it's set against the background of the time in which it first appeared. He didn't mention the atomic bomb, but it lurks as the unnameable monster behind his ideas, and it's not hard to see that after the newsreels arrived from Hiroshima, the notion of the Great Flood or a similar worldwide cataclysm was no longer an abstraction in the popular imagination. Still closer to the present, the landing of humans on the moon in 1969 (not incidentally, the year von Däniken's first book became popular) must have made the notion that the species of one planet could colonize another something less than raw fantasy to a massive (500 million strong) international television audience. Those twin events, with their cultural impact, are the symbolic pillars supporting the popular credulity of crank ideas, making them less fantastic than the investigators of crank-dom are willing to admit. (Since World War II, only two books on science cranks have appeared: Martin Gardner's *Fads and Fallacies in the Name of Science* [Dover, 1952] and Patrick Moore's *Can You Speak Venusian?* [Norton, 1972]. Of the pair, Gardner's is incomparably the better, although even he is given to outbursts of cultural anxiety of the sort that disfigured the decade he wrote it in.) It is the very plausibility of crankishness in this period that makes it significant.

But where the modern Euhemerists completely abandon their claims to reason and science is in their belief that the hyper-technological "gods" who created us are about to return and straighten out our terrestrial act. Here we enter the realm of religion again, to rejoin those age-old human impulses that foresee the end of ordinary history just around the next bend. Before this we might have said that the cranks produce marvelous new metaphorical sparks when they bring together romantic archaeology with astrophysics – that was a new one, all right – Euhemerism with a measurable jolt like a moon landing. But when they claim with no evidence (though with every confidence) that the gods are coming *back*, well, we have a touchdown on very familiar turf indeed.

It doesn't matter how they phrase it, in the end it all comes down to the same millennialism. Sendy discards the term "Judgment Day" for an expression better suited to his rationalist belief: "Today," he writes, "the experimental testing of my hypothesis is near." With equal aplomb, Flindt and Binder once declared that American astronauts would find a message from the stars tucked under a moon rock and are now presumably living with their disappointment (yes, it's quite possible Armstrong didn't look under the *right* rock).

The millennial impulse is so much a part of civilization (although not of archaic cultures, unless they are faced with destruction from the outside) that any historian who could dig up a century or even a short string of decades without its own batch of chiliasts would be making a major discovery. Even the best of times will produce millennial movements. Of them all, Christianity is the most successful (the main sense of fundamentalist Clifford Wilson's at-

Dave Wagner

tack on von Däniken, entitled with polemical gusto *Crash Go the Chariots* [Lancer, 1972], is that the crank millennium is inferior in supernatural beauty to the Christians'. He at least wins the aesthetic argument), even able to find rejuvenation in its adventist roots from time to time, perhaps because its millennial claims are absolute: not only will history come to a sudden halt but the dead will rise, physical bodies will be abolished, and the whole operation on earth will be closed down without notice. By contrast, the cranks (still clinging to their shreds of rationalism) offer a surprisingly pedestrian scenario: both Gerald Ford and Nelson Rockefeller, for example, receive phone calls from a creature who quietly explains that their money is no good anymore and that the Bureau Chief on Arcturus has turned the planet's case over to one of his own people.

It's hard to say who buys this future. Restless Presbyterians? Middle-aged men who tinker moodily in the garage? Unusual florists with tuliplike imaginations? It's impossible to say. The devoted readership of this literature thrives on the esoteric and powerful anonymity of mass culture itself.

When Euhemeros returned from his travels around the Mediterranean to tell his countryfolk that their fine mythology was actually a lot of ancestor worship, he probably thought that he was helping to pull them out of an archaic slumber into the daylight of reason and civilization. And maybe he was. Lewis Mumford has explained that ancestor worship is a characteristic of archaic cultures that usually disappears with the rise of civilization.

Yet now, at the apparent high point of civilization, an advanced form of ancestor worship returns to make its own small thunder in the paperback market. If he were to walk into the present decade, our ancestor Euhemeros, encountering the noise of it all, would probably be startled into reflection about why his method has reappeared to support ideas he was trying to discard.

The answer may be found in the question that burns the crank curiosity into fevers; how is it possible that reason and intelligence would spring forth from the stunted forebrain of an ape, and how could civilizations rise with such suddenness from the detritus of archaic cultures?

It's a good question all right, but we hardly have to turn to extraterrestrial devices for a workable answer. In the first place, the "suddenness" with which early civilizations appeared is largely an illusion. Recent anthropological thinking has come to place just as much emphasis on culture in the process of evolution as was formerly given to biology alone. The rather mechanical nineteenth century determinism of Darwin that bothers the cranks so much is no longer the dogma it once was. Now it is recognized that symbols and ideas were as decisive a part of human development in prehistory as the more muscular principles of natural selection. It took a million years for humankind to get to the point at which culture could achieve preeminence over biology, from which it had never really been separated in the first place, at least over that thousand millennia.

Anthropologist Clifford Geertz (*The Interpretation of Cultures*, [Basic Books, 1973]) puts it this way:

As our central nervous system—and most particularly its crowning curse and glory, the neocortex—grew up in great part in interaction with culture, it is incapable of directing our behavior or organizing our experience without the guidance provided by systems of significant symbols. What happened to us in the Ice Age is that we were obliged to abandon the regularity and precision of detailed genetic control over our conduct for the flexibility and adaptability of a more generalized, though of course no less real, genetic control over it. To supply the additional information necessary to be able to act, we were forced, in turn, to rely more and more heavily on cultural sources—the accumulated fund of significant symbols. Such symbols are thus not mere expressions, instrumentalities, or correlates of our biological, psychological, and social existence; they are prerequisites of it. Without men, no culture, certainly; but equally, and more insignificantly, without culture, no men.

It is encouraging that the cranks are spending so much time squeaking the hinge that joins the Neolithic to civilization, but it is a failure of the imagination to give up the secrets of prehistory to spacemen, especially now, when the elements of the fantastic and the marvelous that were a part of archaic cultures are so urgently needed by a science faced with an incalculably larger universe than it had ever dreamed of. Civilization has narrowed its rationalism so exquisitely to one procedure of thought that a kind of guarantee has been written into its contract: irrational elements of the human personality will be excluded at the cost of one barbarism or another because they will return whether or not they are invited, and their barbarism will either be one that comes as an attack from without (mystical Nazism) or one that emerges insensibly from within the narrowness of reason itself (the atomic bomb).

The dissatisfying aspect of the cranks, then, is not that they are too bizarre or too fantastic but that they aren't fantastic *enough*. All their talk about spacefathers spawning our brainpower is suspiciously similar to the nineteenth-century theological arguments against Darwin that insisted on some sort of supernatural intervention into the evolutionary process to explain the existence of the soul. Now we have intelligence itself accounted for as an injection from the skies.

There is a rationalist's "mythology" invented by Mumford (*Transformations of Man*, [Harper, 1956]) to explain the origins of reason that does more for the imagination than all the crank arguments put together. Mumford sees the quality of reason as deriving, paradoxically, from humankind's irrational capacities: the ability to dream (and to remember the dreams) and the power of the imagination, which are vessels of anxiety, awe, and the "foreconsciousness of death." The power to dream in this case becomes the "forward-moving counterpart to memory" and takes on a planning function that breaks away from the purely adaptive behavior of other animals.

And then, beautifully, ironically, serenely, Mumford plays his ace: sexual desire is the key to the origin of reason because "the erotic impulses play a larger part in men's dreams than sex itself can satisfy," and, as a result, "the dream carries into every act and occupation an image of some further fulfillment, open to his own creation."

Now this "mythology," as Mumford himself refers to it, is not the last word on the question, but it has all the virtues of the ancient art of speculation. It even gives us a way to ponder the question of how intelligence might originate in other worlds. All we have to do is visualize a planet with the necessary fertile fluids and gases, and before long we can see running around on its surface, if it has one, a bunch of oversexed organisms, dreaming dreams that are almost too much for them to handle and planning ways to get rid of all that excess desire. After a million years of fruitful frustration, someone decides to write it down, and before long someone else comes along with an explanation for their mysterious rise out of blind biology into the clarity of reflection: they were abandoned by space-tourists from the Milky Way.

At some point all speculations converge into thin air and are often called novels. But the point here is simply this: when you've explained that the origins of reason are a gift from the outside, you've still got to account for the origins of the intruding reason as well; then the question is quickly sharpened. Unless you devise an explicitly theological explanation, you will have to propose that somewhere, on some planet and in some aeon, reason evolved out of something that was not rational when it started out.

If there was one thing the cranks of the heroic age knew, it was that reason is one moment of many in the harmony of human consciousness and that it won't do to make a fetish of it. Without humor, wonder, or desire, reason becomes an instrument of domination and a club for power. But when it is integrated into the full range and scale of the personality, it is a guide, a mainspring, and coeval source of delight. Science, at this stage of culture, becomes playful.

Charles Fort, our greatest and most playful crank, once put it this way: "There was in these questions an appearance of childishness that attracted my most respectful attention."

Ishmael Reed

Paul Buhle

I felt like starting up a metaphysical bunko squad.
America needs one.

Ishmael Reed

Ishmael Reed, novelist, poet, and editor, comes off as a bitter
man. Christian civilization is definitely his target, along with its
various lay and ecclesiastical, economic, political, and cultural popes
(and lackeys). Now and then Marxists, as well, who are seen as an
extension of that civilization. Sometimes, in passing, even
feminists. "Why are you so mean and hard?" he asks himself in a
1974 essay, and answers, "Because I am an Afro-American male,
the most exploited and feared class in this country." Actually, he
has seen through the facts of his personal existence something
deeper, broader, and more intricately political. As he says, he

*went to the University of Buffalo where I was imbued with Western
culture, myth and ideas. I admired Blake and Yeats, people who
created their own systems, or revived their own national cultures.*

Selected passages reprinted by permission Ishmael Reed © 1972.

*So that's what I wanted to do. When these guys call me avant-garde,
I'm really only using models I learned about in English depart-
ments. I wanted to create a mythology closer to me . . . that's why
I got into Egyptology and Voodoo. . . . Now, if you look at* The
Norton Anthology, *which now goes from Chaucer to me, I'm the
only one in there with Egyptian references. Everybody else is into
European stuff. . . . You should've read what they used to say
when I first came out with these ideas.*

Reed has made it, by this perspective and his skills, as a pulp
heavyweight. But not widely, at any rate, as the political-cultural
revolutionary he most profoundly is. Like Mark Twain, he has a
message, but we want only to laugh.

A literary discussion of Reed's precursors and "school" is
mostly a wasted effort. He writes in places about William Wells
Brown, pioneering nineteenth-century author of *Clothilde* and
about an obscure satirist of the 1930s, Vincent McHugh, whose
Caleb Catlum's America (1936) is one of the most bizarre interpretations of national traditions symbolized in frontier culture. The
celebration of Harlem nightlife in Claude McKay, the careful and
sympathetic observation of Southern blacks' magic rituals in Zora
Neale Hurston's work, the philosophical repose in Ralph Ellison's
legendary account of color and American civilization–all these influences and more are apparent. In an important sense, Reed has
made literary history out of the scraps of popular life that literature
(with a capital "L") almost never took seriously; and he reexamines
them through the pulp literary genres considered in the light of the
present culture. He has all the power of other young black humorists who also surfaced in the late 1960s–Charles Wright, for example, whose *The Wig* (1966) is another too little-known example of
great potential–but Reed went further in placing the narrative at
the service of some larger theoretical scheme and transforming
large segments into stunning prose poems, all the while rolling out
the humor laugh-for-laugh to a climax.

His first novel, *Free-Lance Pallbearers* (1967), grew out of a
Buffalo slum-life setting to lash back at the government poverty
programs of the 1960s. Horror and humor fuse in his description of

the crew around the president Harry Sam: "muscle bound and swaggering attendants carried hand-shaped bottles . . . hooded men with slits for eyes moving their shoulders in a seesaw fashion as they carry trays and towers and boxes of pink tissues." The hapless black protagonist, battered by whites, by his wife, by his neighbors, and by all surrounding circumstances, grows unwittingly to revolutionary stature because he discovers that the "welfare" society cannibalizes the children it can grab. Black nationalism ("rukkus juice and chitlins") is, in itself, no answer: its leaders appear in line with everybody else for the whites' table scraps. The white Left (who publish *Studies on the Flank*) is only vicariously involved in the struggle. Nothing less than the birth of a new generation—those who survive childhood and the collapse of the system—holds any hope.

Reed evolved beyond muck-raking in *Yellow-Back Radio Broke Down* (1969). In part at least, he already had a premonition of the historical reconstruction that America in the 1970s was going to undertake. The "Yellow Back" was a nineteenth-century description of pulp literature; *Yellow-Back* was a rerun of the Western pulp tale with modern stand-ins as well as historical figures. Cowboy star Loop Garoo is a "conjure man," a black magician fighting the traditional corrupters (with all their perversities exposed) across time barriers, like a character in a Capra film gone mad. Loop's straight counterpart, Bo Shmo, was part of the "neo-socialist realist gang" who "had a big reputation in the thirties." He complains:

The trouble with you Loop is that you're too abstract. . . . Crazy dada nigger that's what you are. You are given to fantasy and are off in matters of detail. Far out esoteric bullshit is where you're at. Why in those suffering books that I write about my old neighborhood and how hard it was every gumdrop machine is in place while your work is a blur and a doodle. I'll bet you can't create the differences between a German and a redskin.

What's your beef with me Bo Schmo, if I write circuses? No one said a novel has to be one thing. It can be anything it wants to be, a vaudeville show, the six o'clock news, the mumblings of wild men saddled by demons.

All art must be for the end of liberating the masses. A landscape is only good when it shows the oppressor hanging from a tree.

Right on! Right on, Bo, the henchmen chorused.

That's a measure of what Reed, as a revolutionary, saw himself up against. In *Yellow-Back*, Garoo wins and gives the hippies their paradise to play in, while feminist Amazonians "preferred to do their own thing," and order generally dissolves into a beneficient anarchy of different communities with different styles. Reed later commented that "when a Black writer experiments he gets mugged for it." Irving Howe, reviewing *Yellow-Back*, wrote that it "irresistibly" recalled to him "humor columns in high school papers" and was close to the "commercial cooings of Captain Kangaroo." Even friendly reviews complained of its "gratuitous viciousness," and some young black revolutionaries assailed it as an attack on the Left!

In 1969 Reed clarified his position and laid out a prolegomenon for his future work in a "Neo-HooDoo Manifesto," which he later described as the closest thing to a statement of purpose he was likely to write. Here are some excerpts:

Neo-HooDoo is a "Lost American Church" updated. Neo-HooDoo is the music of James Brown without the lyrics and ads for Black Capitalism. Neo-HooDoo is the 8 basic dances of 19th century New Orleans' Place Congo—the Calinda the Bamboula the Chacta the Bambouille the Conjaille the Juba the Congo and the Voodoo—modernized into the Philly Dog, the Hully Gully, the Funky Chicken, the Popcorn, the Boogaloo and the dance of the great American choreographer Buddy Bradley.

Neo-HooDoos would rather "shake that thing" than be stiff and erect. (There were more people performing a Neo-HooDoo sacred dance, the Boogaloo, at Woodstock than chanting Hare Krishna . . . Hare Hare!) All "Store Front Churches" and "Rock Festivals" receive their matrix in the HooDoo rites of Marie Laveau conducted at New Orleans's Lake Ponchartrain, and Bayou St. John in the 1880s. The power of HooDoo challenged the stability of

Paul Buhle

civil authority in New Orleans and was driven underground where to this day it flourishes in the Black ghettos throughout the country. That's why in Ralph Ellison's modern novel Invisible Man *New Orleans is described as "The Home of Mystery." "Everybody in New Orleans got that thing," Louis Armstrong said once.*

Hoodoo is the strange and beautiful "fits" the Black slave Tituba gave the children of Salem. (Notice the arm waving ecstatic females seemingly possessed at the "Pentecostal," "Baptist," and "Rock Festivals," [all fronts for Neo-HooDoo]). The reason that HooDoo isn't given the credit it deserves in influencing American Culture is because the students of that culture both "overground" and "underground" are uptight closet Jeho-vah revisionists. They would assert the American and East Indian and Chinese thing before they would the Black thing. . . .

Neo-HooDoo is sexual, sensual and digs the old "heathen" good good loving. An Early American HooDoo song says:

> *Now lady I ain't no mill man*
> *Just the mill man's son*
> *But I can do your grinding*
> *till the mill man comes*

Which doesn't mean that women are treated as "sexual toys" in Neo-HooDoo or as one slick Jeho-vah Revisionist recently said, "Victims of a raging hormone imbalance." Neo-HooDoo claims many women philosophers and theoreticians which is more than ugh religions Christianity and its offspring Islam can claim. . . . Neo HooDoo identifies with Julia Jackson who stripped HooDoo of its oppressive Catholic layer—Julia Jackson said when asked the origin of the amulets and Talismans in her studio, "I make all my own stuff. It saves money and it's as good. People who has to buy their stuff ain't using their heads."

Neo-HooDoo is not a church for egotripping—it takes its organization from Haitan VooDoo of which Milo Rigaud wrote:

> *"Unlike other established religions, there is no hierarchy of bishops, archbishops, cardinals or a pope in VooDoo. Each oumphor is a law unto itself, following the traditions of Voo-*

Doo but modifying and changing the ceremonies and rituals in various ways" ("Secrets of VooDoo").

Neo-HooDoo believes that every man is an artist and every artist a priest. You can bring your own creative ideas to Neo-HooDoo. Charlie "yardbird (Thoth)" Parker is an example of the Neo-HooDoo artist as an innovator and improviser.

In Neo-HooDoo, Christ the landlord deity ("render unto Caesar") is on probation. This includes "The Black Christ" and "The Hippie Christ." Neo-HooDoo tells Christ to get lost. (Judas Iscariot holds an honorary degree from Neo-HooDoo.)

Whereas at the center of Christianity lies the graveyard the organ-drone and the cross, the center of Neo-HooDoo is the drum the ankh and the Dance. So Fine, Barefootin', Heard It Through the Grapevine, are all Neo-HooDoos. . . .

"Political leaders" are merely altar boys from Jeho-vah. While the targets of some "revolutionaries" are laundromats and candy stores, Neo-HooDoo targets are TV the museums the symphony halls and churches art music and literature departments in Christianizing (education I think they call it!) universities which propagate the Art of Jeho-vah. Much Byzantine Middle Ages Renaissance painting of Jehovah's "500 years of civilization" as Nixon put it are Jehovah propaganda. Many White revolutionaries can only get together with 3rd world people on the most mundane "political" level because they are Jeho-vah's party and don't know it. How much Black music do so called revolutionary underground radio stations play. On the other hand how much Bach . . . ?

In a poetic stroke, Reed gave the marvelous conception of Negritude a distinctly American perspective (Reed himself says, "Neo-HooDoo ain't Negritude. Neo-HooDoo never been to France"). And he struck harder at Western cultural traditions than any of the contemporary Zensters, to say nothing of the dour, cultureless politicos. Lévi-Strauss has complained that Marxism lacks a steady pivot around which the dialectic moves. Reed has claimed to find that pivot in an irreducibly human potential for a symbiotic-symbolic relationship with nature, the "New Thang" and the oldest thing of all. The combination of this world-old perspective and a sense of the specialness of the New World experience gives Reed the insight for the most astounding combination of humor and philosophy since Twain's later writings. He locates and retranslates popular materials and thereby means to *rejoin* the latent revolutionary aspects of the mass cultural tradition, to shake off the confinements of Old World writing standards, and to realize the implications for literary forms derived as much from movies, television, music, and the other vibrant influences of our times.

All this comes home in *Mumbo Jumbo* (1972), Reed's major "theoretical" work. Reed called it his "straight" book because "I found it necessary to show people that I wasn't one of these 1960s put on people." Just as the purpose of *Yellow-Back* was to complete the cycle of the Western from white racism and pointless violence to race-magic and a universal movement of events, so was *Mumbo Jumbo* to take on the more weighty task of sizing up the "crank" universology of mystics from Madame Blavatsky to Erich von Däniken, to recast it in the shape of the "Neo-HooDoo" mythos, and to create a collage of revolutionary mythology through a specific time period of American history. Reed added to his critique by including drawings and photographs – from medieval prints to 1920s' ads for the Cotton Club to charts of the number of bombs dropped in Vietnam – like the "illustrations" for Breton's *Nadja* or like a crank scientific text.

Reed locates the "great contraries" in world history back to the Egyptian dynasties. On the one side, Osiris, leader of the "Black mud sound," friend of sexuality, boon to agriculture; on the other, Set, who becomes dictator but is humiliated because he can't dance. After innumerable plots, Moses rose to establish civilized (controlled) dancing, a way of meeting the taste of the masses without nourishing their spirit. His misuse of ancient magical texts was a guide to future Western development; and he hid the "Book," Boogie-Woogie equivalent to Lovecraft's *Necronomicon*, which similarly turns up recurrently, threatening to unseat the whole civilization with its "accursed" knowledge. Time passed and Moses' distant successors, the Knights Templar, got hold of the book. Pursued for it, they sought in their gangsterish way to divide their power with the Atonists (Christians) whose coda ends, "Lord, if I can't dance, no one shall." Osiris's successors are the purveyors of the Work; their constant companions are the *Mu'tafukah*, bohemian inhabitants of Sodom and Gomorrah and later scenes.

Reed plunks his forces down in 1920s' Harlem. Transplanted to the West Indies, the force behind Osiris, "Jes Grew," makes ominous advances to the North American mainland. New Orleans is the natural link to the American black experience, and soon the vibrations are being felt across the continent. Harding, known to frequent black parties and rumored to have had a black father, becomes president. Youth culture erupts ("Limbering is the way the youngsters recreate themselves while their elders declaim they cease and desist from this lascivious 'sinful' Buggy-Hugging, this suggestive bumping and grinding, this wild abandoned spooning"). The panic button is hit when news scheduled for suppression gets headlines in a leading New York paper: "VOODOO GENERAL SURROUNDS MARINES AT PORT-AU-PRINCE." While the Knights Templar plot against, then with, the Atonists, who run the country and the police, conjurer Papa LaBas and his Mumbo Jumbo Kathedral continue spreading information, making clear the powers of similarity and analogy in the culture as a whole.

Some of the most critical moments of the novel occur in Reed's description of what he considers appropriate revolutionary activity. While the standard Left piles up tracts, pamphlets, and manifestos, the Work is done through nursery rhymes and science fiction by activists like Buddy Jackson ("while orators and those affected with 'tongues and lungs' were rapping as usual, he sent a convoy to Peekskill and rescued Paul from the Crackers") who are close to the serious popularization undertaken by Marx himself ("Marx came along and removed what was called the ritualistic paraphernalia so that the masses could participate instead of the few") and set out to revive a people (American blacks) in spirit as well as in body. These blacks had their historic sense of humor stolen, had "fallen in love with their own tragedy. Their plays were about bitter, raging members of the 'nuclear family' and their counterpart in art was exemplified by the contorted, grimacing, painful social-realist face. Somebody, head in hands, sitting on a stoop: 'Lawd, I'z so re-gusted.'" But how could they be revived, made to

Paul Buhle

laugh and move in triumph? LaBas is a somber theorist and Old World intellectual. His American followers issue their own solutions: "You ought to relax. That's our genius here in America. We were dumped here on our own without the Book to tell us who the loas are, what we call spirits were. We made up our own. . . . The Blues, Ragtime, the Work that we do is just as good. . . . If your heart's there, that's the thing about the Work. . . . Doing the Work is not like taking inventory."

Or again from the voice of another American activist:

Americans do not know the names of the long and tedious list of deities and rites as we know them. Shorthand is what they know so well . . . they've isolated the unknown factor which gives the loas their rise. . . . Ask those people who be shaking their tambourines impervious of the ridicule they receive from Black and White Atonists, Europe the ghost rattling its chains down the deserted halls of their brains. . . . The dizzying, parodying, punning mischievous pre-Joycean style-play of your Cakewalking, your Calijda, your Minstrelry give and take of the ultra-absurd.

Ultimately, Jes Grew cannot win in this period. The forces of repression are too strong. They put a stop to the removal of "primative" creations from the Museum of Art Detention to their original homes abroad. And, when their choices are narrowed, the rulers move to create the "Depression," "a controlled panic . . . our Panic." Yet the Work cannot be destroyed: shut down publicly by the police, "it will find a home in a band on the Apollo stage, in the store fronts; and there will always be those who will risk the uninformed amusement of their contemporaries by resurrecting what we stood for." It is finally the rhythm of the universe with "no end and no beginning."

Methodologically, Reed confirmed his sweep past the internal controls of the novel as confining art form. He claimed to use "automatic" writing and to listen to voices, psychic entities in touch consonant with black traditions. But the critics seemed almost not to notice. *Mumbo Jumbo* gave Reed new *literary* recognition: front page on the *New York Times Book Review* section, friendly notices in the *New York Review of Books* and elsewhere. Yet there is no evidence that the historic-political content was taken as anything but a particularly well written example of black ranting. (A *Saturday Review* article put it plainly: "With their bubbling imagination and sportive prose, his books can be enjoyed independently of their rather silly ideas.") I have summarized at length because the very opposite seems evident: like the nineteenth-century realist classics that no one would dream of considering politically irrelevant, *Mumbo Jumbo* is essentially a political text. Its message is the supreme literary effort thus far in science fiction or elsewhere to take account of the booming crank universology (whose mainstream contains, as ever, dangerous racist elements that can *only* be combatted imaginatively), and it speaks finally to more than specific incident or specific race.

No one has shown better than Reed himself that method today requires historic and trans-historic evidence, an approach at once poetic and analytic. The moral and economic order of class society – Christianity and capitalism in the West – have had odious results indeed on the general prospects for human survival and happiness. But the people within them have worked with the materials at hand, from gnosticism to trade unionism, locating in negative moments the maximum opportunities for transformation. To push method to its extreme would be, for Reed, to find the hidden relation between those negativities and deeper forces that lay prior to and outside what the business-trained intellectuals call with a straight face "civilization." If the Marxists on the scene would cease to parade their pseudoscientism ("You see, Marxists know all the laws of Nature," writes Reed. "They have the knowledge of the theoretical god of Western philosophy; this is why they can call people and events 'irrelevant' – they're omniscient"), Reed might find it easier to see that the core of that theory intended, at its best moments, to turn history inside out for the sake of a realized "Species Being" that he could call his own.

Three Black Women Writers

C. L. R. James

I have chosen three books to discuss: *Sula,* by Toni Morrison; *Meridian,* by Alice Walker; and *Nappy Edges,* by Ntozake Shange. These three books are by black women, but I didn't choose them because the writers are black women; I chose them because they are very fine black writers. They are first-class writers. I would place *Meridian* and *Nappy Edges* in the forefront of books being published in the United States today. There is another reason why I was particularly interested in these three: they represent a social movement in the United States.

Women all over the world seem to have realized that they have been exploited by men. Marx pointed out many years ago that women were more exploited than the proletariat. (This is a remarkable thing for him to have said.) Now women are beginning to say: "Who and what are we? We don't know. Hitherto we have always tried to fit ourselves into what men and what masculine society required. Now we are going to break through that." These three women have begun to write about black women's daily lives. Black women in America, for hundreds of years, have been scrubbing, sweeping, cleaning, picking up after people; they have been held in the background; kept for sex. And now Toni Morrison, Alice Walker, and Ntozake Shange have taken these black women and made them very visible in American literature. They can't be ignored anymore. So it seems that black people took part in the women's movement, which is not unusual considering their role in other movements in the United States; and they took a part in it which, as I hope to show you, is important not only to blacks but to society as a whole.

I am going to talk about these books one by one, and then I will talk about writing, because that is what you are concerned with; and because it is an important part of the black struggle today.

I will begin with *Sula* by Toni Morrison. *Sula* is a story of black women; this in itself is an unusual topic for an American writer, as far as I know. The story begins with a description of the Bottom, a black slum of the southern town Medallion, and with the story of a World War I soldier who is released from an army hospital while still having problems with hallucinations, who is arrested for his peculiar behavior, and who is finally sent home to the Bottom, which he has not seen since going into the army. He seems to be crazy and doesn't know what has happened to him. He establishes an annual holiday in the Bottom called National Suicide Day; on this day every year it's acceptable for people to let out their anger and their violence. He lives alone and generally celebrates the holiday alone. He supports himself by catching fish twice a week and selling them. This is how the book begins. It begins this way to register that the people in it, and the work they do, and the life they lead, are not normal. But this is the life of the vast majority in the South; from 1971, when the book was published, until this very day.

We are introduced to two girls: Sula and Nell. They are very good friends. The level of their lives is low, and they go through much together. There is something harmonious between them. They are not separated even by the accidental death of a small boy who drowns while playing with them; even by the bizarre incinerations of two of the people Sula lives with. They grow up around and in spite of the daily poverty and tragedy. Nell gets married to a man named Jude. Sula sees that he is a handsome, hardworking, well-meaning young man. She helps with the wedding and reception, and then leaves town.

Ten years pass between the wedding in 1927 and the beginning of the next chapter. Nell is still with Jude; they are living well and have two or three children. Sula returns well dressed, sophisticated, and college-educated. She and Nell seek to rediscover their friendship, but Sula is unable to accommodate herself to the old society. One day, Nell comes home to find Sula and Jude together in the bedroom, and Jude leaves Nell that day. Sula does not particularly want Jude; she begins sleeping with other men in the town and is further distanced from the townspeople. At one point, she becomes really attached to a man; but it is then, of course, that he leaves her.

Sula and Nell see each other only once more in their lives. In 1940 Sula becomes seriously ill, and Nell visits to offer help. She finally asks, "Why did you do it? . . . We were friends. . . . And you didn't love me enough to leave him alone. To let him love me. You had to take him away."

To which Sula replies, "What you mean take him away? I didn't kill him, I just fucked him. If we were such good friends, how come you couldn't get over it?" As Nell is leaving, she asks, "How do you know . . . who was good? . . . I mean maybe it wasn't you. Maybe it was me."

After Nell leaves, Sula dies. At the end of the book, at Sula's grave, Nell comes to a significant and painful realization: that it is not Jude but Sula whom she has missed so much in the year since they all parted.

This is a fantastic book. Now I want to quote a particularly significant passage from the chapter just following Sula's return to Bottom:

It had surprised her a little and saddened her a good deal when Nell behaved the way the others would have. Nell was one of the reasons she had drifted back to Medallion, that and the boredom she found in Nashville, Detroit, New Orleans, New York, Philadelphia, Ma-

*con, and San Diego. All those cities held the same people, working
the same mouths, sweating the same sweat. The men who took her
to one or another of those places had merged into one large personality: the same language of love, the same entertainments of love,
the same cooling of love. Whenever she introduced her private
thoughts into their comings or goings, they hooded their eyes. They
taught her nothing but love tricks, shared nothing but worry, gave
nothing but money. She had been looking all along for a friend, and
it took her a while to discover that a lover was not a comrade and
could never be—for a woman. And that no one would ever be that
version of herself which she sought to reach out to and touch with
an ungloved hand. There was only her own mood and whim, and
if that was all there was, she decided to turn the naked hand toward
it, discover it and let others become as intimate with their own
selves as she was. (104–5)*

Now, this black woman has gone to all of these important
places in the United States, found them to be no good, and gone
back to Medallion. That is a very bold thing to write about. She tells
us why Sula returns—because everywhere she goes the men and
the problems and the emptiness with them are always the same.
The important thing about that is that it could, and would, be said
by women on every level of society in the world today; from the
highest to the lowest. This woman could not find a man who would
treat her as a human being, and she got tired of it and went back
to her hometown. So on the one hand, friendship between women,
which is so often ignored, is really of great importance; and on the
other hand, no matter how hard she tries, she finds that friendship
with a man is impossible.

Now we come to *Meridian*, by Alice Walker, whom I have
found to be one of the finest writers in the United States. Near the
beginning of the book, Meridian is told by a group of her friends that
she can join the movement only if she decides that she can kill for
the Revolution. Meridian is not so sure about this; she is willing to
die but not to kill. It goes against her upbringing and her heart. She
goes off on her own to work and live with the people in the South.
The story goes on and Meridian becomes very involved with a black

man named Truman, who eventually becomes involved with a white woman named Lynne. The personal, sexual, and racial interrelations of these three characters and the context of the civil rights movement are treated very well indeed. They have a lot of difficulties. Again we have a picture of the significance of friendship between women:

As they sat they watched a television program. One of those Southern epics about the relationship of the Southern white man to madness, and the closeness of the Southern black man to the land. It did not delve into the women's problems, black or white. They sat, companionable and still in their bathrobes, watching the green fields of the South and the indestructable (their word) faces of black people much more than they watched the madness. For them, the madness was like a puzzle they had temporarily solved (Meridian would sometimes, in the afternoons, read poems to Lynne by Margaret Walker, and Lynne, in return, would attempt to cornrow Meridian's patchy short hair), they hungered after more intricate and enduring patterns. Sometimes they talked, intimately, like sisters, and when they did not they allowed the television to fill the silences. (173)

This is tremendous. These two women have quarreled over a black man; he has gone with both of them and generally made a mess of things; but they have become friends. This is beautifully expressed. This is a serious and difficult topic; not many books deal with the relationship of a black man and a white woman or even with two women getting together and understanding each other. This is an astonishing thing, but it is not the most astonishing thing in the book by far.

Another part of the book makes it one of the most extraordinary I have ever read. A young man has been killed; a black church is having a service for him, to help his father and so on. Meridian is there, and as she follows the service, and hears the people singing, suddenly, after all her troubles, she comes to this conclusion:

There was a reason for the ceremony she had witnessed in the church. . . . The people . . . were saying to the red-eyed man that

*his son had not died for nothing, and that if his son should come
again they would protect his life with their own. "Look," they were
saying, "we are slow to awaken to the notion that we are only as
other women and men, and even slower to move in anger, but we
are gathering ourselves to fight for and protect what your son fought
for on behalf of us. If you will let us weave your story and your
son's life and death into what we already know—into the songs, the
sermons, the 'brother and sister'—we will soon be so angry we cannot help but move. Understand this," they were saying, "the church"
(and Meridian knew they did not mean simply "church," as in Baptist, Methodist or whatnot, but rather communal spirit, togetherness, righteous convergence), "the music, the form of worship that
has always sustained us, the kind of ritual you share with us, these
are the ways to transformation that we know. We want to take this
with us as far as we can." . . . She understood, finally, that the respect she owed her life was to continue against whatever obstacles,
to live it, and not to give up any particle of it without a fight to the
death, preferably not her own. And that this existence extended beyond herself to those around her because, in fact, the years in
America had created them One Life. . . . Meridian's dedication to
her promise did not remain constant. Sometimes she lost it altogether. . . . But at other times her dedication . . . came back
strongly. . . . On those occasions such was her rage that she actually felt as if the rich and racist of the world should stand in fear
of her, because she—though apparently weak and penniless, a little
crazy and without power—was yet of resolute and relatively fear-
less character, which, sufficient in its calm acceptance of its own
purpose, could bring the mightiest country to its knees. (199–201)*

In other words, these people did not need to be trained or
taught Marxism; these black people in this Southern church had
built up a sense of community, and of right and wrong, so strong
that if the need came, they would join any revolutionary movement
that intended to kill those who were oppressing them. This is a major problem, this feeling that there are certain people who are
revolutionaries but that the great mass of the population is, rather,
filled with God and Christ. Alice Walker shows instead that they,

in their church, with what they have learned there, with their togetherness, with the songs they have sung, and their beliefs, would be ready to join anything to overthrow the mightiest nation on earth: to overthrow the United States. Whether you agree or not, it is a tremendous notion and a successful book.

I lived in the United States for 25 years, and I had no idea that this kind of community could be established in the Southern black churches; but, of course, this was the source of Dr. King's power. It would not be the same in the West Indies. The black church does not have the same role to play, because the bishop of Trinidad is a black man, his son is a member of the revolutionary trade union movement; the result is that blacks do not feel that terrific separation and persecution which has driven blacks in the South to form those churches. The black church also could not have the same revolutionary significance in Britain.

The friendship between women; the impossibility of women getting on with men, as long as men see them chiefly as sexual instruments; the church; the lowest levels of black life in America; these black women are arriving at conclusions that are filling the minds of the most advanced and serious-minded people today.

There is a poem called "Advice," by Ntozake Shange, and it's from her book, *Nappy Edges*.

She says, "I am a poet, and I'm going to be a poet." It can't be better stated, and she says it for you and me and other people; a person who is not educated can easily understand what she writes. She is a very serious and a very funny woman. She can also be very mad. *With No Immediate Cause* is, I think, her finest poem.

She is telling me things that I had no idea of. I read these things in the paper and I pass on, but she says: "It happened to me. That man over there who served me coffee, he might have done it." She makes it personal. She doesn't speak about "it" in general, like a politician; she says, "It happened not to the public in general but to me, and that's what I think about it." Only first-class poets write this way.

I want to say a few words to writers. You must be able to write what you think—and maybe in what you write about your day-to-day, everyday, commonplace, ordinary life will be some of the same problems that the people of the world are fighting out. You must be able to write what you have to say and know that that is what matters; and I hope you can see that you can begin anywhere and end up going as far as anybody else has gone. I hope you are not scared to write about what concerns you, what you know — these things are important.

Write what you have to say, and think about it. Read as much as you can, and don't limit yourself. Gather knowledge. Copy down a phrase that strikes you or a passage that matters. But when you sit down to write something, concentrate on it. That is my advice. Concentrate on it and read it over. And even if it takes you two weeks, you have to settle down and get it right. That is the way to write poetry. But the point is to express your knowledge — to concentrate on special writing.

A Writer's Comment

Marge Piercy

In the 1960s, the cultural work I did was treated by everyone around me as inconsequential and therefore tended to be pushed to the side of the organizing I did, the standard movement office work, the meetings, the writing of pamphlets, the power-structure research. In general, political people in the United States do not express much respect for fiction and only slightly more for poetry. If they have any interest in literature, their taste was usually formed by what they were taught to admire in Departments of English and has not broadened since. Therefore their taste tends either to the naive (Howard Fast fiction) or to the traditional canon of British-oriented modernists.

Most of the time my political comrades viewed my writing in the 1960s as self-indulgence. I can hardly remember any encouragment to such pursuits, although people did like to hear readings and were willing to use readings to raise money. The big change for me came in the strong importance the women's movement placed and places on cultural work. For the first time in years of being active politically, I found myself respected for the work I did, even though what I write always remains controversial within as well as outside the movement.

The women's movement has encouraged cultural work and has also provided a home for thinking and working on the relationship between form and content, between tradition and oppression, between invention and communication. Mostly I have found that people on the Left relate to the poetry more readily and to the novels more slowly, generally two or three behind where I am now. That is, *Dance the Eagle to Sleep* became visible to the Left after *Small Changes*, and *Small Changes* got respectable as a political document only in the last couple of years. Feminists and even futurists picked up *Woman on the Edge of Time* about two years ahead of the rest of the Left; and the only serious attention *The High Cost of Living* has had as a novel about class is in England.

Whenever a novel comes out, it always has the wrong line, fails to contain the moment's slogans, disturbs because it has sex in it—too much sex or the wrong brand of sex—or the characters aren't heroic and simpleminded enough. Fiction seems especially disturbing to political people. Maybe it's a puritan attitude: lies, all lies. What do you want to go around inventing stories for? Is that a good way for a responsible adult to behave? When I think about how the next novel will be received—*Vida*, which is about a political fugitive—I can hear the reviews in advance. Ripping over the underground. She isn't perfect. None of them are perfect. You have written once again about humans. Ugh.

Because I have a very strong sense of what I'm doing, I persist in my dumb way. Fiction that strokes our wish fulfillment evaporates like popsicles with a little sticky wet stain and leaves nothing useful behind. We have to be willing to support art that hurts us, shakes us, moves us into more awareness—not less. I do not believe that reading about the amazing exploits of protagonists without flaws or hesitations or errors helps us to live our lives more usefully.

A lot of what I lived through in the 1960s is inspiring to me, that molten and organic sense of community for instance, the willingness to try to move past the nuclear family and possessiveness and rigidity. The beauty in daily things. I learned a lot about how we learn and grow in crises and stress, how we act when confronted with danger, what keeps us from working together and trusting each other. I know that a lot of what I express in my hopeful vision is based on experiences then that were powerful and moving.

Envoi: Humor as Popular Culture Wisdom

Maurice Kish *The Funeral of an Undertaker*

Humor's Magic History

Paul Buhle

Why do we care about the history of humor? Because when we laugh, something mysterious happens. We step outside the civilized boundaries of polite conversation. We recall a primordial impulse. Like sexuality, the context of humor changes. But when we pull back the covers, a lot of the action smells and feels the same. To try and understand the meaning can be a stifling exercise. Who wouldn't rather watch five good minutes of a Marx Brothers film than read a turgid academic analysis? But we need to seek out the element in our humanity that wants a laugh as much as an orgasm. Everything we have been, everything we might become is now endangered. To recall the strengths and truths of humor from the darkest recesses of our collective history is to help us go on living, so that we may one day laugh with a relief and a happiness that we have never laughed with before.

Comics are the first and last magicians of human history. The Winnebago had a cycle of old, old stories about them. They have magical powers (one of which is voluntary androgyny) but seem stupid about the most obvious things. And, notoriously, they will do anything for a laugh. Finally, a disgusted Deity says about the comic, "You are the oldest of all those I have created. . . . I made you a sacred person . . . you became the butt of everyone's jest. . . . You, although you were given the greatest of powers, made light of my creation." Comics are so unruly that order cannot be established among the peoples and animals of the earth until they die. According to Jung, their mythic origins must be pushed back to the dawn of the society. They are the "forerunner of the savior, and, like him, God, man, and animal at once," both subhuman and superhuman, and above all, *unconscious of moral restraints*.

The Greek joker offers a more intellectualized version. Hermes, the father of alchemy, becomes the mythic keeper of the great secrets from some lost age. He was invented by Hellenic settlers in Alexandria and rather logically merges with the Egyptian deity Thoth, so he is very ancient, even by the standards of the age. According to the recent illumination of Ishmael Reed, Osiris-Thoth had been the fun god, agriculturalist and musician, believer in the "black mud sound" of fertility and rhythm. The ultimate source of hedonist, freelove, guiltless heresies that pester organized religions of repression even today; and the formulator of the "hermetic" mysteries which defy Aristotelean (or Thomist) rationalism and predict dialectical logic. The real-life punster of Greek antiquity, by the way, was Heraclitus, the most famous dialectician till Hegel and Marx.

Jung says that civilization pushes these myths into the background but cannot get away from the shadow they cast because they represent an undifferentiated consciousness we are unable to forget. The source of freedom, and of its child imagination, remains dark, evil and good mixed together and seen through symbol, vision, revelation. If magic can, as the mystics insist, be seen as the original state of nature, humor infallibly offers the expression that is beyond the power of reason (but not beyond the power of the enlightened mind) to comprehend.

Class society conflicts bring humor into action. Oracles, blessed with a special relation to the spirits, deliver extemporaneous gag lines that literally drive violators of the common code to madness, shame, or death. Some scholars think the Druids should

be seen as humor-priest-hitmen. Organized bands of women definitely had a presence, heir to the spiritual powers that nature-
religions, gnosticism, and alchemy attribute to them. Fragmentary
evidence, like the *Song of Deborah* partially preserved in the Old
Testament, shows satiric attack wields the golden sword in the
name of a vision of the just society lost somewhere in the past:
Agrarian communalism that had once existed in ancient Israel? A
neolithic age (Lewis Mumford once suggested) of harmony under
the sign of the goddess and peaceful agriculture? Or that primal
state of consciousness where the mythic god-man-animal signaled
the proximity nature retained to subjectivity—the moment of a
potential evolutionary leap into higher magic that humans did not
take and have ever after longed to achieve? Perhaps the distinction
is not so important. In any case, humorists went on the attack in the
name of someplace outside the existing civilization. Indian culture
reminds us of this other place because the "duplexity," fool and shaman, remain alive in the joker. "The clown's behavior is a vivifica-
tion of his knowledge of *another* reality," Jamake Highwater says.
As we move through class society toward self-annihilation, humor
reminds us of what we may have been and what we may yet become, if only we can set ourselves free.

From the outset, humor faces tremendous repression. Because its militants resisted and mocked the emerging rulers—the
program of expanded exploitation—dangerous humor became perhaps the first ideological enemy of the state. History records the
forced dispersion of organized humorists, in the Middle East, in Europe, in Ireland, and elsewhere, by means of torture, banishment,
execution—especially when the humorists were women. Christianity (Ishmael Reed calls it "atonism") had an especially vicious
role, perhaps because "the laughing Jesus" was one of the major he-
retical claims of the occult and revolutionary Gnostics. A Jesus who
joked had to be a kind of conjurer himself, a leader of a mystic
brother- and sisterhood that would never accept the state religion
preached in his name or the accompanying repression of women's
sexuality after his own erotic embrace (the Gnostic texts imply) of
Mary Magdalene. Christianity had to suppress the revolutionary
elements within its religious background as well as in economics

and politics. It succeeded not only because it wielded state power but because the magic powers of the shaman and the humor hit-squad had already fled. The humorist could threaten only a reputation.

Still, the victory could not be unequivocal. Christianity had to absorb the pagan religions in its path. And when unrest surged up internally, by the twelfth century, it had to give ground, at least symbolically, to the periodical display of mass satire upon everything considered holy. For at least several feast days of the year, peasants and townsfolk elected their own "fools' pope," performed masquerades dressed as animals and mummers, sang ribald songs in the choir, did the dirty boogy in Church, and even brought in a donkey symbolizing Christ and brayed back at his invocations. These customs seem to have ended only at the dawn of the real revolution, Radical Reformation. In any case, the reversal of existing sacred values reminds us of the hayoka, who rides his horse backward; or the funeral mourners at Thelonius Monk's commemoration who wore their hats instead of taking them off in honor of the reversal that Monk had made the philosophical statement of his jazz. The duplexity of life and the consciousness of another and unseen dimension retain a presence for the shaman's shadow.

The Renaissance, the rising European bourgeoisie, the spread of world-scale empire all had the effect of further diminishing folkish humor. In the rising official art, the blood and bowels of human existence, grotesque realism and its cousin, fantastic humor, almost vanished from sight, preserved for the "low humor" mostly used to humiliate women, lower classes or races, and perceived outsiders in the region, group, or nation. Rabelais spoke with the voice of the collective past but to no avail. Real humor could no more be entirely eliminated than could the lower-class oral culture be eradicated without genocide against the people who did the work in society. The individual humorist, playwright, or graphic artist could almost always get along with some artful dodging. The rich and powerful enjoy a good joke, even upon themselves – within limits. But the fact that raw humor had steadily been deprived of its legitimacy had implications in style and content. The jokester who could not transform jests into formal art would get no respect; unlike the poet, who languished financially with at least the illusions of a sacred mission, the humorist internalized his insignificance by avowing harmlessness. This was the making of the anything-for-a-laugh hack.

The appearance of the urban-industrial modern order in the nineteenth century, the ability of working people to spend some money to get entertainment they enjoyed, added another contradiction. The theater, cheap books and periodicals, movies, radio, and television would require a mass audience and, by the same token, needed images that would be readily understood and loved. At the same time, the commercial control of the media both restricted the content and corrupted the contributors—writers, actors, and directors. The contradiction hit no group harder than it did the humorists. They had, and have, a popularity unsurpassed by any other creative sector. But they continue to be looked down on as the bastard children of civilized life. Burt Metcalfe, executive producer of M*A*S*H, said recently that he had the feeling that as far as critical attention went, he and his group might as well be producing some local show. On the other hand, Woody Allen strives desperately to imitate the famous cinema auteurs of the century, afraid he will go down in entertainment history as a mere clown. Many of the great figures, rising out of the masses in some developmental, flexible period of a medium, soon get away from their roots and spend the bulk of their careers imitating their own early creations. Others—Phil Silvers comes to mind—are simply crushed by the pressures of becoming stars, cut off from their live following.

And still the popular culture of humor remains, from the cartoonist on the local labor paper and the stand-up comic in the sleaziest club to the comedian at the topmost level of stardom, tremendously dynamic. Moments of intense pressure upon the society bring forth comedic talents and forms no one anticipates. The strivings of racial and ethnic groups for recognition place fresh candidates in the spotlight; their struggle for existence and dignity has promoted a vigorous if little-appreciated minority comedy in the popular culture shadows. The longer that commercial culture with all its variants dominates society, the more something else very important takes place. An awareness of our culture as history spreads

---

249

Paul Buhle

from the audience to the comic and back again. A new stage is reached, where the prophetic role of humor stands once more front and center.

Red-hot humor has the same message it has always had. The *Stark Fist*, the newsletter of the Church of the Sub-Genius, warns, "If you don't want to broil your brains in the zombie business corridors of empty pinkness OR grinding poverty, if you don't want to feel the meat cook off your bones in a nuclear oven that was once your HOME TOWN, you had better drop your mental candy bars and step out under the blinding light of the sun and make witness to what you REALLY ARE." To separate ourselves from the illusions of appearance is a revolutionary act because we are enabled to return to our real essence, living at a definite point in historic evolution and also living in our biological frame, the age-old *Homo Sapiens*. Humor has seen the truth behind the lies in the ascendance of sex domination, class society, institutionalized religion, the state, official art, and mass commercial culture. If the superpowers show their bankruptcy day by day, if religions go haywire, if the patriarchal family slips, then mass culture begins to turn in upon itself, and humor approaches a new stage.

We are moving toward the collective satire-struggle of the original political humorists; we will soon be taking up conjuring. When we look toward the collapse of the system, the bigger jokes in history or pre-history germinate in the back of our minds. "I guess you can compare it with dying," Imogene Coca said about comedy, "If nothing goes right, you die." The magician's work extends nature's organic powers to enrich life. We fight on the side of life against the death machines, knowing that our humor-spells may yet turn back the course of destruction and help to bring humankind to its full, unrealized potential.

Keynote Address to Radical Humor Festival, New York University, 1982.

Me and My Feminist Humor: All Alone and Feeling Blue

Catherine Clinton

Me: Listen, you wanna hear a good joke?

My: Is it sexist?

Me: I don't know. Anyway, there was this nun, see, and she . . .

Me: Listen, it sounds sexist, so let's just drop it.

Me: You have no sense of humor.

My: Yes, I do. I have a perfectly good sense of humor, I just don't choose to laugh at the degradation of women, and furthermore . . .

Me: Furthermore, you have no sense of humor. You got a great sense of irony, but no jokes.

My: Irony is frequently the weapon of powerless people facing impossible odds.

Me: Smiling through the footprints on your face.

My: Jokes are the staple of feebleminded businessmen who have no television sports show to watch.

Catherine Clinton

Me: Jokes are fine, you just have no sense of humor.

My: Listen, listen, you just gotta get it out of your head that women aren't funny.

Me: No, men are just as easy to laugh at as women.

My: I don't want to laugh at anybody, I want to laugh **with** them.

Me: But you've got to *make* them laugh first. Humor is assaultive – "poking fun at," "pulling someone's leg," "leave 'em rolling in the aisles," "knock 'em dead."

My: Sounds more like Little Big Horn than a comedy routine. Humor is what you make of it and some things just aren't funny.

Me: Like the moron who bought barbed wire to take to his fencing class.

My: No, that's pretty funny, but isn't that a Polish joke?

Me: No, it's a joke, and it doesn't matter who tells it about whom. Like the new resort in Guyana – Club Dead.

My: Now, wait a minute, that's disgusting.

Me: Perversity is just a heartbeat away from a joke. You must astonish, disarm, and, if necessary, sicken with surprise.

My: That's just plain nauseating.

Me: If you'd only develop a sense of humor maybe the women's movement would get more of a following.

My: Like asking feminist comics to perform in Vegas with showgirls on stage behind them? Like asking Gloria Steinem to "drop trou" at a press conference on abortion?

Me: It's better than singing the "Coathanger Blues."

My: I won't put up with any more of this hideous, misogynist . . .

Me: Listen, women have the power to develop their own humor. We've created our own culture, but we're too timid to exploit our resources and too smart not to recognize our own talent.

My: But what are our resources if we continue to mock and ridicule ourselves?

Me: Humor can be defensive as well. Better I should make fun of myself than some pig. Besides, we should go after men not other women.

My: Too much of our time is spent concentrating on men.

Me: And too much of their time is spent thinking about us, but let's just begin at the beginning, haul ass and launch a campaign to do men in at their own racket. Forget the ERA, start an Equal Wrongs Amendment!

My: Bring back bound feet! We'll have a whalebone of a time . . .

Me: But I can see where men provide as much of a butt for jokes as women—

My: *But* the butt is who's the ewe and who's the ram and who's doing the butting. Women have to develop their own comedy, their own targets.

Me: I, for one, am sick of these too-flip hipsters who rumble up to me and say: "Baby, you're fascinated by me." Whereupon I reply, "Drop dead." To which he responds: "Now I *know* you're crazy about me." By the time you've called the cops they're still convinced of their irresistability all on account of you haven't stabbed them with your nail file, a technique they've no doubt learned to interpret as, "I'm into S and M."

My: At least they're refreshingly blunt. The late sixties provided us with a new and even more terrible speciman: male feminist on the make. Women's movements get cluttered with sensitive guys all dying to get laid. They tell you of the oppression of being an oppressor, work themselves up into a good cry, fry you some vegetables in their wok, recite a few Sylvia Plath poems, and they expect to slide you onto their waterbed. There ought to be a law, if not a penalty kick.

Me: What if you fall for a line? Maybe you're *not* falling, you know you're leaping, and you wake up next to some fatuous zombie who wants to know what attracted you to him.

My: Tell him "Nothing, I was just desperate."

Me: But isn't that playing by men's rules?

My: As rules go, they're the only rules. Anyway, you're just practicing up on your honesty instead of on your feminine wiles.

Me: Truth with a ring around the collar.

My: You're still hung up on what these bastards think about you. It's like drinking Drano, you've got to stop it. Reassess, Reevaluate, Revolt.

Me: I was never much good at volting . . .

My: Don't worry as much about waking up next to a chauvinist, as watching one get more pay for less work and an endless supply of smugness.

Me: Maybe women need to start a reclamation program for ego and arrogance.

My: Hang on to your id and let the arrogance goose-step by.

Me: You seem to have worked out all the answers.

My: No, just the problems.

Me: Like husbands who don't want their wives to work but want them to spend their days cleaning, cooking, scrubbing, vacuuming, lugging groceries, picking up dry cleaning, and other unpaid jobs.

My: Like husbands who *want* their wives to work and spend their nights and weekends cleaning, cooking . . .

Me: Like men who don't want their wives having abortions because they want an equal say in the reproductive process. Next thing you know they'll be denying their wives anesthetics so their sons can enjoy a totally natural childbirth.

My: What's worse are the men who happily allow wives and lovers to ingest tons of cancerous, blood-clotting pills so they can have child-free lovemaking.

Me: Cancer-free lovemaking involves women taking the risks, responsibilities, and the rap as well. What about rape?

My: You mean every woman's fantasy of sexual violence. Please, let's not even go into that can of spermatic delusions.

Me: Well, this has been a laugh a minute.

My: Ghetto humor has never been more than a real scream.

Me: Do you really think women are still in a ghetto in 1979?

My: Only five years from 1984, and look around. Check out a secretarial pool, visit a suburban supermarket, observe just about anything to do with children: sexual segregation will slap you up one side of your face and down the other.

Me: But is segregation necessarily bad?

My: Was slavery all that terrible? Especially if you have to live with the enemy.

Me: But men aren't our enemies.

My: They're enemies until proven allies.

Me: Isn't that the opposite of our system of justice?

My: Justice is "just-us-men."

Me: Hey, that's pretty funny.

My: Right, this is supposed to be a comedy dialogue.

Me: But you wouldn't even let me tell my joke.

My: On that note, I think I'll just finish up with a feminist joke.

Me: Like the three great lies: The check is in the mail, one size fits all, and I won't come in your mouth.

My: Too old-fashioned. This is hot off the pages of the *Village Voice*. Did you hear the story of the two morons who saved up all their pay to spend on a big weekend in New York City? So they showed up at Port Authority with their life savings, and before they could get outside to the street, they'd been swindled out of all their money. Pimps, con men and rip-off artists. So one guy says to the other, "What are we going to do? We're here in New York with only a dollar thirty-eight to our names. How can we have a good time?" So the other moron takes the money and goes into a store and comes out with a little brown paper bag. And the guy says, "What's that?" So the other guy says, "Don't worry, I've saved the day. We're going to have a great weekend." Then he pulls a box of Tampax out of the bag. So the first guy says, "Are you kidding, what can we do with that?" And the moron replies, "We can do anything we want. We can go swimming, sailing, horseback riding . . . "

Me and My: Th-th-that's all, folks!

Contributors

Contributors

Mary Bufwack, formerly an associate professor of anthropology at Colgate University, currently works at a YWCA in Nashville, Tennessee.

Catherine Clinton, an assistant professor of history at Harvard University, is author of *The Plantation Mistress: Women's World in the Old South.*

R. Crumb, a founder of underground comics, lives in Winters, California, and draws for *Weirdo* magazine.

Daniel Czitrom, an associate professor of history at Mt. Holyoke College, is the author of *Media and the American Mind, from Morse to McLuhan.*

Ann D. Gordon is director of the Elizabeth Cady Stanton and Susan B. Anthony Project at Smith College.

Bill Griffith, creator of *Zippy Comics*, lives and works in San Francisco.

Sam Hunting, a former factory worker, is now a writer in Cambridge, Massachusetts.

Contributors

C. L. R. James, a famed cricket critic since the 1930s, is author of the semiautobiographical study of the game, *Beyond a Boundary*, among many other works on history, philosophy, and politics.

Angela Keil and **Charles Keil** are musicologists in Buffalo, New York. Charles Keil is author of *Urban Blues* and *Tiv Song*.

Philip Lamantia, a surrealist since the 1940s, is author of *Touch of the Marvelous* and *Selected Poems, 1943–1966*, among other works.

George Lipsitz, an associate professor of American studies at the University of Minnesota, is author of *Class and Culture in Cold War America: "A Rainbow at Midnight."*

David Marc, an assistant professor of American studies at Brandeis University, is author of *Demographic Vistas* and a frequent contributor to the *Village Voice*.

Barbara Melosh, curator of medical sciences, National Museum of American History, Smithsonian Institution, and associate professor of English and American studies at George Mason University, is author of *"The Physician's Hand": Work, Culture and Conflict in American Nursing.*

Jim Murray, current editor-publisher of *Cultural Correspondence*, lives and works in New York City.

James P. O'Brien, a longtime editor of the journal *Radical America*, is a freelance editor in Somerville, Massachusetts.

Bob Oermann is a writer for the *Nashville Tennessean*.

Nancy Joyce Peters, codirector of City Lights Books in San Francisco, is coeditor of *Literary San Francisco*.

Marge Piercy, novelist and poet, is author of many works, including *Vida* and, most recently, *Gone to Soldiers*.

Franklin Rosemont, who formed the first surrealist group in the United States, is editor of the journal *Arsenal/Surrealist Subversion*. His books include *The Haymarket Scrapbook* and anthologies of writings and art by Andre Breton, Isadora Duncan, Mary Marcy, and IWW cartoonist Ernest Riebe.

James Spady, economist and historian, is author of *Negritude, PanBanegritude and the Diopan Philosophy of History, William Leo Hansbery: The Legacy of an African Hunter*, and other studies. He has long been associated with the Black History Museum in Philadelphia.

Bob Schneider is a freelance writer in New York City.

The late **Michael E. Starr** was a historian at Hiram College, Ohio.

Dave Wagner is an editor at the *Phoenix* (Arizona) *Gazette*.

Name Index

Name Index

Adams, Frederick Upham, 28
Adorno, Theodor, xv, xvi, xx, xxiv
Aleichem, Sholom, 40
Alexis, Jacques Stephen, 113
Allen, A. A., 164, 165
Allen, Woody, 249
Anderson, Bill, 85, 87, 89
Anderson, Liz, 96
Anderson, Perry, xxv
Arbuckle, Fatty, 15
Arkoff, Samuel Z., 181
Arnold, Matthew, xii, xiii
Ayrton, William, 13

Bakhtin, Mikhail, xi
Bakunin, Mikhail Aleksandrovich, 177
Baldwin, James, 115–16
Baraka, Amiri, 116
Bare, Bobby, 89
Barks, Carl, 132
Baum, L. Frank, 28
Baxter, Sylvester, 29
Beard, Mary Ritter, 46–51

Bee, Claire, 54
Bellamy, Edward, 16, 17, 26–37
Benjamin, Walter, xi
Benny, Jack, 158
Bergen, Fanny D., 49
Bergier, Jaques, 211
Berle, Milton, 157, 159
Bewley, Marius, 23
Bierce, Ambrose, 24
Binder, Otto, 211
Black, Jeanne, 97
Blackbeard, Bill, 121
Blake, William, 131, 222
Blavatsky, Madame Helena Petrovna, 29, 228
Blazonszyk, Eddie, 81
Bono, Sonny, 169
Boone, Daniel, 23
Boone, Pat, 170, 172
Bosch, Hieronymous, 110
Botkin, B. A., 48
Bowes, Margie, 97
Bradbury, Ray, 208

Name Index

Name Index

Hughes, Langston, xiv
Hugo, Victor, 31
Humbard, Rex, 169
Humphrey, Hubert, 186
Hurston, Zora Neale, 223
Husserl, Edmund, xxi

Irving, Washington, 31

Jackson, Aunt Molly, 95
Jackson, Julia, 226
Jackson, Reggie, 184
Jackson, Wanda, 96
Jagiello, Li'l Wally, 81
James, C. L. R., xxi, xxii, 21
James, Henry, 199
James, Tommy, 84
James, Willis, 113
Jameson, Fredric, xxiv
Jaurès, Jean, 29
Jean, Norma, 97
Jefferson, Blind Lemon, 110
Jessel, George, 97, 157
Jolson, Al, 158
Jones, Ernest, 154
Jones, George, 92, 97
Joplin, Janis, 84, 102-7
Jory, Victor, 142
Jung, Carl, 246

Karloff, Boris, 155
Keil, Angela, 75
Keil, Charles, 75
Kelley, Florence, 29
Kelly, Walt, 132
Kesey, Ken, 57
Kibbee, Jeff, 191
Kierkegaard, Søren, 122
King, Edward, 41
King, Frank, 132
Klein, Paul, 186
Knight, Damon, 198
Kovacs, Ernie, xvi
Krader, Lawrence, 208
Kroeber, A. L., 208-9
Kropotkin, Prince Petr Alecksevich, 32
Kubek, Tony, 184

Kuhlmann, Kathryn, 164
Kurtzman, Harvey, xvi, 132, 133

Lang, Fritz, 177
Lardner, Ring, 68
Lazarsfeld, Paul, xvi, xviii
Le Guin, Ursula K., 205-9
Lear, Norman, 156, 174, 187
Leary, Timothy, 176, 186
Ledford, Lily May, 95
Lehrer, Tom, xvi
Lembeck, Harvey, 160
Lennon, John, x
Lero, Etienne, 113
Leslie, Eliza, 46
Lévi-Strauss, Claude, 215, 227
Lewis, Jerry Lee, 169
Lewis, Matthew, 23, 150
Lippard, George, 25
London, Jack, 25, 29
Longfellow, Henry Wadsworth, 3
Longstreet, Augustus, 23
Lovecraft, H. P., 24, 208, 212, 214, 228
Lugosi, Bela, 151
Lush, Marion, 81
Lynn, Loretta, 97-100

Mantle, Mickey, 183-85
Marconi, Guglielmo, 10
Marcuse, Herbert, xv
Maris, Roger, 184
Marshall, Garry, 188
Martin, Quinn, 182
Marx, Groucho, 124, 158
Marx, Karl, xii, 31, 33, 190, 229, 232, 246
Mather, Cotton, 131
Mauss, Marcel, 147
McClintock, "Mac," 108, 109
McHugh, Vincent, 223
McKay, Claude, xiv, 113, 223
McKay, Windsor, 126
McLuhan, Marshall, xviii, 7
Melies, George, 151, 153
Melville, Herman, 24
Melvin, Allen, 160
Metcalfe, Burt, 249
Miller, Bob, 108, 109

Name Index

Name Index

Paul Buhle is director of the Oral History of the American Left at New York University and also teaches history at the Rhode Island School of Design. He is author of *Marxism in the U.S.: Remapping the American Left* and coeditor with Mari Jo Buhle of *The Concise History of Woman Suffrage*. The founding editor of the journals *Radical America* and *Cultural Correspondence*, Buhle has also contributed to the *Village Voice*, the *Nation, Monthly Review*, and other magazines.